Baby

maneuvers

Baby

Maneuvers

by

Ericka Lutz

alpha books

A Division of Macmillan General Reference
A Simon and Schuster Macmillan Company
1633 Broadway
New York, NY 10019-6705

International Standard Book Number: 0-02-861732-0
Library of Congress Catalog Card Number: 97-071185

99 98 97   4 3 2 1

Interpretation of the printing code: the rightmost number of the first series of numbers is the year of the book's printing; the rightmost number of the second series of numbers is the number of the book's printing. For example, a printing code of 97-1 shows that the first printing occurred in 1997.

Printed in the United States of America

Editorial Manager: Gretchen Henderson
Director of Editorial Services: Brian Phair
Development Editor: Nancy Mikhail
Production Editor: Phil Kitchel
Designer: Scott Meola
Cover Designer: George Berrian
Indexer: CJ East
Production Team: Tammy Ahrens, Michelle Croninger, Toi Davis, Dave Faust, Stephanie Mohler, Angel Perez, and Heather Pope

dedication

This one is for my family.

contents

Chapter 14—Overseas Adventures and Long-Term Travel   181

Appendix A—Alphappendix   193

Appendix B—Recommended Readings   215

acknowledgments

I give grateful acknowledgment and thanks to Bill Sonnenschein—loving support, constructive eye, partner in life, coparent, Numbuh One Fan. To my daughter Anaya Lutz Sonnenschein, for inspiration, joy, adventure, and fun. To my agent Andree Abecassis, who believed in this project before it was one, and, more importantly, believes in me. To my sister, Jessica "Country Bumpkin" Lutz for nieces, shoes, and research assistance. To Tilly "Soulma" Roche for thirty-odd years of friendship (and we ain't that old), and for days and days of writer's retreats.

Gratitude to my extended family, every one of you. Endless gratitude to "Big" Annie McManus for skilled insight and Reese's, my editors Nancy Mikhail and Phil Kitchel, Dr. Lillian Koblenz and Julie Olsen Edwards for technical review and support, Lynn Johnston, and Lettie Lee who asked the pertinent question, "How *do* you get the baby on the bus?"

Love and thanks to Jim "Bro" Higgins, Ailsa "Let's Celebrate" Steckel, Ami "Pomegranate" Zins, Linda "Island Hopper" Marinovich, Peter "Stand Down" Brown, Vicki "Torque Mistress" Gunter, Mark "Handyperson" Hetts, Carolyn "Rolodex" Brown, John Eyles, Alix Kates Shulman, Kyna Marie Snyder, and all the other great people who inspire my life, as well as the numerous parents, babies, and other experts who lent me their stories and answered my questions.

And a special thanks to Arthur and Karla Lutz, without whose parenting I'd be nothing, nothing, nothing . . . .

chapter

1

introduction

> *I should like to rise and go*
> *Where the golden apples grow;*
> *. . . Where the Great Wall round China goes,*
> *And on one side the desert blows . . .*
>
> —**Robert Louis Stevenson**

Baby Maneuvering

Slowed down by a mere baby? Me? No way, that wasn't going to happen. I was one tough cookie, able to balance a job, a passion for writing, and a full social life—and cook a *mean* gourmet meal. I'd masterfully handled border-crossing guards in Asia, built trails in the Wyoming wilderness, penned an unpublished novel, married a wonderful man, *and* lived through morning sickness. I was efficient, I was woman, *hear me roar.*

Then Annie was born. An hour after our new little family returned from the hospital I stood over the changing table sobbing, "I'm *sorry*, Baby," my hair and hormones askew. I stared at my tiny newborn daughter's day-old naked bottom—the same bottom I had just tried three times to diaper in our new, environmentally correct cloth diapers. If I couldn't pin this scrap of fabric around this teeny tush, what would happen to my plan and my resolutions? How would I prevent this child from keeping me penned in and pinned down?

I looked around the tiny closet packed with crib, bassinet, stroller, car seat, changing table, diaper pail . . . . How would we maneuver with all this *gear?* How would we gallivant around the world together when I couldn't even open the stroller? And what would I do when I was alone in the house with this little bitty baby and I absolutely, no-doubt-about-it, had to wash my hair?

ERICKA'S PROBLEM, AND THE SOCIOLOGICAL REASON FOR IT

Here's the situation: In the past, people rarely relocated far from family. New parents relied on Mom or Aunt Martha for tips on the simple logistics of caring for small kids—basic things like how to cook dinner with a colicky baby, or how to survive a cheerful jaunt across the continent. Babies were part of the daily scenery, and wise relatives were easily accessible—often right next door, maybe even right upstairs! In recent years, however, the "Death of the American Family" has meant that many new parents have never even *held* an infant until their own comes squalling into the world. How are we supposed to know what to do?

At the same time, we're a more mobile culture. Mothers travel for business, and traveling dads bring their kids along, too. The mom-and-pop grocery store has made way for the super warehouse store—but (arghhh!) the super warehouse store is a 15-minute drive away. The beaches in Thailand are cheaper and more exotic than the beaches in Florida, if you can survive the 20-hour plane ride. Economics are tight. Most of us have to earn a living. How *do* you fax with one hand, phone with the other, and nurse a baby at the same time? Sometimes the idea of going anywhere or doing anything with your little tax deduction is enough to make a capable grown-up break into tears. We need help, guidance, tips, suggestions, reassurance. We need to know how to maneuver.

THE STORY CONTINUES

I rallied. I learned to diaper, and I fell head-first and life-long into the absorbing, exhausting, and joyful world of parenthood. And three mornings later, Bill and I took Annie to her first restaurant, ordered eggs, and spent the entire meal mesmerized by her tiny sleeping form in its car seat, terrified that somebody would *breathe* on her. "Well, that was pretty easy," I thought, loading her (still sleeping) back into the car. I renewed my resolve. *I* was not going to be trapped in the house (except for the daily, tension-filled trip to the grocery store and the annual, agonizing schlep to a neighboring state) until the kids were in college. Babies *could* gallivant—and even short of gallivanting, babies could and should participate in daily life.

I still believe this. Now, over four years later, Annie is a veteran traveler, at home and abroad. And though restaurants aren't quite so simple when the kid is awake, we've patronized a gazillion of them, and with *rare* exceptions, we're always welcomed back.

This Book Is for You

I'm not alone in my struggles. The baby boomlet of the '90s has created a new breed of parents—brave, resourceful, and resolved to fully incorporate their children into their daily lives. These parents are determined that having kids won't mean the end of their own adventures, near *or* far—but they *may* be overwhelmed by all the logistics of maneuvering with a small child. This book is for *us*.

Baby Maneuvers is a resource guide providing factual information, reassurance, and perhaps some inspiration about the logistics of toting and traveling, anywhere and everywhere, with very young children—from babies through preschool. It's a tool kit that blends general "how-to" principals with essential tips for baby and child care at home and on the road: How do you diaper a baby on a bus? How do you wash your hair while the little screamer is, well, screaming? How do you change a sloppy diaper at a fancy restaurant? What's the best pack for trekking just north of Kathmandu?

This book is for those who have not yet traveled with kids, and for those who have who want their future outings to be easier and less stressful. This book will relieve the minds of new parents, vacationers-to-be seeking specific tips, parents dreaming of adventure, and people contemplating reproduction and wondering if they can ever "have a life" again. It's for those who wonder how two people can get three sleeping children from the car to the apartment when the only parking place is two blocks away.

Packed within these pages is a double-diaper-bag's worth of factual information and encouragement, as well as anecdotes straight from the experts—parents who have done it themselves.

HOW IT'S ORGANIZED

The book is divided into three sections: The Crawling Maneuvers, The Walking Maneuvers, and Advanced Baby Maneuvers. At the end, you'll find the Troubleshooting Alphappendix, which includes first aid information, tips on dealing with large animals, tantrums, illness, and what happens once you go home. Another appendix lists recommended readings and travel and parenting resources.

THE CRAWLING MANEUVERS

No baby begins life as an Olympic runner, and no parent happily gallivants without basic child-care skills. The Crawling Maneuvers, Chapters 2, 3, and 4, covers fundamentals that translate to anywhere on the globe. We'll deal with fears about the safety and hassles of traveling with babies, and try to put those fears to bed. Then you'll learn . . .

🍼 How to put *Baby* to bed.

🍼 How to change a diaper . . . and change a diaper *on the road*.

- All about "baby-proofing."
- How to entertain a toddler on a rainy day.
- How to be "the parent the other kids love"—because you always carry great snacks.
- How to picnic with a preschooler.
- What to do when your baby needs to nurse in Venice and the hotel is three canals away.

THE WALKING MANEUVERS

In Chapters 5 through 10, we'll hit the road . . . slowly. You'll learn how to choose appropriate travel destinations for your family ("No, honey, let's *not* go to Sri Lanka this year; I think the civil war might be a little too *intense* for Lukey.") We'll go over transportation—the ins-and-outs of lugging the little rug rats around town and around the world—and how to shop, hang out, and choose a baby-friendly cafe. There are sections on how and what to pack for the zoo, for the woods, or for a plane ride; how to navigate an airport with both child and wits intact; and where to stay once you get to your destination.

ADVANCED BABY MANEUVERS

Yow! It's the big time, baby! In Chapters 11 though 14, we get serious (though not glum). Here's the scoop on removing beach sand from a toddler's tender bottom, "roughing it" in the woods, traveling as a single parent, and doing business with a baby in tow. We'll talk about long-term travel, and the joys of taking the kids on the traveler circuit to developing nations.

Little Babies, Big Travels

Little children didn't used to *go* anywhere. Neither did their parents, except on rare occasions when they parked the papoose with the grandparents or an obliging aunt and, depending upon their style and circumstances, spent their vacation either wracked with guilt and worry (phoning home every other hour from the beach house or casino floor), or wild with irresponsible abandon (whipping off cheery postcards once a month from the jungles of Malaysia). But mostly everybody stayed home.

Times have changed, and parenting has changed with the times. Many parents want their kids with them when they travel—for work and for pleasure. As the rushing '90s race us to the New Millenium, what better way can you spend both quality and quantity time with your kids?

I should know. At four years old, my daughter Annie has covered more ground than many adults. She's flown coast to coast thrice, up and down the West Coast six times, and to

Mexico, Europe, Hawaii, and Canada. She's camped in the wilderness and dined in fine restaurants, been transported by trains, cars, planes, busses, and boats, and all of us have lived to tell the tale.

Do we have boundless energy? No. Are we rich? Hardly. Crazy? I don't think so . . . . Abusive? Absolutely not. Is all this really good for her, and fun for us? Yes! Can *you* do it too? Of course! (Thought you'd never ask.)

THE FIRST TIME

Some people notch their bedpost for lovers slept with; I spent my twenties notching my passport for countries slept in. My husband Bill also has strong tendencies towards the footloose and fancy free. But with three kids between us (his two big ones and our one little one) we've had to learn to balance our wild desires with hard-core pragmatic reality.

When Bill's kids were teenagers, we all spent time together in Mexico and Southeast Asia. But babies are a different matter—aren't they? For the first few months after Annie was born, we spent every night at home. But having a kid doesn't completely alter your personality. Bill and I got restless. When Annie turned seven months old, we began our adventures with a month-long, modified European Grand Tour.

Our friends with babies were dismayed, "You're so brave!" "What will you do about diapers?" "Can you nurse in a restaurant in Italy?" We had images of quiet walks along Venetian canals, romantic Parisian dinners. But with a baby in tow? Could it be done? Could we *enjoy* ourselves doing it?

Off we went in search of answers, strewing Europe with tiny socks, diapers and lost sun hats. Yes, we had brief moments of exhaustion when we regretted our impulses, but overall, we had a fantastic time.

That first adventure with Annie allowed us to transcend the role of Tourist. The often too-formal French and Dutch approached us with smiles and questions, and the Italians stumbled over themselves in an attempt to get close. Traveling with Annie enabled us to see a side of European culture that had eluded us before—a world of well-dressed children and doting grandparents, where babies hold the central role of attention, and a row of newly washed stuffed animals hangs, pinned in order of size, from a Venetian clothesline over a silent, blue-green canal.

A BABY HAS NO LANGUAGE BARRIER

Little children are natural explorers. They're curious, interested, easily engaged, and open to new experiences. Maneuvering them around may seem daunting, but please don't keep them cooped up in their house or neighborhood. My friend Mary, a psychologist, tells me that flexibility is the key to a well-adjusted personality, and the more positive experiences children have, the more comfortable they will be in the world. The key is your confidence in caring for them wherever you are—if you're relaxed and having fun, they will be too.

Little children also have a healthier sense of pacing than most of us busy people do—they can teach us a thing or two. With a child you're forced to slow down, to look around, to see the world through their eyes. Everything is new, everything is exciting (even the fifteenth hour-long stroll around the block). As companions, children can refresh the tired eyes of the most jaded adult.

THE JOY OF FAMILY TRAVELS

Family travel can and should be more than a dreaded occasional necessity. At its best, it's a liberating, exciting experience. Avenues and adventures you never expected await you. From their earliest childhood, your children will gain flexibility, a sense of adventure, and a healthy perspective about the world. Traveling together, sharing experiences and time, brings a family closer. (Little children are delighted, in this busy decade, to get the in-depth parental attention that a family trip brings.)

Everybody loves a child, and traveling with a child breaks down barriers. Little Anthony smiles and the world smiles back—no longer are you "the other," "the foreigner," "the alien," or "the ugly tourist." Countless times I've witnessed the way babies and little children open the arms and hearts of even the most jaded adult. I've become convinced that traveling with little children, while requiring extra planning and flexibility, provides a gift to the entire family. I don't plan on stopping.

I love watching my little girl learn, grow, and experience the world. I love the looks of warmth she elicits wherever we are. I love, too, that my life has not been impeded, that I am a parent *and* a person. You too can make it work. Join me. Have a baby, see the world.

chapter 2

crawl before you walk

"Meet it, accept it, and let it go."

—San Francisco Self-Actualization slogan, circa 1975

A Child Is Born

Let's begin at the beginning. Your baby has come to live with you, in one of the ways that babies do. He's arrived with a lot of gear, and with an agenda and schedule all his own. You want to travel, but just getting into the car with him takes 40 minutes, what with the gear, the loading, the diaper change, the other diaper change, and now baby is hungry, and "Did I pack that little teeny sweater—where *is* that little sweater anyway? Oops, I'd better start a laundry so we have clean clothes to come home to, and . . . oh no, better do another diaper change. Oh. Shame to take him out when he's sleeping so nicely."

Europe, Florida, Hawaii, the neighbor's house . . . they all seem a million light years away in distance and time. That was a different lifetime when you fantasized about Berlin night clubs and romantic Alpine hikes. That was a different you. Besides, it's too tiring. Forget Paris—let's take a nap.

Whoa—hang on, Sloopy. It's becoming evident that—like the child squirming in front of you—before you walk, you gotta learn to crawl. This chapter provides a brief overview of basic and not-so-basic child-care skills that will translate to anywhere in the world.

- Crawling
- Safety, Fear, and Exhaustion
- Baby Proofing at Home and at Aunt Martha's
- Sleep—How To
- Networking (Parent Support/Child Care)
- Still Life with Baby
- Indoor Water Adventures—Keeping Kids and Yourself from Insanity

Crawling

Travel and parenting require the same three skills—flexibility, good humor, and a sense that life itself is an adventure. These skills take time to learn. Have you watched a baby learn to crawl? She's on her knees rocking, one minute sobbing in frustration, the next, giggling with joy. Developmental Movement experts Peter Brown and Vicki Gunter of Oakland, California, stress the importance of allowing an infant to go at her own developmental pace, and not pushing her into sitting, standing, or walking before she can do these things by herself. "An infant who is crawling on the floor is organizing and programming her nervous system. She is laying the foundation for walking, running, reading, math, and creative thinking."

The same is true for parenting, and for travel. The keys to your successful future travels are found here at home. As a new parent, you don't know how to crawl yet. Don't push it. If you take the time to learn to "crawl" effectively, the next thing you know, you'll have the skills to run around the rest of your life.

REPROGRAMMING *YOUR* NERVOUS SYSTEM

Before your sweet bambino came to live with you, you organized your life one way. Now everything has changed. If you're going to travel with your baby, you need to reorganize—you need to reprogram your *own* nervous system.

The first months of parenting, you'll be deeply involved in the new emotional and physical aspects of being a parent and getting to know your new baby. Many of us spend hours poring over parenting books written by experts, looking for clues. Good parenting is about combining common sense with love. Read the experts (I've included my favorites in the Recommended Readings appendix), and remember that none of them are right *all* the time—they don't know you, and they don't know your baby. The most valuable piece of advice I received from any expert is on the first page of the baby-care classic, *Dr. Spock's Baby and Child Care:* "Trust Yourself."

Though you'll probably stay close to home for the first few months, this time with your baby is the time to build the tools that later on will let you feel comfortable journeying anywhere together.

Safety, Fear, and Exhaustion

Let's get serious for a moment. Sometimes the whole *idea* of planning, packing, and going somewhere strange feels overwhelming—even wrong. The main objections most parents have to traveling with children can be divided into two areas: safety issues, and concerns about the hassles and exhaustion of being on the road.

I understand. As soon as I got pregnant, my sense of what I was willing to risk changed profoundly. The world suddenly had sharp corners—I was no longer Wild Ericka, jaunting around the world, flinging myself into danger and experience. No, I was nervous crossing the street. I felt conflicted—overjoyed to have new life inside me, deeply aware that I was responsible for a life other than my own, and terrified about the restrictions a baby might put on my life.

Traveling with a Newborn

No matter how you slice it, gallivanting for pleasure with a **teeny** infant is not the best idea. Give her a chance to master a small part of the world, and give yourself a chance to rest. If you **need** to travel during the first three months, relax and go with the flow. (I know a woman who hitchhiked from Alaska to Philadelphia with a ten-day-old baby. Of course, it **was** the '60s . . .) For gentle travel, it's **your** comfort that's largely at stake. Remember, for your newborn, home equals you. Cuddle her close.

If you plan on taking your newborn or infant to a medically "risky" locale, make sure you talk seriously with your pediatrician before you go. Babies are not fully inoculated until at least 18 months. Maintain breastfeeding if at all possible—it is the best way to boost your baby's immune system.

MINIMIZING THE HASSLES

To defeat the Voices of Fear and Despair, you have to prepare. The more you prepare, the fewer hassles you'll have. True, maneuvering a baby or young child through life *can* be an exhausting, awful hassle. *But it doesn't have to be!* And while wandering with the teeny ones is not without its complications, once you understand what to expect and how to pace yourself, once you rid yourself of the fear of the unknown, you can change a dreaded experience into a great time. Read on—this book is designed to help you minimize the hassles and free yourself for the joy.

KEEPING YOUR CHILDREN SAFE

Your approach to the world helps determine how your child will live—seizing adventure and opportunity carefully but with enthusiasm; or hiding, timid, from its dangers. Yes, the world has real dangers in it. You keep your child safe by being realistic about these dangers, taking certain precautions, and fostering autonomy and self-reliance. You can't keep a child safe by locking her away from the world.

Educate Them   I believe that you teach small children safety by teaching them not to *fear* the world, but to be *aware* of all the world has in it, good and bad. Teach them how much control they *do* have in their lives by educating them about the world.

Involve Them   Involve little kids in the world, and involve them in decisions about their bodies. Get them active and doing—if they feel physical control of their bodies, they'll be clearer about their own boundaries.

Embrace the World   Children are perceptive; if they sense your fear of the world, they will fear it, too. Better to embrace the world, with all its dangers. After all, the dangers won't disappear just because you close your eyes to them.

Baby-Proofing at Home and at Aunt Martha's

Part of getting comfortable with a baby is feeling safe, and feeling safe means taking certain precautions. Right before Annie learned to crawl, I finally got off my fattening duff and baby-proofed. You need to do this, too. If it feels too overwhelming, do one or two rooms first—say, the room where Baby sleeps and the living room, if you've got one. Wherever you are in the world, you need to be able to relax occasionally, and no parent can be utterly vigilant every minutes of every hour of every day. Creating a space where you know your child can exist in safety and peace will be a boon to you and your child. Then you can barricade the rest of the domicile until it, too, is ready.

The first step is educating yourself about what presents a danger to Snookums—beyond the standard finger-in-plug or "tasty" drink of Drano. There are lots of books and resources available to help you with this venture. Some people with disposable income pay consultants to advise them, or to do the job *for* them. This is not strictly necessary. (You're saving your bucks for travel, remember?)

When you're on the road, you may not be able to arrange everything exactly as it should be, but you can try. The list below will help you assess and baby-proof whatever environment you may find yourself in. (I've put some additional details about baby-proofing hotel rooms in Chapter 10.)

The Hand-Bone's Connected to the Finger-Bone

A six-month-old baby's fingers still function as one unit. He reaches for an object and scrapes it into the palm of his hand. By the time he is eight months old, he is fully "human"—the opposable thumb opposes, that tiny forefinger works nicely with the thumb to create a pincher, and everything small gets grabbed, examined carefully, and, usually, popped in his mouth.

Whoa. Time to get detail-oriented. Haul out the vacuum cleaner. We want our children to fully taste the world, but we want that tasting to be more figurative than literal. Some things were just not meant for mouths.

THE TAKE-IT-WITH-YOU EMERGENCY BABY-PROOFING ASSESSMENT

Get on the floor at baby-eye level. (Come on, I know you haven't been getting to the gym regularly, but you gotta start somewhere!) What looks inviting? Interesting? Dangerous?

- Where are the **cleaning supplies?** Check the kitchen cabinets and remove the substances or secure the cabinets.

- **Medicines.** Get them way up and out of the way. (This is a good time to mention the importance of carrying syrup of ipecac to induce vomiting after ingestion of potential poisons. Call a poison control center or your physician before administering—it's not for use in *all* situations.)

- **Windows:** Are there gates? If not, how hard is it to get the windows open and how far is it to the ground? Do the blinds have accessible cords? Tuck them away.

- Check for **outlets, electrical cords,** and **appliances.** Carry plastic covers for open outlets—they're cheap, small, and light.

- **Sharp objects** lying around on floors or low surfaces.

- **Coins,** shiny and delectable, present a risk of choking. Now is the time to find all that couch change you were saving for a rainy day. Use it on a trip to the

At four, I was a very resourceful, if sometimes stupid, child. One of my earliest childhood memories is of the time I wanted something on my mother's clothes bureau. (I don't remember what I was seeking—secrets, magic spoils, money?) I carefully opened each drawer to fashion a stairway, and began climbing. The next thing I knew, there was an enormous CRASH and I was on the floor, the bureau slammed down on top of me. My screams were followed by the crazed, pounding footsteps of my parents coming to rescue me. Their terrified expressions scared me far more than the light wood bureau hurt.

hardware store—to buy child-proofing safety devices!

- Turn down the **water heater** to a maximum of 120° Fahrenheit.

- **Staircases** are a hazard for the crawling child and the new toddler. Get gates—they come in a variety of designs for all needs.

- **Bookcases.** Your child might suddenly start channeling the ghost of Sir Edmund Hillary and decide to scale the peaks. Is the bookcase attached to the wall? Pull out all the books and reorganize, either putting the largest and heaviest, or the ones you don't mind having strewn about, on the bottom shelf.

- Is the **bureau** stable? Check for **lamps** and other unstable **furniture** that might not stand up to Standing Up.

- **Corners** of tables, bookshelves, etc. Mark 'em, move 'em, or tape 'em.

- Many **house plants** are poisonous. Move all plants out of child's reach.

- Faberge eggs and other fragile **knickknacks** need to be moved *up and away*.

- **Floor heaters? Ducts? Vents?** The **burner knobs** on the stove? Does that **oven, freezer,** or **refrigerator** door open too easily? You may need to create temporary barriers to keep danger areas off-limits.

- Kitchen **knives? Firearms?** Make *sure* these are not remotely accessible.

- Open **toilets** (there are a variety of child-proof and not *too* adult-proof toilet locks on the market.

- The **fireplace.** If you have a wire screen, you might want to wire it shut for the duration (not usually more than a year or three).

- Can baby escape through the front or back **door?**

Once you get used to the routine, it will take you only a few minutes. When traveling, baby-proofing is a good way to accustom yourself to a new environment. We tend to plunge from activity to activity without taking those few moments of emotional adjustment that both children and grown-ups need, especially when we're excited and "on-the-road." Assessing your surroundings for danger provides an extra moment to *breathe*.

Sleep—How To

Whole library shelves are devoted to the subject of baby and child sleep patterns. Through my own copious anecdotal research (i.e., the whining of friends), I've come to the following conclusion: This is child-rearing. Welcome. Get used to the following fact: One way or another, your child will get enough sleep, but *you* may not.

Penelope Leach divides parents into two rough divisions: those who take the Happy-Go-Lucky-Approach, and those who go for the Regular Routine approach. Both have their advantages and drawbacks.

HAPPY-GO-LUCKY APPROACH	REGULAR ROUTINE APPROACH
Pros: 🍼 Take the baby with you anywhere, anytime. 🍼 Don't restrict your life just because you have a kid.	*Pros:* 🍼 Peace and privacy in the evenings. 🍼 A predictable schedule. 🍼 A break from the baby during the day.
Cons: 🍼 Baby will stay up until whenever he's tired—which may be *well* after you have become exhausted 🍼 Not a lot of evening privacy.	*Cons:* 🍼 Only works if you are absolutely consistent. 🍼 Must arrange your life, your evenings, and your travels around baby's routine. 🍼 Some babies determine their own schedules no matter *what* the parents do.

SLEEP PATTERNS

At the beginning of their life, some glorious babies sleep around 15 hours a day. I think of this as nature's way of allowing parents to catch up on life—the problem is that these 15 hours are not sequential; they are spread randomly throughout the day and night as they drift in and out of slumber. Many active newborns sleep as little as 10 hours in 40 minute segments (sigh). With all this up-and-down, it is very difficult to do as the doctor orders: "Sleep when the baby sleeps."

By the time a baby is 12 weeks old, she is awake for longer periods of time and more alert. The good news is that she cries less. The bad news is that her sleeping is still irregular and unpredictable. An older baby sleeps somewhere between 9 and 18 hours a day (13 hours is about average) depending upon her own rhythms and needs.

Once a baby reaches nine months or so, she is able to keep herself awake. This is when a vacation can wreak havoc on the Regular-Routiners—even after you get back home. For toddlers and preschoolers, sleep patterns and problems may vary with each child. What the hell, take the vacation. If sleep isn't easy at home, why should it be any easier on the road?

Sleep deprivation is *not* a foregone conclusion. Many kids go down easily and sleep through the night. Many babies do, too. My lovely daughter, Annie, is not one of them. At the best moments, I cast a lovely light on this: "Wow! She's so *engaged*. She's too excited by life to sleep!" At the worst moments, I hate her guts. "Go to sleep you lousy little insomniac," I mutter under my breath.

It doesn't help that she's probably genetically wired to be a terrible sleeper—Bill and I are up and down all night—trips to the bathroom, jaunts to the office to jot down that pressing thought, journeys to the kitchen for hot milk and buttered toast to soothe the worried mind. So it's probably no wonder we ended up with a family bed . . . without it, we'd probably have just added another destination to our nighttime rambles: "Gee, I wonder if the baby is still alive. I'd better check!"

"COME ON, BABY, LET'S GO FOR A DRIVE!"

There seems to be a strong relationship between movement and sleep. For this reason thousands of parents daily resort to the car in order to get the baby down. No, it is not ecological. Hey, you have to pick your battles.

When you're traveling, there's a tendency to double-up on naps and travel time. If your baby *will* nap in a bed, build in some time for a solid mid-day snooze—not in the car, stroller, or backpack—every few days.

HAPPY-GO-LUCKY OR REGULAR-ROUTINER— RITUALS ON THE ROAD

You may get everything arranged just as you like it and go on your trip, only to find that the sleeping schedule goes south and you spend your vacation in a drowsy fog. You may also find that your little insomniac takes to travel like a duck to water and is solidly dreaming moments after you put him down. Travel and excitement do funny things.

Young children like familiarity, and one way to keep her calm is to establish a bedtime routine at home and perform it every night. When you take the show on the road, take the ritual materials—the toothbrush, Mr. Washcloth, her favorite bedtime books, your songs, even his night-light. Try to recreate the same serene mood as at home—it will help the little one get to sleep even in a completely foreign place.

> For a while, Annie napped only in the car or in her stroller. In desperation on a rainy day when she was maybe six months old, I popped her in the stroller and began pushing her rapidly through the house, around and around the living room, through the kitchen, back through the living room, into the master bedroom until . . . the stroller was silent. After about 10 minutes I thought, "She's down!" and allowed myself to peek. There was Annie, grinning up at me ear to ear, with sparkling, energetic eyes—not even close to sleeping, and obviously wildly amused by the whole adventure.

Networking (Parent Support/Child Care)

New parents can use some support—their lives have changed dramatically, and hanging out with a baby all the time can feel very isolating. Creating a network is *key* to survival for the many parents who have no family around, who have moved, or who have given up jobs. Luckily, having children automatically gives you something major in common with every other new parent. Early parenthood can be a wonderful time to build new friendships—a baby breaks down barriers at home as well as abroad. Go to the playground and chat with other parents—babies are an instant icebreaker. Strike up conversations in children's clothing stores and libraries (I met my pal Ailsa over a rack of miniature rain jackets, and my friend Anna at Pajama Time at the library). You'll meet people you never would have otherwise talked to (it's sort of like school in that way).

PARENTING GROUPS

Parenting groups—female, male, and mixed—often develop out of childbirth-preparation classes. If you are interested in joining or beginning a parenting support group or parent/child play group, you can also try reading the local parenting periodicals. In addition to their articles (some of which are excellent), most of them have extensive listings for parenting resources and schools. Many will run a personal ad for free. Also look for listings on bulletin boards around town. Work the playground "grapevine." Ask your pediatrician for suggestions.

More and more fathers are becoming actively involved in parenting, and more and more are joining fathering support groups. Don't worry—these are not just for the sensitive, New Age, "Let's go drumming in the woods" set. Parenting is hard, and fathers have traditionally had few support networks. It's about time things changed. To find a fathering group in your area, see the suggestions above.

Our Play Group

For over a year, our play group—two boys and two girls—met twice a week for an hour and a half each time. We four moms began with the idea of occasionally excusing some of us and turning it into more of a child-care exchange, but we enjoyed each other's company **so** much, and the support felt so important—we were all new mothers in our 30s and 40s—that we ended up chatting and watching the babies play.

Like all groups, our play group had a natural life span. Happily so, it ended not with a bang but with a whimper as we all eventually went on to other things. As for Bill and me, we've found true, lifelong friends with one of the families—we celebrate holidays together, share child care, take short overnights together, and, now that our kids are a little older, we often schedule play dates where we **do** exchange child care.

SHARING CHILD CARE

Nothing brings families closer than sharing a child-care provider. Especially for "relocated" families, sharing child care can provide a sense of extended family. The kids get close, and the parents get to enjoy an "alternate child." As my friend Susan said, "No one ever told me how important my kids' friends would become to me." (I've got more information about hiring a child-care provider in Chapter 13. Also check out "Child-Care Resources" in the Recommended Readings.)

JOINT VACATIONS

Yes, this chapter is about "crawling," but sometime soon you're going to hit the road. Why not consider doing it with another family? (In Chapter 5 we'll look at this option a little closer.)

Still Life with Baby

Part of realigning your life and reorganizing your nervous system means learning to feel comfortable with having kids in your house. Kids are messy. Imagine this: The house is filthy, you're alone with the baby(s), your cleaning solvents are poisonous and the fumes are dangerous, and you've got company coming over for dinner. Ideally, you would be able to hire help, even a cleaning service once a week, or once a month; however, life is *not* always ideal, and besides, you're saving your money for next summer's dream vacation. Below are some suggestions for dealing with The Mess.

LOWER YOUR STANDARDS

When company arrives, shrug it off, and try not to apologize too much. Those with children will (or should) understand that little ones create enormous messes as a by-product of simply being alive. For guests without children, or whose children are long grown (like your in-laws), if they get huffy or sneer at your housekeeping, try to be compassionate. They don't understand, and they may not ever understand. Their houses may be clean, but they aren't living with the daily joy of a child.

"BIN" THINGS

Babies and small children seem to accumulate detritus—little bits of this and that, small toys, and what about all those photos of the li'l darlin' collecting dust? The solution: "Bin" them. Get some inexpensive, brightly colored plastic bins for toys. Get some inexpensive, classy-and-subtle-looking boxes for your pictures. Label the backs, and throw 'em in. You'll get around to putting them in albums in time to show your grandchildren.

HIDE IT

Company coming? Shove the mess in the closet. One mom confesses to hiding dirty dishes in the oven when friends come over. You can clean later—and feel comfortable *now.*

USE ENVIRONMENT-FRIENDLY, NON-TOXIC CLEANING PRODUCTS

More and more, people are cleaning "green." A variety of non-toxic cleaning products are available in your local health-food store. *Clean and Green: The Complete Guide to Non-Toxic and Environmentally Safe Housekeeping,* by Annie Berthold-Bond (Ceres Press, 1994), has recipes for making your own.

WASHING YOUR HAIR

So you're alone with the babe, you're supposed to be at an appointment in 20 minutes, your hair is disgusting, and the little screamer is . . . screaming. Face it, you're going to be late. Nobody *else* is on time all the time, so just give it up. Time to get Zen about it, baby. Here are your choices:

- Go with dirty hair.

- Beg a friend to come over to watch your kid(s) for half an hour.

- Wait until the little Poopsker is less pissed off, stick her in her car seat, and put the seat in the bathroom. (In an emergency, *don't* wait until she is calm. Do it while she wails. Let the cries spur you on.)

- If Buddy Boy can sit up, spread a towel on the bathroom floor and scatter some toys. Then prepare to *move,* because you'll have a window of exactly three minutes before he starts howling for you again. Before you try this, make sure that the bathroom is completely baby-safe and that the toilet is closed and locked.

- Wash your hair in the kitchen sink. Put baby in her car seat at your feet, or strap her in her high chair next to you where she can watch the soapy action.

If you have a little more time, bring her in the shower with you. Babies usually love the warm misty feel of the water, and the delicious feel of your body against them. You may not be able to actually *wash* your hair, but at least you'll have a good rinse. You can sit a bigger baby on the shower floor while you shampoo. Watch where that soap flies, though. And make sure there aren't any loose "safety" razors around.

Bathe with baby. The author Isabelle Allende says that one of the most sensual experiences in her life is bathing with her grandkids. I have to agree.

Indoor Water Adventures—Keeping Your Kids and Yourself from Insanity

Get enough days cooped up by rain or snow, and everybody goes nuts. If you're having fun, though, "cooped up" becomes "cozy." Even on the road, there are rainy days and "down" days, when you'll want to relax and stay inside. Here are some activities that can all be done in hotel rooms—they're as portable as you and your child will become.

WATER PLAY

Bathrooms and kitchens are potentially dangerous places. Water play must be supervised, but it's a lot less taxing to supervise than to participate. Water play is also engaging enough for your kids that you can usually do something else! (Ah, what did we do before multitasking was invented?) Plan to do your "something else" in the same room until the child is old enough and sensible enough that you aren't risking damage to her, or to any possessions. Options:

Sit the naked child in the empty bathtub with old yogurt containers and other plastic vessels, all filled with lukewarm or warm water. You can sit on the closed toilet and read a book, occasionally refilling the containers.

Stand the child on a chair (with the back of the chair against the sink so it won't tip backwards) in front of a sink with running cold water, and a couple of plastic vessels. In a hotel room, try empty shampoo bottles, or ask for containers at the desk.

THE AQUATIC BABY-SITTER

> *"Annie is a bit of a beast. We threw her in the bath finally, and will now get her out."*
>
> **—Ericka's Travel Journal, Montreal, Canada April, 1994**

There is nothing like warm water to soothe a wild child. Once your child is old enough to sit by herself in the tub, you can pop her in the tub with bath toys and maybe a washcloth or two. Sit on the floor and do your bills or balance your checkbook while she plays (just stay out of splashing range). Out of town? There are lots of lightweight bath games, like finger-paint and crayon soaps, that are too pricey for everyday use but good for a vacation splurge. While she's playing, read your travel guides to plan tomorrow's itinerary.

SHAVING WITH DADDY

Shaving with Daddy is a fine old tradition with a razor-edged line of danger. My cousin Rebekah, now in her mid-30s, still bears a scar on her chin from where she tried to "shave like Daddy" when Daddy wasn't supervising—of course, that was way back in the olden days of the '60s, when people used real razor blades instead of safety razors.

In our house, when Annie shaves with Daddy, her "razor" is an old cosmetic brush of mine. The brush part makes a fine lather, and the handle makes a great (and safe) scraper. Our real razors are stored up high, where she won't be able to reach until she's 12.

chapter

3

bodily functions

> *"Everybody poops."*
>
> —Gomi Taro

The Down and Dirty Details

No sir, there is nothing ethereal about caring for a child. Yes ma'am, many elements are down-right primal. Since babies and little kids spend much of their time ingesting and evacuating, and since *you* are the one who is going to have to deal with it, this chapter presents the hard-core realities of—and solutions to—many of the Bodily Function Situations you may encounter at home and on the road. You'll read about:

- Breast-Feeding
- Formula in foreign lands
- Diaper Changing 101
- Cloth Diapers vs. Disposables—The Great Debate
- Diapering Accessories

- Potty Training and Traveling
- Dealing with dirt

> ## This chapter is rated NS: Not for the Squeamish.
>
> Proceed at your own peril. On the other hand, once you become a parent, even picking your own child's nose won't gross you out. (Ericka, that's disgusting!)

Breast-Feeding

Nursing your baby is healthy, natural, and creates an incredible bond of joy between mother and baby. It's the easiest way to feed your baby when you are traveling. Yet despite what you might see in diaper commercials, nursing is not just a soft-focus, pink and glowing, bonding experience. It is, at times, very . . . leveling. Hang on to your sense of humor. Here are some tips for making your public breast-feeding experiences positive ones. (See Recommended Readings for breast-feeding resources.)

TIPS FOR SUBTLY NURSING IN PUBLIC

Our society has a double standard when it comes to male and female torsos, and whether they should be allowed to be exposed in public. I'm very pro-breast-feeding, but even I get a little uncomfortable with the women who yank their shirts completely up to nurse their babies. Here are a few tips for keeping the public discomfort level down . . .

Wear Appropriate Clothes   Wear biggish shirts that you can pull up. Avoid blouses that button down the front unless you can pull them up from the bottom. By all means do *not* wear a leotard or a body suit where you need to pull your breast up and over.

The Old Magician's Trick   While most of the time, nursing is an important time for interacting with your baby, sometimes you want to be subtle. If you don't want people to notice what you are doing, misdirect them with your eyes. Don't look down at your baby. People will follow your eye patterns. If you are looking around, casually chatting or paying attention to something else, people will assume (if they notice at all) that your baby is asleep. (This technique works best with very young babies. A baby over three months won't put up with your attention going elsewhere for very long at *all*.)

Toss a Blanky Over Baby   Here's another use for receiving blankets—throw one over your shoulder and baby's head, and hide his activities completely.

Readjust Casually When Done   Little draws attention in this society more than a woman playing with her breasts. Wear stretch bras rather than nursing bras and simply pull the material down and out of the way. When you're done, try to whip your bra back up as fast as possible. Readjust later, in private. Don't worry, you'll get the "hang" of it.

Practice, Practice, Practice   Practice in front of a mirror. Have a friend watch you do it. Are you really as hidden as you think, or are you exposing yourself inadvertently?

BREAST-FEEDING AND U.S. LAW

Every couple of years, a case hits the media: WOMAN ARRESTED FOR BREAST-FEEDING IN PUBLIC. The recent cases in New York, Florida, and California terrify me. I have images of a poor mother in leg irons, separated from her sobbing infant, merely because the child was hungry and the mother was feeding her in the most healthy and natural way. It's not that states have laws that specifically prohibit breast-feeding in public; the charges invoke indecency laws—Mommy is a criminal because she bared her breast. As a result of these types of cases, twelve states have instituted laws protecting the right to breast-feed anywhere. Sometimes the lawmakers insert language that specifies that breast-feeding is legal if done in an "inoffensive manner," leaving open the question of "what is offensive . . ."

WHICH BREAST?

The advice books and videos say to start each time with the breast you last nursed on. Some people suggest that you keep track by pinning a tiny safety pin to your nursing bra on the last side that baby imbibed from.

I could never keep track. Either I'd forget to change the pin, or forget whether the pin went on the last or next side, or forget if I'd already changed the pin, or change the pin twice. (Breastfeeding mothers are notorious for their short-term memory loss, and that dazed, blissful look. Those hormones are powerful stuff—bottle it and the world would be a kinder, if spacier, place.) I finally solved the "which side to nurse on first" dilemma by hefting each breast to determine which was heavier, and thus needed to be suckled first. Not a good idea in public—people may understand, but you'll get some strange looks.

NURSING ON THE ROAD

Don't try to wean your baby or child right before, or during, a trip. It's easier to deal with a nursing baby—the breast is always with you, and formula is more complicated, what with bottles and sterilizing and measuring and mixing and warming.

Leaving the breast also presents a big emotional and developmental change in the life of a baby. It is far better to move through that change when you are in a familiar, safe environment and can weather the possible emotional storms.

It's also a big change in the life of the mother—this is true whether or not nursing has been easy and pleasant, or a challenge. Do not underestimate the power of hormones—every time a woman nurses her baby, her brain releases a shot of the hormone *prolactin*, which brings a feeling of balance and well-being. When you wean your child, along with the physical discomfort some women feel (full, tender breasts), you may experience intense, hormone-based feelings. When you stop nursing, your body experiences a prolactin drop. Many women feel like they're in mourning . . . not a great way to enjoy your vacation.

> Sometimes the excitement of traveling will make a child "forget" to nurse. This happened to Brenda and her son, Zev. Since Brenda was ready to wean him anyway, she decided to just continue the process.

HEY, YOU WITH THE BIG ONES, SLOW DOWN!

Though the vast majority of breast-feeding mothers have great success nursing on the road, be aware that stress, exhaustion, and changes in diet and time zones all may affect milk flow. Take your own stamina into consideration when planning a trip with a breast-feeding infant. Allow the baby to nurse when he wants to rather than sticking to a strict schedule. And remember to drink lots of fluids—they are crucial for nursing mothers, and it's easy to get dehydrated on the road.

> In Maureen Wheeler's travel guide, **Travel with Children**, (a must-read for anybody planning to travel off-the-beaten-track or to exotic locations with kids), María Massolo notes that in Argentina, breast-feeding is closely tied with ethnicity and class. In the poorer, more rural areas of the country she observed many women breast-feeding their babies in the markets; in more middle-class Buenos Aires, she never saw a breast-feeding mother.

BREAST-FEEDING IN OTHER COUNTRIES

Just as people in other countries are generally more tolerant of children than people in the United States, most other cultures are also more tolerant of public breast-feeding. When it comes to the boob, however, subtlety is still the way to go. In some instances it may *not* be OK to breast-feed in public, no matter how furtive you are. Watch how residents behave, and follow suit. If you *never* see a baby nursed, then you should follow the lead and save it for the hotel room.

DEALING WITH IT

Sometimes the only solace you can provide a hysterical child is to sit down, wherever you are, and nurse. What do you do when your baby needs to nurse in Venice and the hotel is three canals away? (What do you think they made cafes for?) No, really, I understand that cafes and restaurants are not always an option. Try parks, hotel lobbies, steps. In Venice, where you spend all your time on foot, I ended up occasionally sitting in doorways. This is another reason for keeping that daypack well stocked with things like receiving blankets (see my daypack suggestions in Chapter 8). Toss one over baby, and you're set.

PUMPING, PUMPING, PUMPING . . .

At times you may need to pump and store your breast milk (particularly if you're going out of town and baby is not.) *Dr. Spock's Baby and Child Care* (by Dr. Spock, of course) and *The Nursing Mother's Companion* (by Kathleen Huggins) have details on equipment and techniques.

Formula in Foreign Lands

Let's face it, while breast-feeding provides lots of opportunities for embarrassment, traveling with a formula-fed baby is rougher than traveling with a breast-fed baby, what with the sterilizing and the mixing. If you're attempting it, here are a few things to keep in mind that will make your life and your travels *far* easier.

WHICH FORMULA?

For short trips where weight and space is not an issue, you might want to buy ready-to-drink formula in pre-sterilized, disposable bottles. This option is more expensive than bringing powdered or concentrate, but may be worth it in terms of convenience. For longer trips, or if money or weight really is an issue, you'll need to rely on powdered formula.

Most major American formula companies distribute their products overseas, though often it's only available in a powdered version. If you are traveling

Traffic School

A few months into motherhood, after a particularly sleepless night, I stopped in a bad neighborhood at a red light in the left lane and rapidly turned right, barely avoiding a cop car. The blaring siren woke **me** up. My first traffic violation. My humiliating tears merely made the ticketing officer more condescending. He wasn't even charmed by the beautiful baby sleeping in her car seat. How could anybody look at her and give me, her mother, a ticket? Fine, I thought, I'll do traffic school. But we were bonded, Annie and I. I'd never been away from her for eight hours before and she was the kind of baby that nursed a lot. **A lot**.

Traffic School. Our first exercise was to stand up in turn and intone, "My name is Ericka and I am an offender." By the time we broke for our afternoon break, my breasts were hard and nodular, and I was ready to begin mooing. I stepped into the toilet cubical to express the extra. I'd used a breast pump at home, carefully saving the milk for the rare evening out, but I'd never expressed by hand before. I'd imagined myself like a farmer, deftly milking myself like a cow, with a thin, hissing stream hitting the toilet water. But no, expressing milk by hand takes a little practice, and it wouldn't aim.

So there I was, spraying milk wildly around the cubical. Spots appeared on the walls, toilet, my clothing. The restroom was full of traffic offenders, waiting for the bathroom. The break was almost over. "No more running red lights," I swore grimly, soaking up yards of toilet paper. "Never, ever again."

For half-day trips, mix formula in advance and keep cool in a thermos bottle.

in developing nations, be aware that the formula may have a different recipe and may not have been stored under ideal conditions. Check for tampering and for the pull date—often "expired" products are still on the shelves. Make sure your water is truly safe (see "Mixing it Up"). If you have questions or concerns about obtaining safe formula, call the American consulate for suggestions.

It's vital that you pay close attention and properly prepare your child's nourishment. If and only if you follow the manufacturers instructions exactly—don't add more powder or concentrate or more water—you can treat the formula as if it were breast milk and let the baby feed on demand.

MIXING IT UP

Mixed formula must be made in a sterile container with bottled, boiled, or purified water. The bottle and nipple your baby uses must be sterilized daily, too, as well as any spoons, funnels, bottle brushes, nipple covers, and so on. Boil all equipment in a big pot for 20 minutes (that is 20 minutes at a rolling boil, not 20 minutes from the time you put the equipment in the water). Ellyn Satter's book *Child of Mine* has an excellent section on formula feeding and sanitation.

Hints to minimize your bottle-feeding hassles on the road:

- Carry a roll of disposable bottles and holders.
- Use sterile formula powder and keep the package tightly closed.
- Pre-measure your formula powder into plastic bottles or disposable plastic bags and seal until needed.
- Buy bottled water—it's available in virtually every country in the world.
- Get your baby used to room-temperature formula *before* you go.
- Ask your hotel to sterilize your equipment for you. (Ask nicely, now!)
- Properly-made formula can be kept refrigerated in prefilled bottles for a maximum of 48 hours, so it is best to make it up as you need it.

Diaper Changing 101

For the virgins among us, here's all you need to know about diapers. Diapers come in two basic styles: cotton cloth and disposable plastic. Disposable diapers are self-closing. Cotton diapers are held together by pins, a three-pronged clip, or with a Velcro-closing diaper cover. If you use pins or a clip, you need to put the child in plastic pants. To change a diaper:

- You can use the floor, a bed, the couch, a changing table, or your lap. Never leave the baby alone on a changing table. Put down a cloth or towel to cover the surface.

- Gather everything you'll need in one place—diaper, diaper wipes or damp wash cloth, diaper cover or pins. A toy is usually a good idea, too.

- Talk or sing to the baby. Tell her what a good child she is. Don't rush it. The slower you go and the more you talk to her, the less she'll struggle and object.

- Take off the dirty diaper and set aside.

- Clean the baby's bottom carefully and place the wipe near or on the dirty diaper.

- Put on the new diaper. Make sure any diaper pins are well closed.

- Take baby off changing table and dispose of dirty diaper.

- Wash your hands. Every time. With soapy hot water. Feces are more than yucky, they are a chief cause of the spread of many horrible diseases. Don't take any short-cuts here.

> We were on our way to see my sister in Vermont. The second leg of the trip was in a crowded puddle-jumper flying from Newark to Burlington with not a free seat in the house. In our row, all three seats were occupied by parents with babies. Something happened—an air-traffic jam—and the 45-minute flight stretched on and on as we circled and circled waiting for permission to land.
>
> Two hours into our nightmare, the mother next to me suddenly exclaimed "Oh **no**!" Her baby's bottom turned brown. The air grew thick and unpleasant. The plane wheeled and wheeled. No way to change that baby. As I commiserated with the unfortunate mother, I thought, "At least the humiliation isn't mine. This time."

Cloth Diapers vs. Disposables—The Great Debate

Paper or plastic, to circumcise or not to circumcise, cloth vs. disposable—these are the issues that try people's souls and test friendships. In the interests of world peace, I'll simply present diapering information and leave the lectures to the Pundits of Poop.

The Environmental Case for Cotton Diapers

- Using cloth diapers can save you up to $500 over the cost of disposable diapers during an average diapering period.

- It takes 20 trees to diaper one baby in disposable diapers for two years.

- One baby uses 6,000-10,000 disposable diapers over a diapering period.

Parking in Paris

In Paris, to satisfy Annie's need for rest and exercise, we took to finding parks in the middle of the day so that she could sit on the grass and practice her creeping. In the beautiful Jardin de Luxembourg, treading on the well-groomed lawns is forbidden except for one lawn reserved for children under six and their parents. We spent a blissful afternoon watching the French **bebes** in their $80 navy-and-white outfits playing with their chic mothers. Annie, while less stylish, had a blast. After several hours, I approached a nearby mom: "Is it O.K. to change my baby's diaper here?"

"Yes, of course, eet ees O.K."

"Thanks, I just wasn't sure," I stammered, "I didn't see anybody else changing their baby here."

"Oh, zat ees because French babies only make ze poopy in ze morning."

 18 million disposable diapers were land-filled in the U.S. last year, generating 3.6 million tons of untreated human waste and solid waste.

 Fecal contamination in child-care centers results from poor hygienic practices, not type of diaper used.

DIAPER SERVICES

Hoorah for the times we live in! In most cases, you won't have to buy and wash your own cotton diapers. Diaper services are reasonably priced and convenient—they bring the diapers every week and pick up the soiled ones. Check your phone directory, and phone around for the best deal and service for you.

A DIAPER IS NOT A DIAPER IS NOT A DIAPER

If you're going to be buying your own set of diapers, spend some time researching the product. All cotton diapers are *not* the same—spend the time and money to get the thickest ones. Also, did'ja know that diapers come in a variety of sizes?

Safety-Pinning Tips

If you're having trouble shoving a pin through layers of folded cotton, try:

1. Sticking the pin into a bar of dry soap—the soap will lubricate and enable you to slide it right through.

2. Running the pin through your hair (no, silly, the **side** of the pin, not the tip!) The oils from your scalp will make the pin slippery. Yes, even if your hair is clean!

THE TRAVELING DIAPER SHOW

If you're planning on parking yourself in one locale for two or more weeks, say, at a relative's house or a rental condominium, you might want to set up a short-term diaper service. Most diaper services have a two-week minimum order plus a small set-up charge. Some of this may be negotiable. Call (or have somebody call) in advance and you'll arrive to the familiar stacks of clean, white, fluffy cotton.

MANEUVERING THE MANURE— CLOTH DIAPERS ON THE ROAD

If you bring cloth diapers on the road, you need plastic bags for the dirties, too—small ones for day trips, strong, big ones for general storage.

Some diaper services provide clients with "vacation" cloth diapers. These are older diapers that have been retired from normal service because of wear and tear. Should you lose one or two (easy to do on the road), the replacement cost is less than it would be for a new diaper. Of course, if you're gone longer than a few days, you'll still need to wash these yourself.

WASHING DIAPERS ON THE ROAD

Never use detergents to wash diapers. Carry a plastic bag of real laundry soap (such as White King) and water conditioner (water softener affects absorbency).

Presoak the diaper in cool water to get out most of the soil; throw it in, let the waste leach out, then pop it in a plastic bag and carry to the laundromat or machine. If you do the presoak in the toilet, make sure that there are no chemicals in the tank—bluing, bleach, self-cleaning substances, and so on.

Wash diapers in the hottest water available. Horrible diseases live in feces.

Never use bleach or chemicals of any kind. Even a thorough washing can't remove all traces, and baby skin is hypersensitive to chemicals. In case of diaper rash, add 1/2 cup vinegar to the last rinse.

Be prepared for dingy diapers. Babies don't care. If you hang the diapers in sunshine, the sun will bleach them white again (don't do this in the city where the fumes of industry or auto exhaust might settle.)

> My brother-in-law Jim was in his mid-40s when first-time parenting hit him with a bang. My niece Emma was born five months after Annie. Five months is a long time in the life of an infant, so, as the familial experts, Bill and I were consulted on all matters. Shortly before Emma's birth, Jim called for another informational briefing.
>
> "How do you sterilize the butt?" Jim asked.
>
> "What?"
>
> "My mom told me everything had to be sterilized."
>
> I had a sudden, horrific image of poor Jim, swabbing down his new infant's rear and delicate privates with boiling water or stinging alcohol. "No, no, no," I protested. "Do you sterilize your own butt? Wait, no, Jim. Don't answer that."

IN DEFENSE OF THE DISPOSABLE

There's a lot to be said for convenience, especially when you're traveling with a child in diapers. There's also a lot to be said for hygiene. A day's worth of soiled diapers in a plastic bag on a warm summer day is a health hazard. Disposable diapers were originally designed for travel. It makes sense. They are easy to use and easy to dispose of.

DISPOSABLES 'ROUND THE WORLD

Many of the major U.S. diaper companies sell diapers internationally. Be aware that it's a bit of a crap shoot (groan). Sometimes the product name is different than what you're used to but the diaper is the same, and sometimes the product name is the same, but the diaper is made

Every Family Finds Their Comfort Zone

Some parents stick with cloth diapers all the way through toilet training, some use a combination, some use cotton for the first year or so and then switch, some use disposable diapers from day one. In our somewhat-schizophrenic case, we used only cotton until our first trip to Europe when Annie was 7½ months old. We used disposables on the road, and much as I believe in cloth diapers, **man**, it was hard to go back to cloth. Go back to cloth we did until Annie was a year old, and then we gave in to the powers of the modern world.

to different specifications—thicker, thinner, or made with different materials. Huggies sells an "economy" (cheaper and bulkier) diaper in developing countries.

Diaper costs also vary from country to country—some are pricier, some are less expensive. If you're on an extended trip, you will have little choice but to sample the local merchandise. Let your baby's rear have a cultural experience.

HEALTH CONCERNS

Most disposable diaper manufacturers add super-absorbent materials, such as acrylic acid polymer salts (polyacrylate), to their diapers. This chemical forms into gel beads when wet. Many parents (me among them) have found this gel on their babies' bodies or in genital crevices, raising issues of safety. In 1985, the first year chemical super-absorbent "gels" were used in disposable diapers, 50,000 babies went to emergency rooms with diapering problems. Parents using disposable diapers also need to be concerned about avoiding tears in the outside plastic covering. Ingesting the gel-filled fluff might cause choking. Yucko.

There are now gel-free diapers on the market, disposable diapers filled with cotton and wood-pulp fluff for absorbency. Gel-free diapers are pricier than standard disposable diapers. Some cotton-diaper services are even selling them to their clients (there's a listing for "Tushies Diapers" in Appendix B under "Equipment").

Diapering Accessories

Cloth, disposable, or a combination, you'll need a few other "accessories."

THE JOY OF DIAPER WIPES

I love diaper wipes. Even now, when Annie is out of diapers except for the nighttime pull-up, I buy them by the boxful. (In Chapter 8, there's a partial list of the multitude of things wipes can be used for). Get the unscented kind. Many children are sensitive to scents, and, at least for me, the delicious smell of clean, milk-fed baby is endlessly better than the chemically tinged odor of artificial flowers or baby powder.

THE PROBLEM WITH POWDERS

If you're going to powder your darling's derriere, verify that the product you choose does *not* contain talcum powder. Talc, a mineral, can cause respiratory problems.

OINTMENTS—NOT ALWAYS O.K.

Rashes are usually caused by long exposure to urine. Be careful choosing a diaper rash ointment. Many contain fish oil, and fish oil has been shown to promote bacterial growth—exactly what that wee rashy rear does *not* need. Any ointment containing calendula is good—and then there's the good old "open-air" method. Leave baby without a diaper as much of the day as you can manage.

Rashes *are* more common during travel. Make sure to change your baby frequently. If a rash persists for more than two days, stop using wipes and switch to warm water and mild soap, apply anti-yeast cream mixed with 1 percent hydrocortisone ointment, and put barrier cream on top of the mixture. If you're having trouble cleaning the area with all those creams, remove the creams with unscented mineral oil, swab the little rear down, and then reapply more goop.

> ### Do-Your-Own Diaper Wipes
>
> Even the unscented commercial wipes contain some chemicals that aid drying, and these chemicals can occasionally cause reactions. Here's a recipe for handmade diaper wipes:
>
> Paper towels (thick paper towels folded in thirds, or use baby wash cloths instead of paper towels, and half again more liquid)
>
> 1 cup of water
>
> 1 teaspoon of mineral oil
>
> 1 teaspoon of soft soap
>
> Place towels in waterproof container (Tupperware would work). Mix liquids and pour over towels to dampen.

Potty Training and Traveling

We have friends who are planning to go to Europe once their kids are out of diapers. They don't need to wait—in some ways, it is easier to deal with diapers than it is to deal with the half-trained or newly potty-trained child.

ALTERNATIVES TO STRANGE BATHROOMS

Some kids are nervous in strange bathrooms and unwilling to go; especially common is the child who won't move his bowels other than at home. Some kids get so excited being in a new place that they simply forget. For a child who has some trepidation, or whose patterns are unpredictable even to herself ("I have to go potty, Mommy, and I have to go *now*! Oops."), you might want to revert to diapers or disposable pull-ups for the duration of the trip. Here are some other solutions:

Too Much Time on Her Hands . . .

I know a mom who traveled with a thermos bottle of warm water and soft squares of cotton flannel. Her son had the privilege of never having a cold wipe touch his butt. As my old therapist used to say, people have many ways of living. If you are tremendously concerned about the shock of wet and cold each time you clean your baby, you can buy a diaper-wipe warmer (plugs in near the changing table and maintains the wipes at a steady temperature of 98.6 degrees) but come on, enough is enough! Crumple a wipe in your hand for a moment. It will warm up.

Travails of the Newly Potty Trained

Tiny children are blissfully unashamed of their bodily functions, as it should be. This lovely innocence can lead to embarrassment for the adults—like the time when his grandparents took three-year-old Sascha to a fancy, formal function at the Plaza Hotel, and in the middle of the lowered voices and canapés he suddenly screamed, "Mommy, I have to go potty!" Our pal Joannie (at two, a little less articulate than Sascha) has the bad habit of announcing at the top of her lungs, "Poop! Poop! Poop!" And then there's two-and-a-half year old Mickey, who in the middle of a wedding ceremony shouted, "Momma, the pee is coming out! Hurry!"

- For car trips or around town, keep a potty seat in the trunk of the car

- There's always ye olde jar-in-car trick for boys. For girls, use a bigger jar, and have them practice in the bathtub or shower first.)

- Plan around poop. Some kids have a bowel movement at a regular time each day—try to maintain that schedule.

- Inexpensive portable fold-up seats/toilet seat adapters are available through baby catalogs and stores. These help with the hygiene issue.

MANEUVERING AROUND PUBLIC TOILETS

In many places, public bathrooms are well kept. In other places in the world (or in many U.S. gas-station bathrooms), hygiene is of less concern. What I'm really saying is sometimes public toilets are just plain disgusting.

- Ask to use public rest rooms in hotel lobbies or "better" restaurants and stores. Most places in the world will allow leeway for small, uncomfortable-looking children, even if they have signs posted "For Customers Only."

- If the bathroom is unsanitary and your child cannot wait, hold him above the toilet.

- *Always* carry toilet paper or facial tissue—many facilities are not supplied.

- Travel with disposable toilet-seat covers, but be aware that many places in the world don't have seats. (Squat toilets can be more hygienic anyway. For more information, see Chapter 14.)

- Be aware that in many places, it is OK for a woman to take a small boy into a woman's room, while it is socially unacceptable for the opposite to happen—a man taking a little girl into the men's room. (Dads: In a case like this, you may need to rely on the kindness of strangers. If you do, make the best snap judgment about the quality of the woman you are relying on, and stand right by the door the entire time.)

Dealing with Dirt

Kids get dirty, and they should. It's part of your job to, at least occasionally, freshen them up.

DIRTY BODIES

Bathing is not always a possibility on the road, and you'll need to occasionally excavate their tiny faces from the layers of grime, and de-stickify their hands and feet before they climb into bed. Here's where your ever-useful diaper wipes come in handy again.

DIRTY CLOTHES ON THE ROAD

Much as I've traveled, the dirty clothes thang remains a problem. If you were alone, you could do as my dad did in Europe in the '50s—travel for months wearing a single white shirt. This legendary shirt was made from Dacron, it was thin and gauzy, and it dried in two hours. Each night he washed out his shirt in the sink. In the morning it was dry and he put it on again. With a white T-shirt underneath, and the sleeves rolled up (these were the James Dean years), nobody could tell it wasn't freshly pressed cotton. Now *that's* traveling light.

As a parent, you don't have that option, though you'll still probably find yourself bending over hotel room sinks.

Here are some tips for laundering in Europe:

- Do laundry as you go.

- Bring soap for hand-washing in your hotel-room sink, or buy soap there. Hotels and laundries charge an arm and a leg to do your wash for you, and you won't want to waste precious museum time watching pajamas spin in a Parisian laundromat.

- If you do want to go to a laundromat, you may have trouble finding one. Ask your hotel, or look it up in one of the Europe-on-the-cheap guidebooks *before* you go.

- If you're renting an apartment that is advertised as having laundry facilities (check out my section on house, apartment, and castle rentals in Chapter 10), be aware

Take a Lesson from Us

In Florence, we splurged for a couple of nights at a famous pensionne. When the concierge offered to do some baby laundry, we jumped at the chance. She returned 12 beautifully pressed tiny garments to us the next day (they were practically tied with a ribbon) and presented us with a bill equivalent to 14 dollars. Ouch.

Laundering Clothes in Developing Asia and in India

Hired personal services are usually **very** inexpensive in South East Asia and the subcontinent. In Bali, the local washer-woman scrubbed a hole in my new jeans, trying to remove a coffee stain. In India, the laundry wallahs take your clothes down to the river and pound the bleep out of them before lying them on a rock to dry in the sun. Your clothes will come back stiff and faded . . . but definitely clean.

that European home washing machines are often much smaller than the one you might be used to, and that homes rarely have dryers.

Damp baby clothes can be dried on the back seat of the car as you cruise through the Alps or across the Russian Steppes. Your own under-pants and socks can be too, if you don't mind hearing snickers from the local constables who'll stop you at the occasional road block.

chapter

4

eating with baby

"My fair son!
My life, my joy, my food, my all the world."

—Shakespeare, *King John*

"I do not like green eggs and ham.
I do not like them, Sam-I-Am."

—Dr. Suess

"Feed me, Seymour"

—Little Shop of Horrors

Tips for Eating Dinner with a Baby in the House

The Rocker Take that great infant car seat—the kind that rocks (you'll find out about it in Chapter 6)—and place it in the middle of the table. Diners take turns rocking the seat and all can stare into the blissful face of the living centerpiece as they dine, accompanied by the gentle ka-chunk ka-chunk of the rocking.

The Nurser Of course, only a breast-feeding mother can do this part. A baby with his mouth full of warm milk is likely to be a happy and quiet baby. For a right-handed mom, nursing on the left breast and eating at the same time is a challenge, but doable (same goes for a lefty nursing on the right). What happens when it's time to switch sides? Maybe mom's dining partner can insert select morsels into her mouth. He or she can, at the least, cut up her food.

The Swinger This must be the reason they invented those awful battery-operated swings: The Neglect-O-Matic, for the Exhausted, Fed-Up, New Parent— "Wind it up and let it go, we'll escape to Mexico!" In all seriousness, it isn't good to swing the baby. Many child development people think these are terrible for kids. I'd say that for **very** selective uses (like both parents sitting at the dinner table at the same time once in a blue moon) the swing can be a lifesaver.

The Wolfers If life is too problematic (and sometimes it just turns out that way), you can always just feed yourselves on-the-fly, standing over the kitchen sink, pacing with baby, taking turns, and swearing to try again or at **least** hire a baby-sitter for two hours so you can sit down and eat a meal together. Wolfing should be a last resort.

Chomping the Chow with Children

Every parent spends hours each day thinking about food, preparing food, helping their children eat—and hopefully they get to eat, too. This chapter provides food for thought on eating, everywhere, with babies and small children. Once again, we'll start with the basics—eating at home. By the time you're done, you and baby will be eating everywhere! You'll learn all about:

- Food—It Feeds More Than the Body
- Eating In
- Food and the Older Baby
- Toddlers at the Table
- Eating Out with the Family
- Finding Fabulous Food without Forking Over a Fortune
- Snacks and Snacking
- Food and Dietary Issues

Food—It Feeds More Than the Body

Remember those quiet weekend breakfasts, she with the Sports section, you with the comics? The coffee was hot, the kitchen was quiet save for the rustle of newspaper, the occasional snort of humor or outrage, or the occasional murmur, "Honey, could you pass me the Datebook section?" Remember, too, your romantic candlelight dinners served by the fabulous waiter who anticipated your every desire? (A glass of wine, a single rose . . . .) Remember it well, file it deep in your brain. As you'll learn once you have a child, eating will never be so simple again.

While *all* serenity is not completely in the past (that's what they invented baby-sitters for!), it will no longer be the norm. Eating with a baby, eating with a toddler, eating with a small child—these tend to be noisy, boisterous adventures, sometimes fraught with *issues*. Yet food is far more than fuel for fighting, and eating is one of the sensual pleasures of life, one that you can, and should, share with your kids.

Eating In

In too many families, meals are hastily snatched affairs—little more than stuffing sessions. Three hundred and thirty odd years ago, Samuel Pepys wrote, "Strange to see how a good dinner and feasting reconciles everybody." I don't think it's strange—while the shared dinner hour may have gone the way of the rotary phone in many households, eating together is one of our favorite and most valuable family practices. "Training" kids to appreciate eating *en famille* may take some time, but it's well worth it. At least once a day, you get to share time, attention, and pleasure as a family.

THERE'S A BABY IN THE HOUSE

Start at day one. Baby is part of the family, she's involved in dinnertime, too. That said, don't count on her sleeping through the dinner hour, or even being quiet. For many babies, the evening hour is the time for wailing, not for "reconciling." She's not having any of the Chicken ala King, so why should she be happy? How then, can you eat while the baby is screaming?

TOO TIRED TO COOK?

Especially with a new baby, there will be many times when you have no energy to cook, and no energy to go out. Check out food delivery service (there are more details in Chapter 10). How luscious! Go on a vacation without leaving the privacy of your home! While restaurant delivery goes against my general anti-cocooning sentiment, when you're having "one of those nights," there's no beating it.

THE KINDNESS OF FRIENDS

Set up a network of friends to share or trade shopping trips and cooking responsibilities. It's almost as easy to cook for six or eight as it is for three or four, and that way you have to do it less often. Can't cook? Exchange a night of babysitting for a meal.

Dinner with a Colicky Baby

If your baby is colicky, you're having a hard enough time without trying to be a gourmet chef, too! If there was ever a time to simplify your existence, this is it. Don't try to juggle a bawling baby and cook hot food at the same time. What did they make microwaves, fast food, and marital partners for? Or, cook dinner early in the day before the "colic" hours set in. Don't skip dinner—you need the fuel to get through the nerve-jangling hours of Howling Howie—but don't make it anything special. Just get yourself fed. This, too, shall pass.

Grocery Delivery Services

Sometimes the mere idea of going shopping is exhausting. Pack up the kid. Get the kid in the car. Strap the kid in. Get in the car yourself. Drive. Park. Get out. Get the kid out. Go into the store. Put the kid in the cart. Shop. Wait in line. Leave the store. Get the kid in the car. Strap the kid in. Get in the car yourself. Drive. Park. Get out. Get the kid out. Go into the house. Put the kid down. Leave the kid alone. Unload the car. Put the groceries away.

While it's not as common as it used to be, some grocery stores will still allow you to order your groceries over the phone, and then deliver them to your door. Try the remaining Mom 'n Pops. Of course, you **might** have to pay a delivery fee, you **will** have to come up with a tip, and you **won't** be able to squeeze your own tomatoes. Then again, you won't have to pack up the kid, get the kid in the car, strap the kid in . . .

HOME CATERING

Check your local phone book under "catering." Some catering companies specialize in small dinner parties, or will even bring you dinners for just your family—if you order on a regular basis.

Food and the Older Baby

Baby is getting older, and all of a sudden, "Egads! It *eats!*" A whole new world of culinary adventure awaits you and your little muncher.

AT HOME WITH THE OLDER BABY

Kids start clicking in to the joys of food at different ages—for Annie, though she was introduced to solids at six months, she really didn't *get* food until she was close to a year old. (Food interested her for its texture—we did a point'n'shoot photo series of her little head bathed in stewed prunes, in banana, in cereal . . .) Other kids love the tastes of food from the time they are four months old.

TRAVELING WITH THAT MUSHY STUFF

If you're traveling with a mush-eating little moochie, check out the natural and organic baby foods now available in many supermarkets. (Most of the standard commercial baby food doesn't taste very good, or is loaded with sugar and fillers—read the labels!)

You can create wonderful, tasty meals for your baby with the aid of a food grinder. Much of what *you* eat is O.K. for an older baby. A portable, battery-operated food grinder is good for sharing restaurant food.

Toddlers at the Table

Man, life was eeeaasy back when your kid only drank breast milk or formula. Even that mushy stuff was O.K., though messy. Now your kid is almost, or truly, a *kid,* and if your family is like many families, you've already donned your boxing clothes . . .

"Ladies and gentlemen! In this corner,
wearing the anxious smiles of the desperate-
to-feed, that fabulous duo, the PARENTS!
And in this corner, presenting the not-so-

fresh-from-the-womb, the ever-hungry-for-junk-food, the food-tortuous, TODDLER!"

Typically, when Baby is a baby, she grows at a tremendous rate, inhaling victuals like air. Then suddenly Baby is a toddler, with seemingly no appetite at all, and you, her parent, are freaking out. As our beloved Dr. Mangravite asked me, "Does she have enough energy to play? If so, she's probably getting enough to eat." Trust your child, provide healthy choices, enjoy your own food, and watch her follow your example to the extent that her appetite will let her. Try to provide a balanced diet, but think in terms of the course of the day or week, rather than trying to strictly balance each meal.

Eating Out with the Family

Eating "out," whether in a restaurant, fast-food joint, hotel room, campground, or picnic spot, brings its own agonies—I mean, *challenges*. But as with most things in life, there are trade-offs, and many times eating "out" is just what the doctor ordered to break the monotony or add a little adventure to your lives.

> ### Viva Italia!
>
> At nine months, Annie was far below average on the weight charts. Our pediatrician, Dr. Mangravite, wasn't too concerned—she was healthy, she was alert, energetic, charming, intelligent . . . "Make her a little spaghetti carbonara—bacon fat, cream, eggs—make the noodles soft enough for her to gum," he told us, his eyes growing ever so slightly misty at the thought of what may be for him a childhood comfort food.
>
> The dutiful new mother, I went home, looked up Spaghetti ala Carbonara in my Italian cookbook, and discovered a whole new world of sin. Bill and I enjoyed dinner immensely. Annie looked at the long, coated noodles as though they were a very interesting piece of furniture, nibbled one or two, then patted my breasts emphatically, wanting to nurse.

CUISINE AS A CULTURAL EXPERIENCE

We're a relatively food-oriented family—oh, who am I kidding, eating is our *life*—so for us, a big part of the joy of travel is the thrill of eating. Much of human culture is based around food, and a vital part of experiencing any culture is savoring, and understanding, the local cuisine. From the beginning, introduce your kids to many different kinds of foods. Your own encouragement and enthusiasm will pay off. Your travel experiences will become easier and more rewarding if you show them that food is fun, that adventure is fun, and that new food is an adventure.

- Think long-term. If you're excited about new food and consider it an adventure, Junior will learn to be excited, too.

- Be flexible. Kids love familiar foods, so allow them the occasional lapse into pizza or burgers, even—especially—in exotic locales.

- Have compassion. During travel, food can look and taste different, schedules are askew, even the plates and spoons are unfamiliar.

Escargot, Baby?

Bottled baby food is heavy, but make sure to leave some room in your luggage for an emergency supply. That first day, (or, rather, night) after you arrive, your baby's body (and your own) will still be living in another time zone and he may get hungry at 2:30 a.m. On our first trip to Europe, poor seven-month-old Annie had to make do with a stale rice cracker and tap water—all we could find on a furtive midnight kitchen raid in our friends' house.

The next day you can hit a supermarket, but be prepared for some strange discoveries. The Dutch begin feeding their kids bottled food at three months— try a puree of cabbage, tomato, green beans, and non-iron fortified rice cereal. The French baby food is delicious but filled with sugar and salt. Here's where your newly minted flexibility begins: Take a breath and practice saying, "Ah, what the hell, it's a vacation."

- Use desserts as an entree into new cuisines. ("I don't *like* Indian food." "Try this sweet coconut pudding, Honey." "Yum. I *love* Indian food, Mommy!")

- Tolerate a little whining ("This looks yucky!") and keep trying. Young children are very conservative about food. I like to think of this as a survival mechanism from the hunter/gatherer days, if the little ones were popping everything edible-looking into their mouths, the human race might not have survived to this illustrious day.

- Try not to be irritated when even the youngest toddler begins to pine and sigh within days for his usual food—the food he is not eating this vacation.

RESTAURANT (COUGH!) ETIQUETTE

Restaurant rules and etiquette are the same across town or across the world. Some restaurants are clearly appropriate for little kids, others are clearly inappropriate, and still others are borderline— depending upon your kids, and how you deal with them. The way to teach your little ones how to act in a restaurant is to *take* them to restaurants. If you want to travel with your kids, begin by taking them to local restaurants. Here are some restaurant tips:

- Sit near the door. If baby cries, take her outside *immediately*! (And don't be pissed at her—she's just a baby. Crying is the only way she has to communicate.)

- Order your food and then go for a walk while one of you waits for the food to be served.

- Bring toys, food, or coloring books to keep him happy.

- If necessary, you can use cloth napkins to strap your child to the high chair.

- Make a strict rule: Toddler can toddle next to the table but no further. No bugging "that nice, smiling lady over there."

🍼 If your baby is *very* messy, get a table near the wall and surreptitiously lay a small plastic cloth under the baby's chair. When the meal is over, quietly fold up the cloth and take it with you. Do *not* shake it out until well away from the restaurant.

🍼 When the meal is over, offer to clean up under the high chair. They'll refuse (they can't have other customers see you cleaning up) but they'll appreciate your offer.

🍼 Leave a big tip. You may have been extra work, and you want to be welcomed back.

Engage His Imagination

Food is fun, and involving a kid's imagination doesn't qualify as the dreaded "playing with food." Eating a banana "like a baby monkey" (half peeled, peel draping on small fist) is endlessly more delicious than eating peeled, boring, banana pieces. Pancake "monsters" taste better than pancakes—everybody knows that. If your child wants strawberries and all you have is blueberries, tell them that these are magic **fairy berries**: tiny, blue, and round. It's not a lie—it's **pretend**.

RESTAURANTS WHERE LITTLE KIDS ARE *ALWAYS* WELCOME

You know 'em, you love 'em, you shouldn't be limited to 'em: franchise fast food joints, taquerias, pizzerias, and coffee shops. The pace is fast and furious, there are tons of hyped up little kids and babies, and the food is edible but not (even at a stretch) fancy. Other than the fact that most babies can't handle this much stimuli, there is little wrong with these establishments. The problems occur when you feel you are doomed to eat here, and nowhere but here, until Junior is over five feet tall.

RESTAURANTS WHERE LITTLE KIDS ARE *USUALLY* WELCOME

I've seen some parents peek through restaurant windows and, if they see tablecloths and candles, back away and head for the nearest fast-food joint. "Oh no, my baby would just disturb everybody else!" they exclaim in horror and disappointment.

It doesn't have to be this way. Contrary to your fears, most people don't mind children in restaurants, as long as they aren't too disruptive. Informal but excellent restaurants abound if you behave with courtesy (no, don't whip your kid into shape). You'll be welcomed again and again. These include:

🍼 Moderately priced ethnic restaurants

🍼 Trendy hangouts

🍼 Casual but elegant dining of all kinds

European Restaurants

Can you take your infant to a fine Parisian restaurant? Well, we did. Suddenly, the formal waiter we remembered from three years before, the one with the scornful upper lip, melted into cries of "Coo Coo! Coo Coo!" as he presented our smiling child with spoons, bread, and a tiny plate of her own. Annie spent many an hour sitting under restaurant tables in five countries, and was greeted with, for the most part, joy and pleasure by the restaurant staffs and patrons. Europeans tend to be more tolerant of babies. After all, many of the **other** tables have small dogs sitting politely under them.

How Do You Change a Sloppy Diaper at a Restaurant?

Don't ever, **ever** change a baby or toddler at the dinner table. There are many areas in life where you can push the limits of social acceptability. This is not one of them.

- Are you sure it can't wait? Sometimes it cannot.

- Scope out the bathroom. Is there a changing table? A make-up counter? How wide is the sink? How dirty is the floor? Lay down a lot of paper towels and doo-doo the dirty deed. If the floor is *that* disgusting, do you want to be eating at that restaurant, anyway?

RESTAURANTS *USUALLY INAPPROPRIATE* FOR LITTLE KIDS

Note the word "usually" in the title of this section. As usual, I suggest you use your own judgment. A sleeping baby poses no problem anywhere. A three year old awed by the idea of a "fancy restaurant" may behave just fine. But in general, avoid:

- Anyplace with a formal dress code.

- Anyplace where an entree costs more than your monthly phone bill.

- Anyplace where the music and smoke make it hard to talk without shouting and hard to breathe without coughing.

- Anyplace where the question "Do you have a high chair?" is greeted with intense hostility (some places aren't prepared for a baby, but are willing to accommodate). If the maitre'd stares at you for a long, time-stopping moment and then asks, "Did the nanny take ill?" it's probably time to leave.

- Anyplace where the baby is the youngest in the room by 40 years or more (with the exception of visiting Great Uncle Joe in the nursing home. See Chapter 7 for more).

BORDERLINE RESTAURANT BEHAVIOR (. . . AND YOU'LL SEE A LOT OF IT)

- **The I'm-Too-Big-for-a-Booster Phase** Four-year-old Annie is extremely sophisticated and mature. She's also only three feet tall, a fact that is beginning to cause her problems at restaurants where she's too cool to want to be seen in a booster seat or (heaven forbid) a high chair. However, her nose often barely clears the table. We spend some meals seeing little more than the top of her head and her two busy hands. For other meals she relents, and seated on a booster seat, joins us in her lovely, regal way.

The Make-a-Concoction-from-Condiments Stage Kids love mud pies, kids love ooze, kids love to mix and combine. I personally think it's gross when I see a child making such a concoction (mustard, sugar, salt, pepper, A.1. sauce), but as long as he makes it on a plate and not directly on the table (which I've seen more than once), I have no real complaint. A concocting kid is a quiet kid. (**Note:** If you allow this behavior, be considerate! Glance at a waiter or two—if you see disgust or disapproval, end the project. Take the child for a walk.)

(continued)

How close is the car? Is it worth another buck or two to get the valet attendant to bring it around?

Is there an unused room (perhaps a banquet facility) in the restaurant? How about a staff office? A storage room? (Politely turn down use of the walk-in refrigerator.) Ask! Believe me, it is in the restaurant staff's best interest to help you get this small situation resolved.

UTTERLY UNACCEPTABLE RESTAURANT BEHAVIOR

Yelling and Screaming "Hey, c'mon, pal, shut that kid up! We're tryin' ta have a romantic dinner heah!"

Throwing Food As far as I'm concerned, lack of coordination is acceptable, deliberate rudeness or food throwing is not. Some kids bend towards eating sensibly and neatly, and use a fork at 18 months. My mom, a woman of incredible patience, taught my sister and me to eat with utensils at 12 months, taking a long time at meals and praising us profusely when we managed to get the food into our own mouths. "Children like to please," she says. Then again, some kids (like Annie!) still, at the age of four, require a warm, wet washcloth after a meal for (in this order) hands, face, legs, torso, table, and floor.

Dancing on the High Chair If your kid is in an energetic mood (or is one of those babies that has two speeds: High and Asleep), you may be treated to a little song-and-dance on top of the high chair. Stop this behavior: 1) It is dangerous, and 2) It draws a lot of attention.

The Littlest Stripper in the West

Several months ago, to their horror, our friends Suzanne and Tom were "treated" to their 2½-year-old daughter Sarah's debut as a table dancer. They were in a nice restaurant (not too fancy, but definitely a place you wouldn't be ashamed to take a first date) when they realized that Sarah had escaped while they were enjoying their fresh sand dabs, and was somehow four tables away, standing on an empty table, removing her diaper with a great flourish! A trail of tiny garments led to the aspiring entertainer. The crowd's response was somewhat mixed, and Suzanne and Tom still walk on the other side of the street when they shop in that neighborhood.

FUN FOOD TO ORDER

Scope out the "side order" section on the menu, and try a few selections. In general, little kids often like "discrete" food—food that comes in tiny, natural packages, such as noodles, beans, peas, blueberries, Cheerios, Goldfish crackers, cheese squares, tangerine segments. Many don't like their different foods to touch. And don't limit your kid to the classics (pasta, pancakes, grilled cheese, burgers), give her tastes of your dish and don't be surprised when she likes it.

MAINTAINING MEAL PATTERNS ON THE ROAD

It's not *what* meals, but when. Kids adjust rapidly to time changes, and it doesn't matter if you're eating eggs at "dinnertime" or a burrito for "breakfast." Problems arise when the excitement of the trip interferes with eating at regular intervals. Generally for little ones, the chow should come every two and a half hours or so. If you keep the intervals between meals similar to the schedule at home, you'll reduce grumpiness. Less grumpiness is a *good* thing.

Finding Fabulous Food without Forking Over a Fortune

When you're on the road, you don't have to spend a lot of money on food, even if you don't do your own cooking. Breakfast and lunch can be catch-as-catch-can. If you're on a driving trip, bring a cooler—you can keep milk on ice for a couple of days. Remember that even in the most high-falutin' tourist locale, the locals have to eat, too. Ask a friendly salesperson for a good place to get a bite, "Not fancy, I mean where *you* eat lunch." Follow the off-duty taxi driver to the best alley cafe in Cairo. At LAX (Los Angeles International Airport), we were referred to the hidden employees cafeteria—the same food served in the terminal cafe, at half the price.

PICNICS, TEDDY BEAR AND OTHERWISE

Eating outside is an excellent way to save money on the road. Unless the weather absolutely forbids it, we try to combine our travel experiences with picnicking wherever we are in the world—what could beat the taste of pears and brie on the pier in Vancouver as the seagulls call and the tiny ferry boats dance on the bay? Tote it with you, or buy it at the nearest market. Restaurants can be confining and expensive—eat like the locals, let the baby relax, and enjoy the sights.

SUMMER DINNER PICNICS

Picnics are also a great way to break the hometown monotony of three meals a day plus snacks, day in, day out. Even in the most urban settings there are usually parks and playgrounds, a patch of fresh green grass, and some swings, a slide, and a sand box. In the Summer or Fall after a long hot day, it's worth a little extra effort to get out for a dinner picnic. Exchange your stuffy apartment and chilly air-conditioned office for the clean smell of fresh grass and the sound of birds calling and kids playing. Your little picnics will feel like vacations, even if they aren't.

> The island of Maui in Hawaii is known for its expensive food, yet we ate very well, and quite cheaply. A fish-and-chips stand offered fresh-from-the-water, delicious-broiled-or-fried Hawaiian fishes—ono, mahi-mahi or ahi tuna—plus fries for $5.95. Twice for lunch we sat at a stone picnic table in front of a Bento restaurant in a local shopping center where, to Annie's delight, noisy little birds hopped by to steal scraps of food. Here, for $3.40, we had a lunch plate consisting of a pile of rice, a hamburger patty, and sides of green peas, potato salad, and Japanese pickle.

It doesn't have to be fancy. A few sandwiches, some cold salad picked up at the deli on the way over, juice boxes and a bottle of spring water, some cut-up fruit. The idea is simplicity. Call another family and ask them to join you. Spread a blanket, plop down, and watch the baby crawl and the preschoolers run and swing. The sky gradually turns pink, and in the cool evening air, the grown-ups take turns resolving conflicts, pushing the kids in the baby swings, and leisurely eating their food. The kids check in for an occasional bite, and because there is no table, the stress on manners is relieved. The children go home flushed and happy—for a special treat, stop for frozen yogurt on the way home. Everybody will sleep better that night.

Snacks and Snacking

The world is divided into two types of parents: those like my playgroup pal Bonnie, who travels at all times with a lunch box full of snacks for her kid and other hungry tots; and parents like me. Unless I'm careful, I'll daily knock myself on the head at noon with the realization, "Oh! Lunch!" and then scrounge around the kitchen for something to feed Annie and myself. This wouldn't be so bad except that Bill tends to be that way, too. "Oh! Dinner!" And then we scrounge around again. For people like us, planning is essential—it helps to carry non-perishable snacks at all times, buried in baggies deep in the diaper bag, and in the glove compartment of the car.

Snacks have gotten a bad name, when in reality, they're just food. Yes, the world is full of junk-food snacks that can fatten the little calf and make her refuse her dinner, but most little kids *need* to eat between meals, and healthy foods eaten at "off-hours" are no less nutritious than healthy foods eaten at dinner time.

- Try to select from the basic food groups, and try to offer a mixture.

- Any food that you carry with you should be non-perishable or kept on ice. (You'll find more details under **F** for "Food Safety," in the Alphappendix.)

- Car snacks need a little extra care—avoid cut-up apples, carrots, celery, and other crunchy veggies and fruits—choking danger! Also avoid ice cream—way too messy—and anything with powdered sugar—ditto! Plus, you don't want them bouncing off the car walls, now do you?

- Grapes are great, but make sure you cut them in half for kids under 14 months.

- Cheese squares or string cheese (be careful of spoilage).

- Dried fruit, dry cereal (individual boxes), cereal "O's" necklaces on dental floss, Bananas (but be aware that you might have a major mess on your hands and face, and clothes, and so on . . .), bagels, bread, pretzels (without salt), *Goldfish crackers!*

- Peel an orange or tangerine. If you're in the car, pass back a few segments at a time. Tastes great and fills the car with a wonderful odor. (For babies, cut them into pieces so they don't have trouble with the membrane.)

Food and Dietary Issues

It's easy to get into food battles—our society is obsessed with food and weight, and few of us are free from these concerns. Very early on, your child will internalize your opinions about food, and about his or her body. I've heard 2½-year-olds ask, "Is this food healthy?" or "Will this make me fat?" I once overheard a couple of three-year-olds bantering: "I'm very heavy." "Well, I'm very skinny." (Annie announces regularly, "I'm small for my size.")

It's a challenge for most of us to relax, to present healthy food, and let the children regulate their own intake. As Ellyn Slater, author of *Child of Mine* says, "You are responsible for *what* your child is offered to eat, *where* and *when* it is presented. She is responsible for *how much* of it she eats."

> Let me introduce you to our new family tradition:
>
> "Hey Annie, the Candy Monster is coming to our house tonight! The Candy Monster **looooves** candy, and that's all he eats. The Candy Monster eats candy for breakfast, candy for lunch, and candy for dinner. And then, do you know what the Candy Monster eats for dessert?"

FINDING YOUR BALANCE

Try to balance what you serve not only between the food groups, but with the fats, salts, sugars, chemicals. If you establish a basically healthy eating and meal pattern, then it's O.K. to break it a bit while traveling. We eat organic fruits and vegetables at home as much as possible (not just because they're healthier, they tend to taste better, too), but we're not too rigid about food—the occasional slab of barbecued pork ribs, French fries, gooey chocolate cake, or bright pink cotton candy *does* pass our lips. As I've heard said, "Everything in moderation, including moderation." By not making these less-healthy foods "off-limits," we manage to eat a balanced diet without feeling as though we're missing something deeply desirable in life.

DEALING WITH TREATS ON THE ROAD

Many kids reach an age where the only seemingly acceptable food is buttered noodles. But watch him. What is he really eating? Studies have shown that babies and small children allowed to select their own food from a variety of healthy choices will unconsciously balance the nutrients they receive. Too much sugar in the diet can, however, throw this natural system off.

- Avoid sugary juice or soft drinks—kids should drink mostly water and milk.

- Allow some sweets so they don't become a major power issue.

- Decide on a stance and then stick to it—this will help reduce childhood whining.

- When you're on vacation, relax your home rules.

(continued)

"What?"

"Salad!"

(Wild giggles) "But he's a nice monster, isn't he, Mommy?"

"Oh, very sweet."

"What does the Candy Monster look like?"

"I don't know, I've never been awake."

"Well, **I'll** be awake."

"Nope, the Candy Monster is very shy of people, especially kids, and won't come until we're all fast asleep."

The Candy Monster visits three days after Halloween or **any** holiday in which candy builds up. Our dentist says it takes three days of candy eating for damaging quantities of bacteria to build up in a child's mouth, so rather than fight it, we allow Annie to eat her fill of candy (after meals!) for three days.

On the third evening we decorate a bag ("Write, 'To the Candy Monster from Annie,' Mommy"), put the remaining candy inside, and with great ceremony, place the bag on the porch before going to sleep. The next morning, Voila! The bag is gone! The Candy Monster has been fed, Annie is delighted, the "poison" has been disposed of, and everybody has had fun.

While this may work for three and four year olds, it may **not** work for older children. When the protests begin in our house, I expect that the Candy Monster will take a lesson from its cousin, the Tooth Fairy, and modify its M.O., leaving behind a little toy in trade. As I've said before, I believe in bribery. More so, I believe in fun.

Lila and the Lucky Charms

Three-year-old Lila, much to her parents' dismay, is a sugar hound. A few months before they went to Hawaii, Lila started bugging her parents for Lucky Charms. Anna and Armand began avoiding the cereal aisle, at least while Lila was along for the ride. Anna told Lila, "Lucky Charms are not the kind of food we have for everyday eating, it's vacation food."

Lila is a smart child. Lila has a memory. A few months later, the family went to Hawaii and as soon as the plane hit the runway, Lila asked for Lucky Charms. True to their word, Anna and Armand's first stop after the car rental agency was a supermarket. Lila had Lucky Charms for breakfast everyday of the vacation, enjoyed herself immensely, and on the last morning happily dropped the three-fourths empty box into the trash can. "You can have Lucky Charms again on our next vacation," Anna promised.

FAST FOOD—OVERCOMING MCDONALDITUS

We, personally, use fast food as a last resort. Part of this is because of health concerns—fast food tends to be fatty, salty, and chemically processed. Part of this is aesthetics—I only enjoy fast food if I eat it less than once every three months. Writer David Owen says "pizza . . . along with Big Macs and Whoppers has become a sort of culinary lingua franca." Almost anywhere you go, you'll be able to find those familiar foods. And even Groovy Ericka often finds herself beating down the door of the nearest McDonalds after a couple of months overseas.

The advantages to fast food are that it is: fast, familiar, inexpensive, and standardized. Yes, fast food is a boon for the parent on the road, but don't fool yourself—it is not good food. Food is part of the poetry of existence, and part of our responsibility as parents is to educate and cherish our children's palates. Fast food doesn't do that.

If your family struggles with McDonalditus:

Substitute other fun activities for that trip to the fast food joint, like dinner at home and then an evening jaunt to the playground.

Ethnic restaurants offer a wide variety of good quality, healthy, and inexpensive fast food. You can feast like royalty on burritos, Asian noodles, or good-quality pizza.

Remember that kids like to eat what the big folks eat. If you keep a watchful eye on sugar and salt content, offer lots of healthy choices, and don't make a fuss about it, your kids will end up eating healthy!

DEFEATING THE PICKY EATER

Serve your child very small portions; don't overwhelm her with large amounts. If she wants more, she'll let you know.

🍼 Let him serve himself as soon as he can get food from the serving plate to his own.

🍼 Encourage her to try everything, but don't force the issue. It's her body—respect it.

🍼 It takes a long time to learn to differentiate between *not* liking something, *liking* but not being in the mood for it, and being *tired* of something. I've watched children gleefully wolf down most of a plateful of something, and then, full to the brim, push the plate away saying, "It's yucky!"

> Well, it was another one of those days. Annie and I had sinned and hit McDonalds for lunch. As we were getting out of the car in front of our house, Happy Meal toy clutched in one of Annie's hands, cup of Coke clutched in one of mine, an acquaintance, we'll call her Organic Olga, and her son Olaf happened to walk by. Olaf, at the age of three, had never so much as tasted white sugar or played with a plastic toy. Olga cast one horrified look at Annie and me and our booty, grabbed Olaf, and strode away from us. She's never spoken to me again.

🍼 Avoid commenting on how much or how little he is eating. I know, it's hard. You got the food on the table, now your job is over. Enjoy your own meal. Bite your tongue. Little kids have little power in their lives except over what they ingest. If he understands how concerned you are, he may choose to make food into a power play. He'll eat when he's hungry.

chapter 5

where to, baby?

> *"Where are we going to, my pretty maid?"*
> *"I'm going a-milking, sir."*
>
> —Old nursery rhyme

Geography Is Destiny

O.K., let's get to the meat of the matter. You've got the basics down, now you're ready for the big stuff. Getting on a plane, maybe, or spending some nights away from home. Here's the $40,000 question—*Where are you going?*

Choosing a destination is vital to ensuring that you and your little ones will have a good time. In the Hugh Lofting *Dr. Doolittle* books I read fervently as a young child, the good doctor-who-talked-with-the-animals and his pals Dab Dab the Duck, Gub Gub the Pig, and the two-headed Pushmepullyou chose their next adventure's destination by gathering around the map of the world, throwing a dart, and going wherever it landed. (One time the dart landed in the middle of an ocean—and off they sailed!) Though romantic and adventurous, this is *not* a recommended approach for traveling with babies and small kids. This chapter covers:

The Four Steps to Choosing the Perfect Destination:

1. Discuss what *type* of trip you'll enjoy

2. Consider your kid(s)'s *temperament* and *development*

3. Take a look at your family's travel *style*

4. *Gather information* and *decide*

Planning your Trip—Travel Agents, Planning Itineraries, Reducing Conflict in Advance

Imagine Maui . . .

Smooth white sand stretches in either direction; children cavort, chase each other, tumble, and fall giggling into the frothy waves. Beaming adults read bad novels. The green surf purrs. Leave your baby with your partner and float over glowing coral reefs and deep canyons, waving seaweeds, colorful fish, sea turtles, eels, the warm sun on your back. Or, stand waist deep in the blue green waves holding your frightened two year old. Look down—a small school of colorful fish is visible through the clear water, swimming through your legs, nibbling gently at your knees. A little foot slides down, and your daughter slowly relaxes her lower body into the ocean. Delighted, she looks at you. "It's warm and cold at the same time!"

Step 1—What TYPE of trip?

The world is a huge place, full of different types of destinations. Are you in the mood for excitement and adventure? For relaxation? Do you want to hang out with other people, or are you sick, sick, *sick* of the teeming masses? Does your small one vomit on winding roads? Do you *really* need to shower every day? The short descriptions below should help you get the destination discussion started.

Urban   In any city, there are activities for children, and often they are low-cost or free (see Chapter 7). If you need relaxation, look somewhere else; a busy city's pace can be infectious and stimulating. Might be just what the doctor ordered to cure your baby blahs.

Rural   Especially for city toddlers, a rural setting can be more exotic than a trip to Sao Paulo or Cairo. Toddlers who've only known cats, dogs, and pigeons will love watching cows being milked and eggs being gathered—and learn important lessons. Digging potatoes, harvesting cherries or pumpkins; all those activities that are chores to kids who live in the country are *adventures* to city kids and their parents. Enjoy a slower pace of life. Stand under a night sky in all its starry glory. A trip to the country can also require a great deal of adult energy—farms are not childproofed, ponds don't always have fences, horses kick—be prepared to watch your child like a hawk.

The Road Trip   With the right preparation and mental attitude, a few days in a car can be a fun family adventure. Watch out—too much driving and grown-ups get crabby, kids get restless, and siblings fight. But all that time together is a great way for a family to create or renew bonds. And who knows what you might discover around the next bend in the road?

The Beach   Oceans and lakes. The classic family vacation—the little kids spend their days running and digging in the sand, the adults relax and contemplate the idea of wallowing in a trashy novel. Kick back, soak up the rays, but be prepared! The sun can easily burn your baby's delicate skin, and the water is deep and strong. However, at the end of a busy, wet, sandy day, your toddler will sleep like a log.

Organized Fun   Family resorts, theme parks, cruises—while most tours are not appropriate for children, family travel is big business these days, and many areas have travel agents who specialize in family vacations (I listed some in Appendix B). Some cities and universities sponsor inexpensive family camps where *they* do the cooking and *you* do the relaxing. There are real benefits to the organized approach: you'll meet lots of other families, the activities are geared towards kids, you *know* kids are appreciated, and somebody else does all the planning for you!

Outdoor Adventure   Backpacking, skiing, or camping with your children is a wonderful way to incorporate them into your interests. Logistics can be rough—no amenities. But exposing your child to nature early can lead to a lifetime of love and respect for nature (you'll find many more details in Chapter 11).

Foreign   Visiting other countries can provide educational and stimulating adventures. Unless the foreign country is very near, make sure you have enough time to balance out the hassles of long flights, jet lag, and culture shock. Some developing nations provide great value for the dollar—once you get there. Read Chapter 14, and strongly consider climate, and medical factors. Then go—and have a great time!

The Family Reunion   For little kids, spending time with extended family provides a sense of their personal history as well as an opportunity to just hang out with relatives they may rarely see. For you, it may provide an opportunity to pass the baby to your aunties-with-the-hungry-arms. (And it may be a nightmare of well-meaning but inappropriate advice.) Family reunions can be a great choice when traveling with more than one child. Siblings tend to do their *best* at family reunions, since there are lots of adults to connect with and often cousins their own ages. The kids disappear to play, checking in only occasionally, and for a moment or so, you remember what it's like to be an adult!

The Joint Family Vacation   Joint family vacations can be wonderful, or they can ruin friendships—so think carefully about who to travel with, and make sure that . . .

- You discuss your plans and expectations
- You are operating on a similar budget
- Your travel "styles" are compatible (some people are early-risers, some are lazy-bones; some like to "hang," some need to see everything; some buy everything in sight, some are thrifty . . .)
- If your styles *aren't* compatible, you all know it and are comfortable with that fact.

Step 2—Consider Your Children's TEMPERAMENT and DEVELOPMENT

Each age has its complications and its joys. Now might a good time to pull out those books on child development and review your child's developmental stage. Step into Jenny or Joey's teeny-tiny shoes and think, "Would I want to spend four days strapped into a car seat as my parents drive across country? Would I *like* the ocean?"

INFANTS AND SMALL BABIES

Babies can enjoy a trip to any venue as long as their needs for food, shelter, comfort, and love are met. In some ways, the best time to travel with a baby is before the squirmer is mobile. For nursing mothers, travel can be a breeze (as you learned in Chapter 3.) Many people recommend very short trips with an infant. Always consider your fatigue factor and don't push it. If your infant is colicky and you are delirious with exhaustion, you might want to wait a few months. On the other hand, car travel is an age-old remedy for soothing colicky babies. Babies sleep a lot—especially in planes, trains, and cars. This can be a bonus!

THE OLDER BABY

Traveling with older babies can be fantastic. In the second half of their first year, babies are often at the peak of their baby cuteness—little ambassadors who provide great entertainment for you and other baby-friendly adults. They'll love having Mommy and/or Daddy with them at all times. Rarely are they so mobile that they can get away from you—but be cautious! The baby that walks early has physical abilities without common sense. Take extra safety precautions. And babies can be overwhelmed by too much stimulation. Build in a lot of "down" time.

TODDLERS

Toddlers are entranced by the world, and what fascinates them may surprise you. Travel with a toddler and you'll see the world through refreshed eyes: the twist of an ornate fence, the puppy in the window of a shop. Toddlers are self-centered. They work hard on internalizing their own veto power—a fancy way of saying they love to say "No!" As they become more aware of the world and their place in it, stranger-anxiety becomes common.

Toddlers like to walk *sometimes*. Luckily, they're not too big to pick up, and they're sturdy enough to put down. (Though when you try to, they have a bad habit of retracting their legs into their body, thus straining your back irrevocably . . . .) Plan to go slow. Build in "down" time, and provide opportunities for daily physical play.

PRESCHOOLERS

Three and four-year-olds can be great travel companions—old enough to enjoy learning about new places, and fun to talk to about them. Many of them are past the stormy two-year-old tantrum stage, but be prepared for nagging and whining. The famous quote, "Are we there yet?" was invented by a three-year-old. Like toddlers, kids this age need plenty of exercise every day. Sleeping in strange places can be scary for preschoolers—maintaining bedtime rituals and providing lots of reassurance is important.

MORE THAN ONE

It's a challenge to travel with kids in different stages of development. Gear the pace of travel to the youngest, but make sure activities will be available for all the kids. Travel is definitely different with two or more, and it's best to be prepared. Read the sibling material in *Becoming the Parent You Want to Be* by Laura Davis and Janis Keyser (this book is listed in Recommended Readings), and talk with other parents with two or more kids. And then *go!*

KNOW THYSELF, KNOW THY CHILD

Modify all advice you receive from guidebooks, friends, or me with self-knowledge. Don't expect yourself, or your child, to become a different person once you're on the road. If heat makes you grumpy, try to avoid heat. If your kid has a hard

Consider Mobility

Richard Langer in his classic book, **The Joy of Camping**, divides children into three distinct categories: Carry-Alongs, Anchors, and Catch-Me-If-You-Cans. Carry-along babies are the easiest to lug—they fall asleep in slings and backpacks and can follow their own rhythms most naturally.

Anchors (otherwise known as the Toddler and Preschooler set), are too little to walk all the time and too big and restless to be constantly carried. This is a good era for base travel—choose a lovely spot, get there, and venture out briefly.

Once your child is seven or so, she'll become a Catch-Me-If-You-Can—you'll be eating her dust up the mountain trail.

Sibling Stress

Travel can be stressful. Over the course of any trip, make sure to take some focused time alone with your kids every day. Try an outdoor activity. How about the local playground? Be prepared for fur to fly—they may very well take their added stress out on each other.

Sometimes the stress is displaced. Say Emma's feeling a little jealous—at the family reunion, Cousin Annie got the biggest cookie at dessert, and Grandma Karla whispered a secret in Annie's ear! Rather than take it out on Annie, Emma might bonk her little sister Alexandra for no reason at all when they are alone at the playground.

(continued)

Remember: Your kids will feel most comfortable with each other. They'll "clear" their emotions with each other. Doesn't mean you have to put up with it, just understand that it might occur.

ID bracelets or dog tags are a good idea for all children, especially mobile ones (check Appendix B under "Other Resources"). As soon as they are able, teach kids their full name and phone number. Leave an emergency number on your answering machine or service at home—that way, if your kid is found, you can be located.

time with strangers, either modify the trip or expect the behavior that too many strangers elicits in your child. You cannot force a boisterous child to be silent in a quiet setting. You can't force your child to enjoy Disneyland if she flips out in large crowds.

What if your child is firmly set in her routines and howls if something new is introduced? Go slow, but go. Take as many routines with you as you possibly can—the "Morning song," the "Bedtime story," the "This-is-the-way-we-wash-our-face" poem. These rituals are the bedrock of your child's existence. With a few key rituals that she can rely on, your child will learn to be flexible. Flexibility is one of life's great coping mechanisms. Better to teach your child to be flexible *now* than to watch her suffer later because she is unable to cope with a swiftly changing world.

Be kind to your less-stalwart child; show patience and compassion, but get them into the world. *You* become their home, their security, their routine. Pack extra loveys and plan to spend a lot of quiet time in hotel rooms or quiet country pastures with little stimulation. Calm their fears. Love them enough to show them the world.

CHILDREN WITH SPECIAL NEEDS

Kids with medical problems or mental or physical disabilities can travel, too. Plan to modify your activities to fit your kid's needs. Consult your pediatrician for any special advice, and choose a destination where those needs can be easily met. (Many resources exist for travelers with disabilities; I've listed a few in Appendix B under Disability Resources.)

WHEN TO GO WHERE

Not all vacations, or "travels" are age-appropriate with small children. Think long term (maybe not the Himalayas this year; wait until Angela likes to hike.) You have many years of parenting and travel ahead of you.

Step 3—Establish Your Travel and Budget STYLE

Reality can be painful—how much money do you have, and how much time? There are many ways to have a fabulous time with a limited amount of both money and time. Sometimes money is short, sometimes time, often both.

INDEPENDENT TRAVEL ON-THE-CHEAP

When you're broke, just getting out of your own environment can do a world of good for your mental state. Visit friends or family in a nearby city for a weekend. Inexpensive "Street" food (hot dogs and pizza slices in this country, you name it in others) can be as delicious and more fun (though not always as sanitary) as dinner at the Ritz.

Or throw in the towel, put the furniture in storage, grab your kid and head for Thailand. It is possible to travel the world on pennies and take your kids along, too; we've met people shoe-stringing with young kids and babies all over Asia (see those inspirational stories in Chapter 14). Not ready for something that extreme? Camping is cheaper than hotels, and often more fun for little ones too. Even nearby state parks can provide cheap camping facilities (more on the Joy of Outdoors in Chapter 11).

Pros: More bang for your buck. On-the-cheap travel makes adventure affordable for just about anybody.

Cons: Less comfort and more potential travel hassles than a more organized, structured family vacation.

Caution: Don't *ever* be thrifty when it comes to safety and medical care.

GOING THE EXTRA DOLLAR

When Bill and I traveled in India, the difference between a dump and a decent bed, between rancid, inedible food and a delicacy, was often little more than a single dollar. An ounce more comfort—and a little more money—can often make a tremendous difference to a young child. We're still budget travelers, but we've learned our lessons well. And a trip with a little kid is no time to fool around. We watch our budget, but spend more than we used to. We buy little, and opt for comfort.

Follow the Business Traveler

From our travels in Mexico and India we've learned to stay in business traveler hotels where the amenities and costs fall between tourist hotels and dumps.

Pros: Makes travel affordable without *too* much stress.

Cons: Often takes more time to seek out the good deals.

THE CLASSIC MIDDLE CLASS VACATION

You'll probably spend too much, but you'll have a great time. You'll come home relaxed, having let somebody else do much of the planning. You'll have memories, souvenirs, and probably too many slides to torture the neighbors with. Since you probably only take a trip like this once a year, what the hay!

Pros: Somebody else is doing a lot of the work. You're free to enjoy.

Cons: So, you come home broke! So what?

THE TOTAL TREAT

What a life! Bring along a baby-sitter, schedule massages and daily facials, enjoy breakfast in bed as you lie in your penthouse suite overlooking the warm ocean. Be pampered. Have it all done for you.

Pros: Everything.

Cons: Unless you are *very* wealthy, vacations like this will, by financial necessity, be very short and rare.

Going Home Again

Visiting the homestead? Even if you own a palapa in Yalapa or are off to visit lonesome family in Laredo, there's probably lots you **don't** know about the old hometown. Now that you are a parent, you're returning to old haunts with new eyes. (I've been to this park 60 times; I never realized there was a **playground** here!" or: "Our zoo has the finest collection of wombats in the world? Amazing!")

Step 4—GATHER INFORMA- TION and DECIDE

Talk to friends, visit the travel section in your local library and bookstore, contact Chambers of Commerce, call a travel agent. For every destination, consider what there is to do, for you *and* your kids. Ask lots of questions. Take it all with a grain of salt. Relax, breathe deep, don't stress . . .

WORKING WITH A TRAVEL AGENT

Many travel agents specialize in family travel and will understand—maybe even anticipate—your special needs. It's helpful to have a general sense of the type of experience you'd like for your trip before you make that first call. Don't feel apologetic for asking questions and making certain you get exactly what you need. Travel agenting is a service industry—they are there to help you. (It is not nice, however, to spend hours getting information from one agency and then buy the tickets from another agency, or from the airlines themselves.)

The Right Place

Once you decide on the type of trip you'll take, get a general sense of your travel style, analyze your family's needs, and do your destination research, all you need to do is decide. Choose a destination that will delight all of you, *including* the adults. Don't skimp on yourself—you have to have a good time too. Enjoyment is infectious and so is tension. If you're relaxed and having fun, your kids will have a good time, too.

PLANNING AHEAD

Whoa, Nellie, there's more work to do! Now that you *know* you're going, you need to make some plans.

PLAN AN ITINERARY TO MINIMIZE FATIGUE AND CRANKINESS

Children need to play. Build in "down time" every *day* of the trip. You may not cover as much territory, but you will all be much happier.

Try not to drive during rush hour. Plan to leave early, stop early, and enjoy relaxing afternoons.

Rule: With a baby or small child, places are farther away than they look on the map. Here's a good guideline: The number of hours it takes to reach a vacation destination should not exceed the number of days you stay there. That means no four-hour car rides to visit friends for a two-day weekend, and don't brave that 20-hour flight to Thailand unless you've got at least three weeks to relax and eat tropical fruit (yum!).

Schedule your days, but build in flexibility. Spontaneity is the spice of travel—don't schedule the trip so tightly that you can't pull over to watch the cows eating, pick up berries at a fruit stand, or spend 20 minutes at a cool bookstore you happen upon next to the restaurant. When planning your trip, *always* make reservations for at *least* the first night. If you hate the hotel or motel you can make changes in the morning, when you and the baby are fresh.

Build in private time for the adults—alone and together. All-day-every-day togetherness can be oppressive, no matter how much you all love each other. Partners can take turns doing separate activities—one plays, one has private time with the baby. Hotels often provide sitting services (and you'll find out about *that* in Chapter 10). Adults traveling alone with kids deserve a break, too.

Try not to expect perfection. Aspects of traveling with little ones can be hard. Your other option is to stay home and not have a life . . . .

REDUCING CONFLICT IN ADVANCE

On the road, normal routines and rules are often disrupted. Before you leave, discuss with your traveling partner (or, if you are traveling alone with the kids, decide for yourself) what you'll do about special food treats, buying souvenirs, bedtime, TV. Some parents relax their normal rules, others feel it's important to remain consistent on the road. Work towards finding policies that are comfortable for both parents. Knowing where you stand on these tricky issues *before* you go may help you avoid uncomfortable policy fights.

Three Things to Help Ensure Happy Travels:

1. A sense of humor
2. No tight timelines
3. Flexibility to (radically) change your plans

If you can't have the last two things (and, as Mick Jagger says, we can't always get what we want), concentrate on the first thing ("it's funny, it's funny, it's funny, it's funny . . . .)

THE LAST WORD

And go *now*. When your children are babies and toddlers you have a certain flexibility that you may not have again for years once school schedules come into play.

chapter

6

lugging the little rug rat around

You can go by balloon or broomstick OR
You can go by camel in a bureau drawer.
You can go by Bumble-Boat or jet.
I don't care how you go, just get!

—Dr. Suess

Hitting the Road, Jack

All right . . . ready, set, go! Travel is about traveling, not just about the experiences you'll have once you get there. The minute you leave the house, you begin dealing with transportation systems—feet, cars, buses, subways, boats—you name it. This chapter is about managing the "moving around" part of traveling with babies and little kids. Some sections are broken into "local" and "long distance" travel but, as you'll find, the same tips and information often apply both near and far from home. After all, walking with your toddler from home to the post office involves some of the same issues as walking from *l'hotel* to Notre Dame. And, a crying baby in a car seat won't know whether she's cruising the highway near Cleveland or Rio de Janeiro. This chapter's subjects include:

- Hoofing It
- Choosing Your Tote Mode: Backpacks, Slings, and Strollers
- In the Car—Short Trips and Long Travels
- Boating with Baby
- Riding the Rail—Local Travel
- Long-Distance Trains
- Bus Travel
- Resources for Disabled Parents—Toting and Traveling

Hoofing It

Wherever in the world you are, you will probably be doing some walking and, at least part of the time, bearing the burden of Baby.

Obsessions!

At about 14 months old, our friend Jesse became obsessed with parking meters. He'd point and moan and fuss until his stroller was wheeled over to it and he could pat the cold metal pole. Only then would he be satisfied—until his stroller was wheeled past the **next** meter. Since meters are usually only a few feet apart, navigating commercial streets became a bit of a challenge.

Annie, on the other hand, was entranced by key holes. I'd never noticed how many small, low key holes there are on any given street—commercial buildings with glass doors locking on the bottom, garage doors handles, and so on. As she toddled along, Annie wanted to, no, **needed** to touch each and every lock with a single, tiny index finger.

THE LONG MARCH (AROUND THE BLOCK)

You start small—you leave your house for a walk. Terrific!—a trip around the block is an adventure for a toddler. The very smallest walkers may spend hours getting from point A to point B. Kids with another temperament might take off and be somewhere around point Q while you're still getting off the front stoop.

"CARRY ME, DADDY!"—SAVING YOUR SPINE

For the next few years you will be bending and lifting a constantly inflating bundle of wriggling flesh—your baby. Remember to bend your knees when picking your baby up, and try to alternate which side you carry Baby on. Strollers have saved many a spine. When actually *walking* with your child, consider a front pack for a small baby and a backpack for a larger baby (I'll discuss backpacks in a bit). Once your toddler outgrows the backpack, you may still be able to negotiate a stroller. Or you may simply have to negotiate: "Honey, you are big enough to walk now. I'll hold your hand."

HERDING BEHAVIOR OF THE HUMAN YOUNG

Remember the sheepdogs in the movie *Babe*, how they raced 'round and 'round the sheep, underfoot, nipping at their heels, until the sheep went the way the dogs wanted them to, baa-ing all the way? Toddlers often act like sheepdogs. They'll run in front of your feet and stop, refuse to move, and start yapping, "Pick me up, pick me up, pick me up, pick me up!" At two and a half, Annie began her sheepdog behavior. At four and a half, the end is not in sight . . . .

> Annie doesn't walk. She operates in two modes: Running and Carried.

"DON'T PICK ME UP!"

And if your kid refuses to be carried? Recite today's mantra: "His agenda is different from my agenda, his agenda is different from my agenda." Then either put up with his behavior, or put up with the evil looks of strangers who think you're killing your child as you forcibly pick him up and haul him away . . . .

> Sometimes people with very active children use wrist bands—two rubber wrist bands with a stretchy cord between attaching parent to child and child to parent. You may get a few glares from strangers, but your child won't get a sore back from walking with his arm in the air, and the alternative (a child in traffic or a lost child) is far worse.

Choosing Your Tote-Mode: Backpacks, Slings, and Strollers

Until they are well into their preschool years, children will often need to be toted. Luckily, many options are available to save your back and free your hands.

FRONT CARRIER OR SLING?

For infants, front carriers provide a good way to keep your little baby close to your body—since that is where she wants to be—and enable you to move around and actually *do* stuff. I used the classic Snugli, but there are many brands available.

Slings—swaths of wide fabric that strap over one shoulder and down your side—are also very popular. Wait until Baby is born to buy a carrier or sling, then borrow a friend's to try it out. Many babies like to be carried in a particular way, and you won't *know* that way until you have your particular baby. Make sure to alternate sides. With some brands, it is even possible to nurse your baby while on the go. Talk about subtle!

Warning: Never carry your wallet in the back pouch of a baby backpack. It's an easy target.

Packing It through Europe

In Europe we opted for a lightweight backpack. Annie was able to view the world from her perch and we took turns toting the well-balanced load. In Italy, our pack was looked at longingly by many Venetian mothers who spend their days pulling strollers up and down the four hundred bridges of Venice. What many people don't know is that the famed Venetian bridges are all steps.

Note: Packs and strollers are not always welcome in all European locales. In both the Rodin museum in Paris and in the Van Gogh in Amsterdam we were requested to check the backpack. Be prepared to argue your case (we won in Amsterdam) and be prepared to lose (we lost in Paris).

BACKPACKS

Once your baby gains the strength to hold her head up (usually around four months), you can carry her around the neighborhood or around the world in a baby backpack. Babies and toddlers usually love being so high, and you'll enjoy the freedom of movement. If the backpack is the proper fit, your child will be able to look over your shoulder to encounter the world, yet have the warmth of your body in front of her for emotional support, and the back of the pack for physical support. Many babies prefer to nap while in the backpack. Go ahead, take a hike! Get in shape while baby sleeps! Stroll around the neighborhood. If you poop out, take a bus home.

Baby backpacks can usually carry up to 40 pounds (when your baby is approximately four years old), though some top-of-the-line models can carry up to 60 pounds. (Do you really want to carry 60 pounds of child on your back?) In addition, most baby backpacks come with rear pouches for carrying diapers, wipes, clothing, and other supplies. Some also come with sun, rain, or wind screens. Accessorize!

There are many types of backpacks available, depending upon your needs. A good children's store or camping supply house should have a broad selection. Ask for help—the fit matters!

Baby backpacks have somewhat-wobbly retractable stands for loading and unloading your child, leaving him asleep in a restaurant (braced by the wall), or putting him down (with your support) for a short break where he can see the world. Practice getting the backpack off and on before you go for a jaunt alone with the baby. There are at least two techniques:

- Try putting Baby in with the stand extended, lifting pack and Baby onto a higher surface, and backing into it.

- Put Baby in, cross your arms, grasp the straps, and swing the backpack (with Baby) around onto your back.

No matter how you get the pack on, make sure to always attach all the straps to yourself—both belt and chest restraints. This will help save that back of yours. You only get one.

UMBRELLA STROLLERS

There are strollers and there are *strollers*, and they range in price from $15 to $300. For travel, the most useful stroller is usually the collapsible "umbrella" stroller. They are small, light, and inexpensive. They can easily live in the trunk of your car or be checked through at the airport. Umbrella strollers are more suitable for the "older" baby through small preschooler, as they don't provide enough head or body support for infants.

If you have a large, clunky stroller and are going on a short trip, consider renting or borrowing a light-weight one. Many children's stores rent them (also check out Babies Away, listed under "Equipment" in Appendix B).

AND LET THAT BABY CRAWL!

No matter which tote method you decide on for your little one, be careful that you don't rely on it too much of the time. A child must move her body—she needs lots of time on the floor learning to crawl, and, once she can walk, she needs lots of time to run and walk unrestrained.

According to Developmental Movement experts Peter Brown and Vicki Gunter, "a child whose exploration of the world in this way has been inhibited (whether due to accident or health, or due to spending his infancy in playpens, backpacks, walkers, etc.) . . . will look perfectly normal, but is quite likely to experience problems such as confusion between left and right, difficulty working through problems independently, poor eye-hand coordination, . . . difficulty walking or running smoothly, . . . and may have problems learning to read or write."

In the Car—Short Trips and Long Travels

If you're an average American, you're gonna spend a lot of time in the car. Most children learn to like, or at least tolerate, the car from a very early age. Many won't nap during the day anywhere else. Riding in the car is soothing and entertaining—as long as the ride isn't too long. The information below is applicable to short, local trips as well as trips abroad.

INFANT AND CHILD SAFETY SEATS

There are good reasons that safety seats are now a requirement in every state—they save lives. They are designed to keep the baby or small child from being thrown forward during a crash. They also distribute the crash force over the child's body so that no single area takes the full brunt.

Here's the problem: Little kids *must* be strapped in for safety, and little kids *need* to move their bodies. Neither is optional. Here's the solution: Keep the car trip short, and/or keep the breaks frequent.

Buying Car Seats

Used car seats can be risky—are you sure it's never been in a crash? Are the instructions included? Are all the straps in place? Don't accept a seat unless you are sure it meets all codes. If you can, before you buy a particular brand, ask friends with babies who have the same model how they like it.

Here's a bit of scary not-so-trivia: Not all car seats fit all cars! In the Resources Appendix, I list the number for the National Auto Safety Hotline—call them before purchasing a car seat for your car. They can also give you complete installation information.

INFANT SEATS

Infant seats are the law—you won't even be allowed to take your new baby home from the hospital until a nurse verifies that you have an infant seat installed in your car. Infant seats face backwards in a reclining position. They attach with the usual, car-equipped seat belt. Most infant seats can double as baby carriers for the first couple of months, until your kid gets too heavy and your arm feels like it's about to break off. Just undo the seat belt holding the infant seat in place, and *voila*! No need to wake up Baby. There are infant seats with and without bases, seats that turn into strollers, and seats that are round at the bottom and rock.

We had great success with the model we used for Annie as an infant—the rounded bottom enabled us to get through dinner for the first three months. (Remember "The Rocker" in Chapter 4?)

TODDLER SEATS

Once a child grows to 18-20 pounds, he can go into a toddler car seat. Toddler seats face forwards so the child can see out of the windows. They, like infant seats, attach using the car's existing seat belt, and are safest when installed in the middle of the back seat.

Make sure to periodically check the car seat's adjustments to accommodate for your child's growth. Also remember to adjust the straps for different climates. A strap that is snug and reassuring on a sunny autumn day may be tight and binding in winter, with all those extra layers.

BOOSTER SEATS

At four years old *and* 40 pounds, your child can technically leave all that behind, and take their risks like the grown-ups in a regular seat belt. Technically. Legally. But for safety and comfort's sake, you might want to check out the new family of booster seats. These look enough like a regular seat to satisfy most children that they are a "big kid," yet the best ones retain their 5-point harnesses for kids between 30 and 45 pounds, and provide an over-the-collar belt for kids from 45 to 60 pounds.

EMERGENCY/FIRST AID KIT FOR THE CAR

Fill a cardboard or metal box with the following items: A list of emergency phone numbers, some coins, a flashlight, a couple of flares, two diapers, a baggy of diaper wipes, Band-Aids, antiseptic, safety pins, tweezers, children's Tylenol, a thermometer, sunscreen, gauze pads, scissors, washcloth, a small bottle of water. Keep it in the trunk or the back of the car. Forget about it. You'll remember it someday when you need it, and you'll be happy it's there.

Bonus: Transfer this emergency kit into a travel bag for quick getaways!

EATING IN THE CAR

Warning: You're gonna get good at the back-hand back-seat pass maneuver . . .

True meals in the car are not a great idea—you need mealtime to stretch the body. However, it's a good idea to have snacks with you during car travel (go back and review the car snack suggestions in Chapter 4), and it's a *must* to carry water—in sippy cups, baby bottles, or, for the over-three crowd, in small plastic bottles or cups with straws. Avoid juice in the car—it's sticky when it spills (and it *will* spill), and the sugar will get your child wired (you don't want *that* in a confined space) and may even get them thirstier. If you're determined to do juice, try juice boxes. (Check the sugar content—there is a great juice scam going in this country, and sometimes "juice" contains very little juice at all . . .)

Be aware of the dangers of choking. Avoid small hard foods, ice, and anything that could possibly plug a weeny-teeny windpipe. If possible, have an adult sit in the back with the child during munch sessions.

Babies and Air Bags

Babies, children, and airbags don't mix well. In fact, the federal government is currently reviewing the laws on airbags. Rear-facing infant seats are not designed for use with passenger-side airbags **at all**. Baby rides in back. The force at which an airbag is released in an accident can severely injure or kill a small child. **Do not** seat your toddler or child in the front passenger seat of a car with an airbag (not only is this dangerous, it may be illegal in your state.) If you have no choice, be sure that the seat is correctly installed and that the child is properly strapped in.

So how **do** you carry three sleeping children into the apartment when there are only two of you and the only parking place is two blocks away? In theory, it goes like this: The strongest adult gets dropped at the door, and totes the two smallest sleeping kids up the stairs. The other adult finds the parking spot, and totes the remaining snoring child. In reality, unless you have the brawn of Arnold Schwarzenegger, or progeny who sleep like Rip Van Winkle, somebody is going to wake up—usually in a cranky mood—and that one will wake up the others. Oh well, sleep is overrated anyway.

The Case of the Missing Hamburger

It was one of those days—too many errands and I'd forgotten to budget time for lunch. On the horizon loomed the Golden Arches and so, with pangs of P.C. guilt and regret, I pulled into the drive-thru line, ordered a Happy Meal for Annie (Burger, Apple Juice, Toddler Toy) and a Filet O' Fish for me. No sooner had I unwrapped her burger, placed it in her hungry fist, wolfed my own morsel and gotten back on the freeway towards home when three-year-old Annie let loose a mighty wail:

"Mommy, I lost my hamburger!"

With my right hand I felt behind me onto her lap, careening for a moment on the freeway. No burger. I cast a quick glance at the floor. No. The windows had been, and still were, closed.

Annie howled. "I'm hungry! I want my burger!" Finally, I pulled off at the next exit, stopped, and tore the car seat and car apart. Annie's burger was nowhere to be found. Though she denies it to this day, I came to the only conclusion possible: She'd eaten it. Or . . . hamburger-eating fairies protecting her from the evils of fast food? We'll never know for sure.

SOOTHING THE SCREAMING LITTLE BABY . . .

Depending on how adept you are, you can even learn to nurse your baby in a moving car while she is still strapped into her car seat—as a passenger, not a driver, of course (I don't even want to try to visualize *that* picture). If your child is in a rear-facing infant seat, sit in the back seat next to her, and lean forward and over. Try bracing yourself on the front seat. This won't work for long (unless you are a circus contortionist).

. . . THE SCREAMING BIGGER BABY

Talk sweetly, sing, play with him. Offer him a snack. If you need to nurse a child in a forward facing seat, you'll have to be even *more* adept, and some physiques will never be able to accomplish it. Try it a few times when the car isn't moving. Make sure the neighbors can't see—they may think you've gone totally bozo. Believe me, if your family is cruising down the German autobahn at 160 kilometers an hour without an exit in sight with a screaming baby, you'll be glad you figured this trick out, neighbors be damned.

. . . AND THE SCREAMING TODDLER

Sometimes you can reason with them ("Breathe, honey, use your words, I can't understand what you want when you are screaming like that") and sometimes you cannot. Try to change the mood by playing a tape, or by offering a treat. Try ear plugs (just kidding). Try a "stretch break." Then try another one. Some folks stop more often for their *dogs* than their kids (no, I'm not talking about *you!*)

CRUISE WHILE THEY SNOOZE

For driving long distances, try leaving late at night or early in the morning (depending upon your temperament) so you can get in many solid hours of driving while your children blissfully dream of sugar plums, being forced to *share*, or whatever else little ones dream about.

When Bill drove from Oakland to Los Angeles alone with four-year-old Annie, he left at 9:00 p.m. and drove into the night. Annie fell asleep after an excited hour of chatter, and Bill, who usually hits his stride after 10:00 anyway, was free to drive and ponder life in glorious silence.

RENTAL CARS AND CAR SEATS

Most U.S. car-rental companies rent car seats (usually for about $5 a day). You'll need to reserve it in advance, and you probably will need to return the car seat at the same place you picked it up. Ask if any of their rental models have built-in car seats.

Here are some reasons why you should bring your *own* car seat, rather than rent one:

The Booga-Booga Method

This is a method developed by my Aunt Kathie in which the whole family gets out of the car, once an hour on the hour, and runs three times around the car, waving their arms high in the air and screaming, "Booga, booga, booga, booga!"

This method has the added bonus of amusing drowsy fellow motorists, causing them to perk up, and thus preventing any number of accidents caused by sleeping at the wheel.

 If your seat is FAA approved, you can use it on the airplane.

 Familiarity. Babies and little kids get very accustomed to their car seats, and very territorial. In a strange place, familiar items help keep them calm.

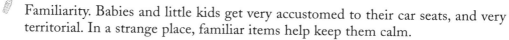

WHAT SIZE CAR SHOULD YOU RENT?	
Advantages of a Smaller Car	*Advantages of a Bigger Car*
If you're traveling with just one child you probably won't need more space.	If you have more than one kid (especially more than one in car seats) you will need the extra room.
You'll save money (rental fees plus gas can add up).	Generally a more comfortable drive.
Parking (in cities) becomes easier.	Power—You don't want to be driving a sewing machine on wheels.
Keeps you from packing—and buying—too much stuff.	You can take as much stuff as you like, and fill the trunk with souvenirs for Dear Aunt Martha.

You'll know it fits your child. Every brand of car seat has a different "fit." When you rent a seat through a car rental, you don't know what you're getting until you get there, and you may not have the choice of changing.

You'll have the option of a one-way rental.

You'll even save some money. Five buckaroos a day starts to add up.

Keep in mind that "rest stops" are not always that restful for the parent. If you've stopped near a stream, you won't be able to simply flop down on your back in the grass and shut your eyes as you would if you were alone, or childless. No, you have to make sure that Petite Petunia isn't throwing herself into the foamy brine, or falling down into the dog doo-doo, or eating that strange looking plant over there. Remember, pace yourself! Stop pushing! It's the journey, not the destination.

KEEPING SUN OUT OF EYES

Sun in the eyes is one of the chief complaints of little kids in the car (even if they can't verbalize it). And who can blame them? You don't like it either.

There are several suction-cup attached window shades on the market, some that pull down and roll up with the snap of a wrist. Check 'em out.

Several infant car seats on the market now come with built-in umbrellas.

Bring extra pillows in the car and rearrange them as needed (best done by the non-driving adult). Extra pillows are also useful for solving sibling squabbles.

Sunglasses and sunhats can help.

Keep a couple of old receiving blankets to drape—close the car window over one end and stretch to the appropriate place. Or sew Velcro strips to an old blanket and attach to the car interior.

Sometimes the combination of car direction and sun position is just *bad* and you may need to combine a couple of solutions.

Boating with Baby

Babies and little kids usually love ferry boats and cruise ships. Perhaps the gentle rocking motion reminds them of the womb . . . .

FABULOUS, FABULOUS FERRIES

Ferry boats are cool. The kids can stretch their legs, the air is wonderfully fresh, and you don't have to do the driving. Ferry boats provide relaxation for the parents and fun and excitement for the kids. Take the usual safety precautions depending on the ferry boat, its size, its setup, and your kid's climbing proclivities (keep them *away* from the railing).

Some children may experience seasickness. See **S** in the Alphappendix for motion sickness advice; if sickness is a pattern (and you use boats regularly), have your pediatrician prescribe medicine.

> The ferry from Swartz Bay on Vancouver Island B.C. to the mainland is great for kids. We crossed on **The Spirit of Vancouver Island**, a tremendous boat that carries 2,000 passengers and 470 vehicles, and offers fancy buffets, a snack bar, and several children's play areas, as well as changing and nursing rooms. Annie and the other kids played wildly all the way across—sliding, climbing—it reminded me again how much children **need** to play. Through the large windows, we enjoyed the view of leaping dolphins. They seem to **need** to play, too.

CRUISE SHIPS

When Annie was 16 months old, Bill's dad took the whole family on a three-day "Carnival" cruise from Los Angeles down to Mexico. Annie spent a lot of time staring at the other nautical vehicles through the porthole window, pointing with a crooked index finger and yelling, "Boat! Boat! Boat!" Our cruise was also memorable for two reasons: It was the first time Annie had her own plate of food in a restaurant, and it rained the entire time (I'd even bought my first post-pregnancy bathing suit for the occasion). Despite the weather, Annie had a great time hanging with her relatives and being entertained by the singing restaurant staff.

Some cruises are definitely not appropriate for babies or little kids—many are marketed primarily to seniors, or have reputations as floating singles bars. Find out as much as you can about the tone of the cruise before you book passage, or contact a family-oriented travel agent for advice.

Riding the Rail—Local Travel

Chug-a-chug-a-chug-a-chug-a-CHOO-CHOO! Everybody loves trains, especially little kids.

SUBWAYS, UNDERGROUNDS, METROS, ELS

Crowded city trains can be a hassle for parents. Be prepared to move *swiftly* through those sliding doors, and be prepared to have to stand.

> The best place to be in the New York subway is the front of the first car. Peering through the front door, you have a great, eerie view as the train careens down the tracks. Fascinating for any toddler or preschooler—or grown-up.

- Make sure you're able to pick up all your belongings and your child at the same time—you won't have the option of loading a little at a time, and you won't have time to practice.

- The loud noise of subways may actually put a small baby to sleep (too much input, and baby tunes out . . .).

- Kids are too little to reach the straps. Have them hold on to you, or to a pole, at all times. Subway cars lurch and come to sudden stops. Your unrestrained child can easily become a flying projectile. This may be hazardous to his and other passengers' health.

- Be extra-careful when moving between train cars. This is where the train hinges together and there are lots of moving, sliding, bending parts where little fingers can get caught and injured. The area between train cars is noisy, too—the booms, clangs, and scraping noises can easily frighten a small child.

Long-Distance Trains

Many people who travel with children consider the "getting there" part to be the worst part of the trip, a nightmare to be gotten through, so they try to minimize the amount of time they spend actually traveling. Train travel is a different approach—part of the joy of the trip is the travel time. Many toddlers become enamored of trains. For them, a trip by train *is* the dream vacation.

Here are some advantages of train travel:

- Train travel is slow-paced and romantic, a wonderful way to truly *see* this, or any other, country.

- Train travel often provides beautiful views and the advantage of being able to relax.

- The kids can stretch their bodies and not be strapped into a seat the entire time.

- Since the adults don't have to focus on the road, they can give more attention to the child.

- There's lots to see, many people to meet, and you can always visit the dining or observation car (again).

- In some countries, trains offer another advantage: safety. There are some countries where I'm *not* about to drive those roads, and where I take my life in my hands every time I get on a bus. I'm not willing to risk Annie's life. Trains are often a good, safer, option.

BRING IT ALL

If you're going by train, tote it all with you. In the U.S., snack food is limited to a selection you may or may not like, and you won't be able to pull over to hit the local convenience store for diapers. In other countries, vendors may work the aisles with terrific food (sweet tamales in Mexico, sticky rice and mangoes in Thailand), but you *still* won't be able to hit the local convenience store for diapers. (The nearest 7-11 will be 5,000 miles away!)

PACK FOR PORTABILITY

Assistance isn't always available. If your destination is not a major station, you may experience a moment of panic as you try to grab all the luggage and your kids and hop off quickly before the whistle blows and the train moves on down the line.

Smaller pieces of luggage are easier to swing up into the luggage bin or stash under your seat. Practice the counting method: Add up the number of people and items ahead of time, and do a rapid count before you embark or disembark. One kid, two suitcases, two adults, a purse, and a diaper bag equals seven—make sure you always reach seven before getting off.

BLANKETS AND PILLOWS

Once you board the train, ask the porter for pillows and blankets, even if you are traveling during the day. The temperature on trains fluctuates. You can also use blankets and pillows to pad the seats—the "fit" may need to be adjusted for young, small bodies (or older, not-so-small bodies—but we won't go into that).

FOOD SERVICE

Find out in advance what kind of food service will be provided. Many trains have snack and/or liquor bars; some have full sit-down dining cars. In this country, long gone are the days of dining cars with heavy pewter plates and a single red rose on each table, but dining cars can still be fun, and the food can be quite tasty. Whatever food service is available, remember to bring lots of your own, especially if you're traveling on a budget.

SLEEPING ARRANGEMENTS

Sleeping in a moving train can be one of the most pleasurable experiences in life. The gentle rocking soothes and deepens sleep—you'll wake up refreshed, and at a new, exciting locale. Babies usually sleep well on trains. If you're traveling with a mate, you might even find an opportunity for a little romance.

Sleeping cars and couchettes are expensive (from a price perspective, it's usually far cheaper to fly or drive). In this country, Amtrak offers family fares—rates are reduced for kids under 15, and kids under two travel free, if on your lap. Consider whether you want your 18-month-old on your lap for two days.

EUROPEAN TRAIN TRAVEL

We've taken trains through Mexico, Thailand, Malaysia, and Java with Bill's kids, and they're usually a great experience—the old-fashioned railway dining, the all-day voyeuristic peek into steamy jungles, drowsing to the coconut vendor's song. The slow, steady pace makes you aware that you are really traversing the earth in a way you cannot experience traveling by air.

Remember that summer abroad in Europe during college? The ragged Eurail pass; the endless swinging movement from country to country; the overnight train rides to save youth-hostel fees; fog-bathed castles on the hills; the time the train from Italy back to France was so crowded that you spent the entire time in the bathroom to get an inch of breathing space? And the people you met—the peasant family from Cantal who fed you the finest bread and cheese of your life; the cute blond guy from Cambridge who kissed you between train cars; the "ugly Americans" who induced you to hold your face in a Parisian kitten pout and speak only in a thick French accent to hide your embarrassment at being "one of *them* . . ."

Going back as a parent will be a different experience—the blond guy may not be making eyes at you from Paris to Lyon, but you can still buy passes good for unlimited rides within a certain time period. (If you're over 26, you'll be paying "adult" rates now). That family from Cantal (and the family from Turin, and the family from Breve) will adopt your baby for the duration and still share their meal with you—and the bread and cheese will be even better because the good will will be even more sincere.

If you do any overnights on the train, resign yourself to spending more money than you did as a student. Rather than trying to tough it out on a seat, consider reserving a first-class bedroom (sleeps two plus a baby) or a couchette (six bunks in a room—good unless your baby cries all night). You can book through a travel agent on this side, or at the train station on that side.

Here are some other tips for European train travel:

- Don't try to pack in too much. Limit your destinations, and plan several days in each place between train trips.

- Make reservations whenever possible to assure yourself seats (that two year old isn't gonna like hanging out in that toilet cubical for eight hours.)

- As with any train travel, you'll need to accomplish the near impossible—packing everything you need for the trip, and packing lightly.

- Food on the train is expensive and unpredictable. Bring your own bread and cheese (and, this time, share some with the family from Cantal . . .).

- Some European trains have special cars geared to family travel. Ask at the station about the Baby or Family car or train.

Ask your travel agent about the pass options: EurailPass, EuroPass, and FlexiPass. Many travel options exist; we once combined a few days' car rental with a FlexiPass on the trains.

Bus Travel

Buses are one of the cheapest travel modes—they can also be one of the most challenging.

> ## Diapering Baby On a Bus?
>
> You may need to change your baby on your lap; just hope for an understanding seat partner. Get your ingredients ready, and do it during a stop, if possible.

LOCAL BUS TRAVEL

Negotiating a city bus with a baby, a stroller, and a bag full of groceries requires some patience—from the bus driver and the other passengers. If you have trouble getting all of you aboard, ask for help from a fellow passenger, or tell the driver you need to make a few trips. Holding the baby, leave the groceries and stroller on the sidewalk, board the bus and pay, then, *holding the baby the entire time, first* get the groceries aboard, *then* grab the stroller. This is a chance to practice your "Bleep 'Em All" attitude—take your time, and assert your right to courtesy. And *never* put the baby down. If somebody says, "I'll hold the baby," politely say, "No thanks, but you could help me by getting this stroller up the stairs . . . "

Another option is the baby backpack, though this probably dooms you to standing the entire time, as swinging a "loaded" baby backpack off your back on a lurching bus might produce tragic results. Better to keep baby on board, brace the shopping bags with your feet, grab a pole, and hang on tight.

LONG-DISTANCE BUS TRAVEL

Long-distance travel on buses can feel frustrating—you know those dreams where you're running and you feel like you're chest-deep in mud? If the bus makes a lot of stops, it can feel like you're going nowhere fast.

Pack everything you need—you won't have access to your luggage until you reach "the other side." Be prepared to hold your baby on your lap the whole time, unless you paid for another seat. If there's room, let the baby or child sit next to the window—this keeps them from escaping down the aisle or falling into the aisle and rolling to the front or the back of the bus. (For some hints on bus travel in developing nations, turn to Chapter 14).

Resources for Disabled Parents—Toting and Traveling

In this country, 10.9 percent of all parenting families have one or more parents with a disability. For families of color, this statistic is even higher, and the number of disabled parents in all populations is growing. If you use a wheelchair, the issue of how to tote your baby and small child may loom large. Traveling becomes more logistically sensitive—not only do you have to carry your baby, but many places locally and worldwide present access problems.

There is no single easy solution for parents who use wheelchairs and who have young children. Each disabled person's abilities and limitations are highly specific, and there are no products currently on the market *specifically* for disabled parents.

However, if you are permanently or temporarily disabled, contact Through the Looking Glass, a national organization for families of adults who have disabilities (see the listing in the Appendix under "Disability Resources"). They publish *Adaptive Parenting Equipment: Idea Book 1*, a book describing and displaying 50 items of equipment and ideas for caring for babies and toddlers ($10 for consumers, $25 for professionals). The items listed focus on ways to carry, hold, and keep kids nearby. Many are helpful for traveling.

day tripper

> *She was a day tripper, a one way ticket, yeah . . .*
> *It took me so long to find out, and I found out.*
>
> —The Beatles

Navigating the Grocery Store—and the City Zoo

The world is filled with things to do, see, and explore. And so many of these things are easy, fun, and cheap. The possibilities are endless. Go on a day trip! Just 'cause you have a baby is no reason to stay home—almost everything you did before you had a child, you can still do now, and there are millions of activities you may not have thought of in *years*.

This chapter focuses on small, daily activities and adventures away from the house or hotel, and the adjustments you should make on account of Baby. We start with the most common (and dreaded) form of day trip—the errand. Too much to do and you've got the baby, too? You can successfully lug your little one with you and have a good time doing it. Then it's on to the cafe, the zoo, the farm, and beyond! (For nature-based activities, see Chapter 11.)

Here's what's included:

- The Joy of Running Errands
- Hanging Out
- Urban Activities and Entertainment
- "Parking" It
- Zoos and Natural History Museums
- The Littlest Culture Vulture
- Rural Activities
- Sporting Events
- High Energy Activities
- Nightlife?
- Kids in Retirement Communities and Nursing Homes

For the World Weary . . .

It's been said that there are no geographical solutions, that problems follow you wherever you go, and that—for better or worse—wherever you go, there you are. I've got news—for a cranky, bored child and a cranky, bored parent, there may be no geographical solutions, but there **are remissions**. Getting out and going somewhere, just for the day, can entirely change your frame of mind.

The Joy of Running Errands

Kids like running errands, especially if you establish a ritual: "First we go to the bank, then we stop at the bakery and get bread and a few samples. We always stop at the post office and the Flower Lady before we go home." Rituals provide security. And don't squeeze in too many. Always keep in mind your child's personal Errand-to-Play Ratio: the exact number of errands allowed before complete baby meltdown occurs. Some babies and toddlers have a limit of two, some three, some can go all day. You'll know.

THE SUPERMARKET

The supermarket can be fun, or a trip through a chamber of horror. When you and Baby are fresh, there's a lot to see, Baby is sitting up high near you so she's happy, and you're getting things done. And other times . . . well, supermarkets are *the* classic place for toddlers to throw tantrums, and for parents to completely lose their cool. (For more details and tips on tantrums, see **T** in the Alphappendix.)

"SAFEWAY'S GOT COOKIES, BILLY, IF YOU'RE A GOOD BOY."

Oh, Mama, can you bribe your way through a supermarket—the key is to avoid having to do it every time.

> Keeping your kid occupied with a snack is not necessarily a bad idea. Avoid the candy and chips by opening a bag of crackers or raisins and allowing your child to munch (saving the wrapper, of course, so you can pay for it.)

> Figure out how you want to deal with shopkeepers who hand your child goodies or food. Although, in general, you don't want your child to accept food from strangers, store samples are not always a bad thing. (I still fondly remember the butcher at my neighborhood market, gruffly handing out slices of bologna to children when I was growing up. He didn't make a fuss or ask for the things grown-ups usually want in return for a gift—a smile, or a thank-you. Because he was undemanding, we loved him.)

SHOPPING CART/CAR SEAT COMPATIBILITY FACTORS

Infant car seats fit in the top of most shopping carts. Some supermarkets provide carts fitted with vinyl infant seats. Make sure all the straps are there, and *use* them. It's a long way down to that hard, cold floor. When Baby can sit up, she can ride in the front of the cart, facing you. Carry an old belt in your diaper bag and strap her in. If she's still wobbly, prop her up with sweaters—don't let her droop into the lettuce.

World-Wide Markets

As far as I'm concerned, food shopping around the world is one of the finest forms of family entertainment. Once experienced, who could ever forget the baskets of spiky red rambutan in the Chiang Mai, Thailand night market? The delicate samples of salmon roe and green tea in the Tokyo basement supermarkets? The pungence and colors of the Mercado Libertad in Guadalajara? The haricot verts that Bill practically cried over for lack of a stove in Paris?

Recently I was in Berkeley Bowl, our local market, watching a patient yet exasperated mother try to shop with her wild two-year-old boy. He was in the back of the basket dancing—no sitting down for this child. Every item she placed in the basket was either chewed or stomped on, so she finally solved the problem by handing Sonny a bagel and putting all the groceries underneath the basket on the rack usually reserved for laundry detergent and 10-pound sacks of potatoes.

SHOPPING WITH A STROLLER

Sometimes you'll shop with a stroller. In this case, you'll need to do one of the following:

- You may be able to balance a hand basket on top of the hood of a standard stroller.

- Fold the stroller, place it on the bottom rack of the shopping cart, and put Baby in the front basket.

- Fill a shopping cart, dragging Baby and stroller behind.

Remember that you have to wheel the stroller while carrying groceries. Have them double-bagged in plastic. (I know, I usually ask for paper, too.) Hang the bags over the handles and make tracks.

Warning: If you pick up Baby with bags hanging on the handles, the back-heavy stroller will fly dramatically backwards and smash your eggs. If the bags are *too* heavy, the stroller will fly over backwards with Baby inside!

Special Note: A longtime "child watcher" told me that one of the primary risks of gym child-watch services is the potential of infection from sick children—that is, children too ill to be in daycare or school but well enough to be out and about with a bored parent who is tired of being cooped up and runs in to use the gym for an hour.

BABY AT THE GYM

Many gyms have on-site child-watch services. Baby plays while you sweat. Please note the semantic difference between child *watch* and child *care*: Child watch doesn't change diapers, feed your child, or do much at all besides watch the kids play. If there are altercations between kids, the child-watch person may or may not handle the situation effectively.

When checking out the gym, make sure to find out if the child-watch providers have regular schedules (or if the center is staffed by bored aerobics teachers between classes), and try to meet the "regular" person who will be there at the times you plan to exercise. Always tell the child watcher where in the gym you plan to be in case your child gets distressed. If you're taking a class (usually an hour long), plan to hurry on both sides the first few times—come in your exercise clothes and take a quick shower afterwards. Later, once you see how your baby does, you can soak in the Jacuzzi, hang out by the muscle men, or give yourself a facial.

BABY AT THE DOCTOR (YOURS)

Sometimes you just have to drag li'l darlin' along. Though you'd no doubt like privacy during your doctor visits, the day may come when you don't have child care and you urgently need to be seen. Remember that to your kid, you are Everything, The World, Immortal, and that your being sick or in pain can be a terrifying experience. Besides your attempts to be reassuring, you can do something else—be entertaining. Bring toys, books, coloring supplies (if age-appropriate), and non-messy snacks. With toddlers and preschoolers, you can talk about the doctor's tools. Maybe little Jenny can even *help* Dr. Matthews hold the stethoscope (check this out with Dr. Matthews, first).

BABY AT THE DENTIST (YOURS)

A mobile baby can be challenging at the dentist. Ask the staff in advance if it is appropriate to bring your baby or toddler with you. Some family dentists suggest bringing the children in even before it's *their turn,* to familiarize them with the strange and potentially scary equipment. A non-mobile baby or an easily distracted child can sit or recline with you while you have your teeth cleaned—if the dentist or hygienist is amenable. If you *know* none of this will work for your child, beg, borrow, or steal a baby-sitter and pretend that you are getting a massage or a special treat. You are, at least, taking care of your body.

Hanging Out

The fine art of hanging out is deeply under-appreciated, but much of what adults do with babies and small children comes under this category. These years fly swiftly by. Appreciate the opportunity. You may never get this chance again!

THE MALL

Mall hanging doesn't always require shopping—many malls are also entertainment centers, good in good weather or bad. When the playground is soggy or frozen, the mall may provide a good place to stretch little legs (but be aware that the floors may be hard and slippery). Some malls even have ice rinks. (Some rinks rent skates as small as size six, for toddlers. Call to find out before setting up little expectations.) Food courts provide food to please all palates, ranging from "junk" to "healthy." If you're mall-crazy, there is a mall to end all malls in Edmonton, Canada. There—practically at the North Pole—you can shop, eat, skate, browse, people-watch, and, if you bring your swimsuit, indulge in the water slides and gigantic wave pool in the basement.

THE LIBRARY

The public library is too often underrated or forgotten as a great place to hang out with kids. Some parents are nervous about taking their kids to a library because they're incapable of keeping voices to a whisper. Don't fret—most public libraries are set up with separate children's rooms. While it's *not* all right to act out and scream, children's librarians understand children, and are happy to help them learn appropriate library behavior as well as find wonderful books. Visiting libraries on a regular basis helps introduce kids to the joy of books and reading. It's never too early to do that. (Also see "Story Hour," later in this chapter.)

CAFE CULTURE

Paris, Rome, Vienna, New York, San Francisco . . . hell, nowadays *every* university town is filled with coffeehouses and cafes. Long before I became a harried, multitasking mother, I used to be cool. I was an art student with pink streaks in my hair. I wore black and sat in Parisian cafes sipping espresso and smoking unfiltered cigarettes as I wrote long journal entries about men, love, and angst.

I still love cafes and cafe culture, though sometimes I think I've forgotten how to truly "hang out" . . . renting a table by the hour with a cup of bottomless coffee or a slowly sipped latté, staring at cute guys, and dreaming of the future. Now I glare at smokers, I tend towards decaf in the afternoon, and it's hard to fantasize about men with dark, soulful eyes when your right shoulder is covered with white goo—the remains of Baby's burp.

But as I learned early in Annie's life, you *can* have it all! Kids are natural hanger-outers. You, too, can be a cafe parent, and your child can be the Cappuccino Kid—cool before her time, ready for adventure, ready for the world.

Here are tips on choosing a baby-friendly cafe:

- Listen to the music: If the atmosphere is too "classical" or the hip-hop is too loud, try somewhere else. My ideal musical choices are jazz, blues, swing, eclectic rock, or eclectic anything else.

- Highchairs or booster seats are bonuses, but not a requirement. Your kid can sit in the stroller, eating a snack. In our area, most cafes serve Madeleine cookies, soft vanilla sticks just the right size for grasping in a toddler's hands. (For the more organic among you, try the Oat Cakes.) Shake out the stroller before you put it back in the car or house.

- A too-crowded cafe means you have to get in and get out. Avoid peak hours—people getting their morning caffeine fix or trying to pull out of their afternoon slump. You wanna be able to *hang* at that table without being subjected to the vulture-like gazes of table-less customers, clutching hot cups of espresso.

- A too-empty cafe means boredom for Baby. Might as well stay home and stick the tea kettle on the stove. The idea is people-watching. Baby is fascinated by the parade of people and the sound of the espresso machine and milk steamer. Baby is not fascinated by the dull sight of Daddy trying to read a newspaper for once in his life. (Exception: You're on a stroll, and Baby goes down for a nap. *Now* you can park at a cafe and catch up on Dear Abby.)

🍼 Avoid square tables. André will automatically want to go round-and-round-the-mulberry-bush, and square or rectangular tables with corners are dangerous. You're here to relax, to *haaaannng* out. Search for round, or at least rounded, tables.

🍼 Look for places to play. Cafes that are truly serious about being kid-friendly provide a small play area or (for the older-than-baby set) kids books near the communal newspapers, or crayons and paper at the counter.

🍼 Check out the lighting. Some cafes have great overhead light fixtures that Baby can fixate on while you practice your Poet's Pout.

🍼 The best places (and this might be your funkiest corner cafe) provide, on request, "baby foam," an inch or two of milk foam free for your child. The correct way to ask for baby foam is to add to your own coffee order the semi-apologetic request, "May we also have just a little bit of foam in a cup for the baby?" Beware the barista who asks, "Will that be a large or a small steamed milk?" You don't want steamed milk—you don't want to pay for it, your kid won't drink it all anyway, and it's a production that often involves too-hot milk and lots of spilling. You want an inch of foam in a cup. (Unless you do want steamed milk, in which case, order it!) A truly classy establishment will give your two year old an inch or two of foam in a demitasse cup and saucer with a tiny demitasse spoon. Watch those eyes grow wide.

🍼 And finally, the cafe should be smoke-free. Finding one in this country shouldn't be too difficult, but you may run into trouble when traveling abroad. It may not be possible to completely eradicate second-hand smoke from your child's environment, but at the least choose a well-ventilated spot by a window or door.

Urban Activities and Entertainment

Check the local periodicals; there are lots of organized activities and entertaining events for kids.

CONCERTS AND THEATER FOR KIDS

One of most thrilling moments of my childhood was being taken backstage at a Pete Seeger concert to meet the great man himself. Annie is growing up on the music of Pete Seeger, Gary Lapow, Ruth Pelham, Tim Cain, Julie Olsen Edwards, and other wonderful musicians who play music that children enjoy. There are many musicians, puppeteers, clowns, and acting troupes who specialize in entertaining kids. You'll find performances listed in newspapers, baby shops, bulletin boards, and so on. The best children's performers engage the children and get them standing, clapping, and singing. Your toddler or preschooler may want to run around; restrain her gently (even if other parents aren't as attentive) and draw her focus back to the stage—too much activity is impolite to the performer and other audience members.

Sometimes theatrical performances and concerts can be overwhelming to a little one. That doesn't mean don't go—gentle, short-term exposure to crowds will get her acclimated.

STORY HOUR

Many libraries and some bookstores offer regular story hours for babies, toddlers, and preschoolers. These can be wonderful experiences for both young children and their parents.

- Most story hours last less than an hour—attention spans are short.

- Some story hours incorporate music and may end with stickers or pictures to take home and color.

- If you go often enough, you'll build a regular relationship with other kids and parents who also value the written and spoken word.

GOING TO THE MOVIES

We love going to the movies wherever we are. It's inevitably a cultural experience. In Thailand, before the movie, the entire audience stands and sings the national anthem (written by the king) as a movie clip of the king saluting is shown. You wouldn't see that here! Going to the movies is not a foolproof adventure—judge your child's development before you decide to worship before the silver screen. Things to keep in mind:

- Make sure the movie is appropriate for your child. Very few are—even PG-rated films can terrify little kids. Child-care staffs see a marked increase in "acting-out" behavior (pun intended) every time a new adventure film hits town.

🍼 Some brave parents take their infants to grown-up movies. Depending upon your particular little baby, this may, or may not be a successful outing. The intense auditory sensory input puts some infants to sleep, and makes others scream.

🍼 Some theaters have nursing rooms. Call in advance to find out about facilities.

"Parking" It

Strolling on the promenade, visiting the arboretum, rowing on the duck pond, feeding carrots to the buffaloes, flipping a Frisbee, visiting the horse stables, zooming through the zoo . . . . Parks and outdoor recreation areas everywhere are fun, energizing, and restful for every member of the family.

PLAYGROUNDS: A CULTURAL OPPORTUNITY

Playgrounds provide the basics—a place to run, a place to dig, and something to climb or slide on. Babies and small children need the outdoors everyday. And for the adults, part of having a child is enjoying the life of a child again—guilt free. Playing in the sand with your two-year-old son, you can simply enjoy the sensations of the sun, son, and sand. There is nowhere else you have to be.

Playgrounds also provide an opportunity to meet people. One of the surprises of becoming a mom was my new ability to meet women my own age. When I traveled alone or with Bill, we'd meet lots of men (many of them in the tourist industry)—but where were the women? As a relatively late-starter (almost 32 when Annie was born), I guess they were off with their babies, not accessible to travelers or tourists. (If I'd known then what I know now, I would have gone to the playground and admired babies.) On the cultural level, when you're involved in child-rearing, the child-rearing of other cultures and subcultures becomes fascinating. What better place to see child-rearing practices than a playground?

Playground Survival Skills

🍼 Lots of babies like to eat sand. Our little friend Shoshana had a particular passion for the substance. Is it the texture? Is it the flavor? (Since I haven't tasted sandbox sand myself in thirty-odd years, I can't explain the appeal.) Stop your baby from indulging. A little clean sand probably won't harm a child—but most sand is not clean, and some sandboxes can be terribly contaminated.

🍼 Old kitchen utensils make good, inexpensive sand toys. Consider strainers, ladles, plus the ubiquitous plastic yogurt containers. Bring a few to share; your kid may get to play with other things, too. In most playgrounds, kids are pretty generous.

🍼 Balls and other age-appropriate sports equipment are also good things to bring to a playground. Some kids develop the ability to throw and catch balls at an amazingly early age. Others are slower. Much basic sports ability is based on years of exposure and practice.

In addition, in any playground, home or away from home, you will find people with whom you have something very basic in common—you both have kids. It's easy to strike up conversations, and a good way to beat parental isolation.

One of our favorite nature museums in the world is the Biodome in Montreal, Canada. Visitors walk through four "environments," complete with climate, plant, and wildlife changes. We learn best through visceral experience. How better to teach your two year old about a tropical rain forest than to walk through the double-glass doors into hot, wet air echoing with the sounds of parrots flying overhead? (I **can** think of another way—Thailand, Mexico, Maui . . .)

Zoos and Natural History Museums

Zoos and Natural History Museums are fun for all, and they have the added bonus of exciting your little ones about science and nature early on.

MEMBERSHIPS

Natural history museums and zoos are designed with families in mind, and often offer yearly memberships. If you like zoos or museums, and think you might go more than three times in a particular year (a year is a long time!), consider a family membership. The initial outlay may be expensive (and may feel hard for parents on a budget), but if the museum or zoo is reasonably local, you may save a lot of money in the long run.

- Membership enables you to take it slow, not make it a chore. It's counterproductive to have your kid identify museums with what I call "museum feet," the fatigue that makes your feet feel as swollen as your thighs, and makes you feel liiike yoou aaaare mooooving innnnn ssslowww mmmotion. I get that feeling when the morning hit of caffeine has worn off—or I've been in a museum with hard floors and too much visual stimulation.

- Memberships also allow you to be casual about visiting. With entrance fees as high as they are, there is a tendency to try to get your "money's worth." With a membership, go for an hour, go for a single exhibit, go visit the ducks. Then move on. Incorporate it into your life.

- Many museums and zoos have reciprocity with other facilities across the nation, so when you travel (as you're gonna do, right?), you'll be able to stop by the local zoo or museum and get in free! (Free is good.)

ZOOS AND ZOO ETIQUETTE

People have mixed feelings about zoos. Are they freak shows of strange animals for kids to gawk at, or educational centers? The answer depends largely upon the zoo itself. Good zoos are active players in the environmental movement and active centers of scientific research, stressing respect for their inhabitants. Here are some tips for navigating through the zoo.

- Stay on the path.

- Don't touch the animals—they bite, and some carry diseases.

- Never feed the animals. You'd be surprised how many people ignore signs and throw candy, peanuts, and popcorn to wild animals. It can make them very ill.

- Have respect. Be considerate of their ears. Yelling and tapping on the cage is cruel—and it sends a bad message to your kids.

- Try the "off" hours—mornings, weekdays. On foggy, slightly rainy days, the animals are active and the people are few. A visit to a quiet zoo when the animals are awake and active is far more gratifying than a visit when thousands of families are crowding around the lion's den.

- Be prepared for changes in weather. Try the layered look, and bring hats for sun and cold. Always tote along the sunscreen (get the "dirt" on the sun in Chapter 11).

- You'll be doing a lot of walking, and toddler legs may give out early (usually in front of the second animal enclosure). Bring a stroller. Even if you don't use it for your kid, you can use it to push the day pack, extra sweaters, and any souvenirs you give in and pony up for. Some zoos rent strollers—call in advance.

PETTING ZOOS AND CHILDREN'S ZOOS

Most zoos have petting zoos, though they can also be found in city parks, at country fairs, and so on. Goats, sheep, rabbits, guinea pigs, chickens, and pigs are often featured. Sometimes animal food is available for a small fee. What charms can also chasten—goats are gentle animals, but their insistence on crunching and gobbling the pellets a little one clutches in her hand can be intimidating. Be prepared to carry your child. For the first visit, you might want to observe, rather than feed. Then practice at home, offering food from a *flat* hand. First you offer and Baby nibbles, then *he* offers and *you* nibble.

> Babies love babies. At the Beacon Hill Park petting zoo in Victoria, B.C., baby goats scampered, rabbits hopped, guinea pigs squealed, peacocks paraded, and an 11-day-old pot-bellied pig nursed from her mommy. Annie spent a lot of time brushing the baby goats.

The Littlest Culture Vulture

Values and a sense of "culture" are instilled early in our children. Part of your task as a parent is to expose your child to some of life's highlights—remember that just because activities are

"Hungry, Little Michaelangelo?"

Art-going is hungry work. Once the head has been fed, you might want to feed the stomach. Museum cafes often serve inexpensive, excellent food in a "family-friendly" atmosphere. Replenish!

"cultural" doesn't mean they aren't fun. Taking your kids to museums from the beginning helps incorporate art into everyday life, and ensures that they won't single it out as something separate from normal life.

Art museums can be boring for small children, so I'm talking moderation here, not a steady diet of Mattisse, Rembrandt, or Picasso. Ethnic art museums can give children a sense of family and world history. Call ahead and see if they have resources for kids, and check stroller/backpack policy (see Chapter 6). There are even museums that focus specifically on children's art, and often have activities and projects geared for young visitors.

Town Clerks in Small Towns

Want to know the skinny on the small town you're visiting? Call the town clerk's office. In rural America, the local town clerk can often provide regional information—what to do, where to go, historical facts, road conditions, gossip.

The town clerk is often elected by community members and is usually someone who has been in the area forever, often a native, sometimes an older, garrulous person who can trace their own history in the area back for generations. Everything that happens is officially noted here—births, marriages, deaths. It's where people pay their taxes and vote. Often the small office is connected to the post office. Look for "Town Clerk" in the phone book under Government Offices. The number listed is often a home phone number.

Rural Activities

My sister Jessica and her family live in Central Vermont, in a renovated barn up a dirt road seven miles from the center of Plainfield, population 1,301. What a far cry from our urban, Bay-Area existence in Oakland, California! Yet when we visit, our days are filled with activity. Here are some suggestions for rural day trips. Adjust for your locale and season.

- Drive around looking for cows. Don't laugh—it's fun! When you find a pasture of cows, pull over and practice mooing over the fence at them. They may even moo back. Be polite. Do *not* refer to the pasture as a steak orchard.

- Call a farm ahead of time and ask if you can visit a small dairy farm in action. Even two year olds are fascinated by the sight of cows being milked. Look in the Yellow Pages under "Dairy Farm" or call the town clerk (see the upcoming sidebar).

- Visit a "Pick-Your-Own" farm—pumpkins at a pumpkin farm, apples from an apple orchard, baskets of juicy, ripe raspberries.

- Visit the local waterhole. Is there a wide bend in the river, an old quarry, a beaver pond where the locals swim?

- Even toddlers love to visit rural Farmers Markets (particularly fabulous in European countries). There are usually free samples, delicious baked goods, and sometimes a local entertainer.

- General stores have everything—forget snow boots? Need a hat? A leg of mutton?

- And—particular to New England winters—visit the local maple-sugaring house for sugar on snow.

LIBRARIES IN SMALL TOWNS

Libraries can be lifesavers, especially if you're visiting a small town. Once you've walked Main Street three times, hung out in the cafe, and imitated bulls in the local china shop, what is there to do? Hit the library. You won't be able to take out books, but you can sit in the kids section and read to your baby in a quiet voice. No matter how limited the selection, there will be more than enough for one day's entertainment. Libraries provide a good opportunity to slow down.

Sporting Events

Attending baseball, football, basketball, hockey, and other professional sports is an American tradition. Can you take a baby or little kid? Sure! (Will they appreciate it? Maybe.)

> We brought Annie to a baseball game when she was in utero—every time the crowd cheered, she thumped inside me in perfect rhythm to the hand claps.

- Infants are easy to care for at a ball game, though the noise factor might be a bit much. Imagine 60,000 people screaming at a high-scoring football game. Imagine your baby there.

- Once a baby can crawl, trapping him (and you) in the small space of a few seats with steps and concrete flooring is *not* a great idea.

> My cousin Karl regularly brings little Mark to Candlestick Park to watch the Giants play. Mark enjoys the game, Karl says, as long as he's fed often enough. They have a rule in the family—Mark has to eat a hot dog before he can have any ice cream. Mark doesn't understand the Rules of Baseball yet, but he sure knows the Rules of Ice Cream.

- For football, basketball, and other sports where the seats cost a fortune, take the babe-in-arms but don't throw your money away on a seat for a toddler.

- Three or four year olds have a short attention span, but are usually good for a couple of hours at a baseball game, as long as you keep the goodies coming. Be ready and willing to spend time wandering around the stadium.

🍼 You're in luck if your team doesn't draw big crowds—it's easier to wander around with a restless kid if you aren't constantly tripping over and bugging people.

🍼 Some stadiums and coliseums have a "game room" for kids, complete with video games and TV monitors broadcasting the game on the field below. But as my friend Dave says, "What's the point of spending all the money and hassle of going to the game? We could stay *home* and watch the show on TV!"

High-Energy Activities

Life isn't—and shouldn't always be— like a calm, serene Summer day. Sometimes the wind is gonna come and shake things up! The world is filled with high-energy family activities. Be aware, but be there!

ACTIVITY CENTERS

WOW! ZOWIE! CRAASH! BANG! BOOM! Indoor, high-tech activity centers are better for older kids than the toddler set, though many of them have small areas set aside for the little ones. Babies and infants may feel completely overwhelmed. Activity centers are good for bad weather, decent for birthday parties, and usually fairly inexpensive. If you join your child in the shoe-less zone, be prepared to feel like a mouse in a maze. Bins of balls to jump in, ropes to swing on, mazes to maneuver in, tubes to tunnel through—yes, the place will exhaust your kid, but be prepared: your child will nap, but so will you.

AMUSEMENT PARKS—THE PROS AND CONS

When should you start taking your children to amusement parks? Consider the pros and cons below:

The Pros:

🍼 **It's fun designed by pros.** Professional fun often has a compelling, frantic pace that will rev up and excite every member of the family. Fun is fun! Amusement parks, theme parks, and water slides can all be thrilling, engaging, and give a pure sense of escapism.

🍼 **All-in-one entertainment:** You don't need to leave the facility to find food or a bathroom. The large amusement parks supply everything from pet kennels to aspirin.

🍼 **Great people watching!** The crowds at amusement parks are usually multi-racial, of all ages, and kid-friendly!

Everybody's happy! There's usually something for every member of the family to enjoy.

The Cons:

They're expensive. Surviving a trip to consumerist America with at least a portion of your wallet intact is sometimes a tricky proposition. If you can pack in your own food and limit the number or cost of souvenirs, you may be able to escape with a few solitary bucks.

> Try to eat **before** you hit the amusement park. Some parks prohibit bringing in your own food—but they won't search your pockets for the spare apple, package of nuts, or fruit roll-up. Food for sale is usually fun—but full of sugar. Try to balance your child's intake with something reasonably healthy—their energy level, and yours, is less likely to spike and then wane.

Dazed and confused: Though you may be eager to relive your childhood and your love of Mickey Mouse, consider your child's age before flinging yourself into the exhausting proposition of a theme park where nothing and nobody stops, where the noise and crowds and larger-than-life figures and garish colors can overwhelm a sensitive little one.

Size matters: Many rides have height limits; for children small for their age, this proposes a particular problem. If she can't go, you can't go. Solution: Bring another adult and alternate turns.

FEAR. Rides are often geared to be scary—and it's that intersection between fear and fun that grown-ups love, isn't it? Kids don't always understand how to process those emotions. Don't denigrate his fear by saying, "There's nothing to be scared of." If your child is likely to be terrified of the ride (the mechanical aspect) or the special effects, go slow. Test the waters on something tamer. Time will pass.

Nightlife?

Remember the happy-go-lucky parents in Chapter 2? They're the ones who try to incorporate their children into their own lives as much as possible. If these parents go out on the town, they'll often bring their kids along, too. These are the babies you'll see riding on their parents' shoulders at night-time carnivals, or carried to the movies in slings.

Other parents feel that schedules are more important, and have babies and toddlers who go to bed early. If these parents get out, it is only with the services of a baby-sitter. Everybody has different styles.

Since Annie is a "night owl" by nature, she does well when we take her out at night. Since I am a "morning dove," I often do not. Here are some ideas for evening prowls with a baby, at home or abroad:

BOOKSTORES

Bookstores are particularly great on a rainy evening when everybody has been cooped up all day. More and more, bookstores are staying open late to catch the evening crowds. Some incorporate cafes. More sponsor readings or author appearances. We'll sometimes head to a bookstore where I'll attend a reading (not appropriate for a baby or a chatterbox of a kid) while Bill and Annie hang out in the children's book area. Then we'll all indulge in a little sweet something-or-other at a cafe.

Like Father, Like Grandfather

From the time Annie was a little baby, my dad has taken her on early-evening strolls down College Avenue in Oakland, our local trendy commercial strip featuring cafés, restaurants, bookstores, and charming boutiques. They have their usual route: They stop at the pizza maker to watch him toss the dough. If it's early enough, Mr. John's, the dog groomer, is still open, and they go in to watch the furry proceedings. They stop to read a book or two at DIESEL, a bookstore, or further down at Pendragon Books, which has the added panache of the shop cat, Cookie.

The regularity and ritual of these walks brings fond memories of being a small child myself, clutching my dad's pinkie or riding on his shoulders down to Cliff's Hardware in San Francisco for penny candy, or burying my face in his hair in intrigued terror at the sight of Laughing Sal, a huge, roaring mannequin at now-decades-gone Playland-by-the-Beach.

THE EVENING STROLL

Anywhere—near your house after dinner to stretch your legs, downtown, or down near the Bay, getting fresh air in the evening helps to calm that inevitable last burst of energy that spikes up before bath and bedtime.

Kids in Retirement Communities and Nursing Homes

Babies and children should be incorporated into the rhythms of life, and those rhythms include aging and dying. Given the right approach and locale, babies and toddlers usually get along very well with the elderly, who in turn, are delighted and moved by the beauty and fun of new life.

Be sensible about it—children should not be exposed to an adult in extreme pain. There is also a big difference between retirement communities, where relatively healthy older people live independently, and nursing homes, where residents are often ill, in pain, bedridden, or close to dying. And consider the physical layout. Some locales are not appropriate for little ones. A crawling baby in a room with bedpans on the floor is not a good idea.

If you decide that the locale and your older relative's condition are appropriate for a visit, be sensitive to any fears or reactions your child might have—odd smells, wheelchair contraptions, and so forth can be scary.

Developmentally, children at around four and five become interested in—and sometimes frightened of—death and dying. Depending upon your responses, a visit with an ailing great-grandparent might terrify them. But don't keep away just because your child *might* be scared. Listen to, talk with, and hold your child, and allow him to get to know his family.

Some retirement communities have small rooms available for family reunions. It might be worthwhile to reserve one if you're bringing a little one along. Older people can sometimes become agitated by little ones playing with their belongings, and baby-proofing could be quite difficult.

The Cult of the New

Before they made the flight from Vermont out to California to see the family, Jessica introduced the subject to Emma. "We're going to meet your Great-Grandma Dolly. It's going to be her 95th birthday. That means she's a very, very old lady."

Emma looked seriously at her mother. "Do we need to throw her away?"

chapter

8

tote that barge, lift that bale: packing for Europe (or the grocery store)

> *What's the use of worrying?*
> *It never was worthwhile,*
> *So, pack up your troubles in your old kit-bag*
> *And smile, smile, smile.*
>
> —George Asaf

Packing Up Your Troubles

When you have a young child, even getting out of the house for the afternoon can feel daunting. So much to remember, so much to carry, so little time. I know parents who refuse to travel just because they don't want to pack! Relax. Once you get organized, packing for the zoo or a longer trip will be a snap.

This chapter gives guidelines and suggestions for what gear to take, wherever you are going. It includes:

- The Perfect Day Pack
- Luggage for the Longer Trip
- Ericka's Seven-Step Planning System
- So . . . What Should You Bring?
- And Don't Stress

The Perfect Day Pack

Your basic piece of equipment for daily adventuring is the day pack. Do you remember Mary Poppins' magical bag? In the movie, it's a large, ordinary-looking purse that somehow magically contains everything she could possibly need including a full-length coat rack and a mirror. Can anybody tell me where to get one of those? Short of that, for around town, your day pack can be a large diaper bag or light back pack—filled with the normal motley assortment of gear (see below). For hikes and beaches and trips to the zoo, consider a more heavy duty pack with bottom straps. We try to keep our day pack partially ready to go, adding last-minute items and food right before we whisk ourselves out the door.

WHAT'S IN THE DAY PACK?

What should go in it? Here are some suggestions (modify for your circumstances):

- Essential documents (if in a foreign land, your passport and papers). Documents should include a note card of emergency information—biographical/medical sketch of child.
- Money, wallet, camera, and film
- At *least* one change of clothing per child
- Four to six diapers, if applicable, or an extra pair of underpants
- Portable wipes (commercial or moistened terry cloth—see Chapter 3)
- Tissue and/or a roll of toilet paper
- Plastic bags
- Medications as required. Consider a first-aid kit (see the Appendix).

- Sippy cup or drink bottle (for a half-day trip, you can pre-mix baby formula and store in a thermos).

- Plastic (Tupperware) container of rice cakes, crackers, Goldfish, or other non-perishable snacks (see the suggestions in Chapter 4)

- Pocket knife

- Spare set of house keys

- Small toys for emergency entertainment (spare keys can double)

- Thin paperback children's book(s)

- Sun hat

- Sunscreen—15 spf or higher (sunscreen information is in Chapter 11)

- Something warm to wear (sweater, jacket)

- Old receiving blanket (for nursing privacy, changing diapers, impromptu picnics, or instant shade)

Crossing Borders?

Yes, even your eeny-beeny infant needs her own passport. Children's passports are good for five years. I agree there **is** something ludicrous about trying to identify a four year old from a photo taken when she was three months old. Even sillier is trying to fill out the application, gazing into those cloudy newborn eyes to discern what color they will be. Blue? Green? Brown? (For Annie, we guessed gray—they ended up hazel.) For information on how to get your child (or yourself) a passport, see Overseas Travel Resources in the Recommended Readings appendix.

Luggage for the Longer Trip

Your requirements will vary depending on number of adults, number of children, destination, planned activities, and length of stay. Bill, Annie, and I usually share one big and one medium-sized suitcase. Plus, we carry an assortment of carry-ons—at least one per person (including Annie). Make sure you can lift it all, and the kid, in one swoop. The time may come when you'll have to.

PUT 'EM TO WORK YOUNG

Children love to be involved, and involving them in the packing process helps you gain "buy in" for the trip. Toddlers and older children can carry (or load

Sturdy As She Goes

For a trip to the Pacific Northwest, Annie, almost three, spent two days loading and unloading her tiny carry-on suitcase. A wide variety of items were selected and discarded before she settled (with our encouragement) on very sensible choices: a sweater, a small spinning top, two books, a brush, a comb, a tube of sunscreen, a sun hat, an extra diaper, and her stuffed Kitty and Pooh Bear.

The suitcase had a loose clasp with a habit of opening and causing Annie's prized possessions to tumble out. (Get a

(continued)

sturdy one.) Bill and I lived in terror that her two favorite stuffed animals would be lost, so Annie's suitcase became the first thing we grabbed each time we made a move from airplane to car to motel to car.

Annie took her job seriously, enjoyed her responsibility, became distressed whenever she didn't know where her suitcase was, and staggered through the Seattle-Tacoma airport dragging it behind her along the floor, yelling, "It's not too heavy! It's not too heavy!" until we rescued them both and praised her for a job well done.

How To Pack Light

Ah ha ha ha ha ha ha ha ha ha ha! OK, I'm done laughing now.

and unload) their own little tote bags. Start your child with the idea a couple of days before you go, and let her (with your gentle suggestions and veto power) choose what to bring.

If you have more than one child, the older one can help pack for the baby. Make sure to review and edit all suggestions.

Ericka's Seven-Step Planning System

Organization is not always my strong point. I tend to be of the grab-and-run school of parenting ("What, you're hungry? Oh. Let's see, are there any cafes around?"), but for a trip, I *rely* on advance planning to smooth the way. It took me a few trips to develop this comfortable planning-and-packing system.

1. The week before departure, I carry around a yellow pad to jot down a list of items "To Bring."

2. When making the To-Bring list, I consider various possible weather scenarios and social situations.

3. As To-Bring things get collected or bought and piled amidst the general chaos on the couch and living room floor, I put a check mark next to the item on the To-Bring list.

4. On the same pad I create a separate To-Do list (cancel diaper service, water plants, do neglected laundry, notify day-care provider, stop paper, change answering machine message, call neighbors, and so on).

5. As the things-to-do get done, I cross them off the To-Do list. Eventually this list can be thrown away (or saved for a future trip's reference).

6. As I pack each item into the suitcases, I put a single fine line through each item on the To-Bring list.

7. As the suitcases go out the door I review the still-legible To-Bring list one more time to ascertain if we've forgotten anything truly vital.

So . . . What Should You Bring?

There is no one definitive packing list. The general list below includes all the items I either always take or regret not having, plus some more obscure ideas and suggestions. Use this list as a jumping-off spot. Your own list will reflect your child(ren)'s proclivities, activities, and developmental level, and your own. Trim down if you'll be lugging everything by hand—load up if you have room in the car.

TONS O' BABY CLOTHES

An hour before leaving for the airport on our first big trip *avec bebe,* Bill and I sat in the middle of a living room littered with baby clothes, road maps, two suitcases that seemed to have shrunk to gym bags, and seven-month-old Annie, rocking back and forth on her knees, thrilled by the chaos.

"Don't crawl," I told her. "Wait a few weeks. Please?"

She smiled with glee.

"What clothes shall we bring for Annie?" I asked Bill.

We looked at each other mystified. We were off to a different continent for three weeks. What kind of weather would we face? What social situations?

In a flash of brilliance, Bill said, "Let's bring it all!"

It worked then, and that's what we always do now, though as Annie's body gets larger we're getting a *little* more selective.

For a baby, I suggest bringing as much baby clothing as you can cram in the suitcase. Doing laundry can be a drag (there are laundry tips in Chapter 3), and your little dirt-ball won't become neat just because you're on the road. In most cases you'll be able to replace whatever you need, but you don't want to waste your

Clothes	A roll of toilet paper
Laundry soap	Diaper wipes
Snack food	First Aid kit
Day pack	Sunglasses
Kleenex	Chewing gum
Bathing suit	Socket protectors
Sturdy toys	Plastic bags
Sunscreen	Receiving blankets
Books	Camera and film
Fluids	Flashlight
Lovey toys	Baby tote gear
Toiletries	Lovey blanket
Brightly colored	Distractions and bribes
Band-Aids	Documents

Just How Many Outfits Does One Kid Need?

Evaluate your child. Be honest, now. Some little angels never seem to get wet or messy. Packing for them is easy—pack up to seven little outfits—one per day of trip up to a week. For longer trips, plan to wash as you go, or hit a washer/dryer on day six.

Some kids, on the other hand, are like Annie, whose enjoyment of the world is based on sampling substances with more than one sense or body part. We're well acquainted with ice-creamed shoes, jellied T-shirts, and a little face that looks like it went nine rounds with Jackson Pollack. We pack every outfit she owns, tote our own laundry soap, and scope out laundromats with fierce radar.

valuable vacation schlepping from store to store for necessities. (Note for the continental traveler: Though shopping overseas can be fun, the beautiful clothes in Europe are far too expensive for everyday use.)

- Toddlers and preschoolers need a lot of clothing, too. Dark clothing and denim can be worn until filthy without much visual evidence—kudos for using an item more than one day without washing!

- Bring at least one sun hat, and for cold climates, a winter hat that covers the ears.

- Extra shoes (lightweight, inexpensive tennies) are good insurance against puddles, deep gutters, or toilet-training accidents. They can double as wading shoes.

- Extra clothing to consider (depending on season and destination) could include bathing suits, rain gear, wool sweaters (sturdy, warm, and slow to show dirt), one "fancy" outfit, a winter coat, maybe a windbreaker, a warm hat, and light gloves. (For camping and snow clothing, see the lists in Chapter 11.)

LAUNDRY SOAP

Get the soap you can use in sinks as well as in machines. For a short trip, pre-measure load-sized scoops into plastic bags and seal with a twist-tie. In Hawaii, the condominium we rented had a washer and a dryer, and several times I found myself on my knees in front of the machines, grateful, grateful, *grateful*. (At Lake Tahoe, the condo was similarly equipped; unfortunately, the power went out in a blizzard, leaving a machine full of wet, soapy clothing—but that's another tale.) Generally when we're on the road, we do a lot of washing by hand.

TOILETRIES

Don't forget the things that you don't use every day, like the baby nail-clippers. Another important item: diaper ointments (even if your baby is not usually rashy)—keep in mind changing climates and all (review the rash procedures in Chapter 3).

FLUIDS

Bottles, sippy cups that don't spill, canteens, juice boxes—bring some or all. At three, Annie became adept at drinking from a commercial bottle of spring water—the kind with the squirt top. Whatever form it takes, don't forget the liquids. Nothing is worse than searching for fluids with a screaming, thirsty child. Of course if you're a nursing mom you have it easier—but bring along a canteen of water for *you.*

SNACK FOOD

Bring a small amount of something high-protein and non-perishable for emergency situations—delayed flights with no food service, terrible traffic jams . . . anything can happen. Bring an eensy jar of peanut butter, a protein bar, fruit roll-ups . . . just try not to casually munch on it yourself, or you may find yourself sorry!

THE BASIC BABY FIRST-AID KIT

You don't need to buy a special kit. I suggest customizing your own based on your destination. A call to your pediatrician explaining your destination and circumstances is always a good idea. I've included a "starter list" of first-aid items in the Alphappendix.

Each family's customized first-aid kit will illustrate a particular "slant": Our accident-prone little friend Jay's parents suggest suture glue and butterfly bandages. (At three, we already call the poor guy "Scarface.") Of course, they're the ones who call the emergency room at every destination to find out what the pediatric procedures would be should something happen.

My personal weak point is skin, and I highly recommend the new anti-itch Benedryl ointment stuff available over the counter in your local drugstore. It is my friend. I'm the type that mosquitoes love. On any given rural twilight, Bill will get a mosquito bite—*one*—while I'll get swarmed. Then my bites swell, pop, ooze, and eventually scar. Annie, poor dear, has inherited my skin. This ointment, with a little cortisone chaser, is great.

SUNGLASSES

Available for you and Baby in a variety of styles, colors and (ouch) price ranges. Don't forget that Baby needs them in the snow, too.

KLEENEX

This is the kind of thing I never, ever would have thought about packing in my premotherhood days. Long ago, it was me, my carry-on, and the road at my feet. But ever since Annie was an infant, I go *nowhere* without one of those little plastic pouches. Wow. I feel like I've finally become a grown-up.

CHEWING GUM

For airplane rides with kids three and up. Annie tried gum for the first time on a flight from Oakland to Seattle and did pretty well . . . hey, by the way, did you know that you really *can* remove chewing gum from hair using peanut butter?

BATHING SUITS

They're small—pack one just in case, even if you don't think you'll be swimming. You never know when it will come in handy, and buying a swimsuit on the spur of the moment can ravage your wallet. In Maui we learned the hard way—children's swimsuits were hard to find on the mainland in January, so we cast our fate to the trade winds, and the bitty scrap of Hawaiian orange-and-green fabric set us back 20 bucks.

SOCKET PROTECTORS

Quick baby-proofing for hotel rooms—small, cheap, and worth their weight in worry.

STURDY TOYS

Not too small, and not too many. Especially if you're spending time in a natural setting. Picture yourself traipsing through the underbrush looking high and low for Sammy's one-inch-tall favorite doll. Sammy is sobbing, you're contracting a fierce case of poison oak . . . no thanks. Let Sammy enjoy the sticks, the rocks, the leaves, the dirt.

PLASTIC BAGS

You can *never* carry enough plastic bags. Tote a wide selection of all sizes: large garbage bags for dirty clothes; medium bags for dirty diapers *or* food *or* shoes; small baggies for found objects (feathers and rocks); and all size gradations in between. They weigh almost nothing and take up limited space.

SUNSCREEN

Our little friend Jakob's parents call it "Sun Scream."

On the road, we're outside more than we usually are at home, so it's easy to catch a few too many rays. Daily deployment of sunscreen is a good habit to get into, especially as the ozone grows thinner. Slather it on yourself and your loved ones before you get dressed in the morning; that way it won't be an issue when you hit the beach and the little one wants to run . . . (A more detailed discussion of sunscreen is included in Chapter 11.)

BOOKS

Bring some for all family members—though there's a good chance you won't find the opportunity to read yours. Reading books at bedtime is a good way to help settle kids who are still a little too hyper from the excitement of the long travel day. Paperback children's books are small and very lightweight. Have your toddler help decide which five she wants to take—then stash away an extra few for on-the-road surprises.

CAMERA AND FILM

Inexpensive, light, point 'n' shoot or disposable cameras are a boon to society. In general, I suggest never bringing anything on a trip that you're not prepared to lose or have damaged, but there may be times when you'll *want* to take your video camera. Weigh the stress of worrying about it against the pleasure of having it with you (and having the videos later), then decide.

RECEIVING BLANKETS

My friends Ailsa and Stephen swear by these. They always bring along at least three to use for car sunshades, extra towels, or in case Shoshi or Ellie throws up in the car.

DIAPER WIPES

Wipes for all ages! You'll need approximately one box more than your normal allotment for every four days on the road. This doesn't mean you necessarily have to lug them all—they are available (with slight variations) all over this country, and in many places around the world. (Diaper wipes come in handy for the adults, too. Get the unscented type, unless you *enjoy* smelling like a clean baby's butt.)

FLASHLIGHT

Useful outside when you're camping. Especially useful inside for reading in the motel room if you're having one of those awful nights where the baby tosses and turns and wakes up every time an adult switches on the light. What—your kid always sleeps through the night? I hate you.

BABY TOTE GEAR

Backpack, stroller, what do you need? No easy answer to this one. Where are you going? How much walking will you do? Weigh the benefits of having the item against the drag of lugging it around. Factor in the size and ages of your children. Can they walk? *Will* they walk? What's your primary source of transportation? If you have a big car and are doing a car trip, why not bring the stroller? A stroller is less manageable if you are going Greyhound. (Go back to Chapter 6 for a more in-depth discussion of tote modes.)

Alternative Uses for Diaper Wipes

Wipes can be used for far more than little bottoms. Some other applications:
- Sticky hands
- Grimy faces
- Filthy feet (before climbing into bed at night)
- Backs of necks (saves wear on shirt collars!)
- Damp underarms
- Assorted other body parts

In addition, we've used them for:
- Dusty windshields
- Washing dishes in the stream (more effective than a sponge, and reusable)
- Cleaning picnic tables
- Arts and crafts paper (dry flat)
- Shoe polishers
- Emergency coffee filters (just kidding)

How Much Stuff Do You Really Need?

A friend of ours recently returned from beautiful Costa Rica. Bus travel in Costa Rica, though cheap and convenient, often entails changing vehicles. Busses arrive at one side of an unsafe, rickety bridge, the passengers disembark, carry their luggage across the gently swaying bridge, and board another waiting bus, which carries them 10 or 15 miles—where the same thing is repeated.

On the day our friend traveled, her bus was filled with locals traveling light, tourists with backpacks, and an intrepid family of five Americans—two parents and three children aged five years, three years, and eight months. Each time the bus stopped, the hassled mother hustled the cranky children out of their seats, down off the old bus, over the bridge and into the waiting (even older) bus. Meanwhile the father, sweating furiously in the tropical heat, unloaded and trekked back and forth over the bridge, lugging multiple suitcases, strollers, a baby backpack, and a playpen.

The family did not look like they were having fun.

She's Got A Stuffed-Animal Jones . . .

Our family lore includes a story of my step-daughter Rachel, aged five and seriously addicted to stuffed animals. The family was on the way to Mexico and traveling "light" (car to the border and the train to Mexico City), so a strict,

LOVEY TOYS

Familiar friends are a welcome touch of home for sleepy children wanting comfort in a strange environment. We have a rule that stuffed animals are for inside cars, hotel rooms, and tents—just imagine dear little Lambykins, covered in creek mud, clasped to the tiny chest of your just-bathed tot.

LOVEY BLANKET

Bedtimes in strange places can be scary for toddlers. Bring a blankie from home. Annie's travel quilt is a zillion different colors and cheery prints. It has accompanied Annie on all of her journeys. (If it was a person, it would wear a bored blasé expression: "Europe? Hawaii? Been there, done that.") From one corner of the quilt peeks a little bear. Annie and I used to play a game checking each of the corners for it. "Is it here? No. Is it here? Yes! Here's a little guy who wants to say, 'Hello, Annie, Hello!'"

Now that Annie is in day care, the quilt lives in her cubby and rests with her during naptime. She doesn't remember all the places it (and she) has been, but it brings a sense of security. On trips, the quilt still comes with us. In a strange place it is one more environmental factor that remains familiar.

BRIGHTLY COLORED BAND-AIDS

Not strictly a first-aid item—carry a few in an easily accessible place. "Preventive medicine," says my friend Ailsa, whose little girls Shoshi and Ellie (ages three and four) often arrive at destinations with their legs and arms plastered. Stickers work too.

DOCUMENTS

Don't forget your tickets! You may need some or all of the following: birth certificate, immunization record, passport (yes, your baby needs one), medical information, prescriptions, and insurance forms.

You might also consider family zoo or museum membership cards (if you're a member of your local zoo, you may be eligible for entry into other zoos). For security reasons, some parents travel with photos and fingerprints of their kids to help in the *very* rare cases of natural disasters, lost children, or abductions.

DISTRACTIONS AND BRIBES

Since we're exceptional parents who never, *ever* lose our cool or our sense of control, and Annie is a perfect child who never cries or whines, and never, *ever* throws tantrums, we don't need to stoop to such things as little gifts for distractions and/or bribery when nothing else is working. (Give it up, Lutz.) But we've heard from people who aren't as perfect as we are that it's always a good idea to keep a few hidden gems to pull out in dire circumstances when you absolutely need the little buggers to shut up. Things like tiny dolls, trucks, books, or even . . . no, *I* didn't say it, Mom . . . candy.

TOILET PAPER

Bring an extra roll. You never know.

And Don't Stress

It's always best to take what you need, unless you *like* unpleasant surprises, hassles finding things, or spending lots more money than you should. But you can always make do. In our global economy, replacements for almost anything are available (unless you're in the wilderness or deep in an under-industrialized nation). Children really need very little to survive. Ultimately, all they require is food, shelter, clothing, and you. When you're on the road, you are their home, and their security. Little else matters.

(continued)

two-animal limit was imposed on the poor girl. How she agonized over which friends would accompany her! Finally, Owly and Betsy were carefully bedded down amidst Rachel's clothes and toiletries. The journey was long, but eventually the family arrived at the hotel. Out of the duffel bag came Owly and Betsy. Then, much to the family's horror, out came the stowaways: Donder, Rainbow, Kissy Bear, Sheepy, Sealy, Moosy, Big Moo, Little Moo, Dolly, Molly, and Spot!

Annie isn't old enough yet to be quite so devious, so to honor the grand family tradition her sister began, we always pack at least one unexpected stowaway that we keep hidden until bedtime the first night. At the grand unveiling, her face inevitably lights up with joy and amusement at the sight of her unexpected friend, and at the silliness of it all.

A Final Note to Despairing Moms

When you feel desperate that last day before you leave, with the floor strewn with items and the baby teething on the first-aid kit, and you're biting your lip to keep in the **screams**, remember, moms, it's just like labor and delivery. It's just one day (albeit one painful day) out of your life.

chapter

9

up in the air

> *Up in the air you go flying again,*
> *Up in the air, and down!*
>
> —Robert Louis Stevenson

Up Where the Air is Clear

I love listening to parents recount their recent airline trips with the little fruits of their loins. "It wasn't bad at all!" they usually tell me, amazed that everything went so well after all their nights of worry. "Sophie *loved* the airplane!" or "Henry slept during the flight and the grandparents were *so* happy to see him!"

Yet sometimes their voices hush as they tell me a nightmare story of screaming kids and frantic parents. Airplanes can provide trying times, and airports can seem like giant pinball machines—and you're the ball. Knowing what to expect, planning ahead, and taking a few precautionary steps can help assure a positive experience.

What follows is a step-by-step breakdown of everything connected with air travel—from making reservations, through airports and flights, to collecting the baggage and getting the rental car. (If you're flying alone with the small one, read this chapter first, then get additional survival hints in Chapter 12.) We'll cover:

🍼 Making Reservations

🍼 Negotiating Airports

🍼 On, Off, Up, and Down

🍼 In-the-Air Survival Skills

🍼 "We're There, Honey!"

Making Reservations

You can make flight reservations through a travel agent, over the Internet, or by telephone directly through the airlines. Package deals are available through tour companies as well—check newspaper travel sections for bargains.

Some things to consider when planning flights:

🍼 Try to schedule flights during your baby's nap time. If you have a non-napper, avoid flights late in the day when your child is exhausted and cranky.

🍼 Ask about off-hour, mid-week travel. The rates are often cheaper.

🍼 Be aware of this difference between direct and non-stop flights: Direct flights stop at least once. You might have a layover, though you won't change airplanes (use the layover as an opportunity for your toddler to run around). Non-stop flights are preferable because (like the name says) you don't stop.

🍼 Build in "buffer zones"—ask how much time you'll have between connecting flights. There is an FAA minimum layover time between connecting flights, but if the buffer zone is too short and the first flight is too late, you might have trouble making your next flight (I've got a horror scenario for you in Chapter 12).

Special note: Airplanes are germ-factories. The air is recycled and the oxygen content becomes reduced. To reduce your chances of getting sick, drink mass quantities of non-carbonated water, take Vitamin C, echinacea, and zinc lozenges before, during, and after the flight (consult your pediatrician for advice on dosages for little ones), and wash your hands frequently with soap and water. If you or your child are especially prone to contracting viral illnesses, get flu shots, consider wearing disposable paper surgical masks, and **avoid flying** during the height of flu season (drive, take the train, take a boat).

SEATING ARRANGEMENTS

Center bulkhead seats face the walls at the front of each section of the plane. They provide more leg room and a small play area right in front of you. I swear by them, though they have a few disadvantages: You have to stow your carry-ons in the luggage racks above you (no seats in front of you to stow stuff under), sometimes the armrests don't move, sometimes the seats don't recline, and sometimes you have to fend off other passengers trying to use the space between you and the wall as a shortcut across the plane. (This can be a particular drag when your baby is napping on the floor at your feet.

> Not all airlines allow families to sit in the bulkhead, and those that do don't allow you to reserve the bulkhead in advance. You can try! Call early and often, to have requests entered in your record; arrive at the airport with time to spare; and, if necessary, throw a small tantrum yourself.

> If you have an infant, your plane is equipped with bassinets (ask the ticket agent), *and* the bassinets are the type that attach to the bulkhead (see "Bassinets and Sleeping Bags," coming up), you can try to land the bulkhead by reserving a bassinet. You'll still be bumped if other passengers have more need for the bulkhead than you do (the lady with triplets, the man in the wheelchair).

SO, THE TANTRUM DIDN'T WORK?

If the airline won't allow you to sit in the bulkhead, try asking for the front seats of a section. The other approach to seating is reserving an aisle seat. Sitting on the aisle guarantees access to the rest of the plane, a necessity with a toddler. If you're trapped in the middle of the middle with an antsy kid, you may be in for a miserable journey; and even though window seats provide a nice view (for *you*, your baby won't care), they can be a hassle as you try to get to the bathroom yet again. ("Excuse me . . . I'm sorry . . . excuse me . . .")

If you're traveling as a family of two adults and a child under two, try reserving the aisle seat and the window seat in a row of three. Unless the plane is very full, they'll probably keep that extra seat open.

CAR SEATS ON THE PLANE

Here's the dilemma—pediatricians insist that the safest way for a baby to experience take-off and landings is strapped in her car seat. But where do you put it? If your child is under two, you're probably not paying for her seat.

When you make your seat reservations, ask the ticket agent to enter in your record that: 1) You're traveling with a baby, and 2) That you want to bring your car seat. Ask them to try to leave the seat(s) next to you open (try the aisle/window trick above). When you call back to reconfirm (coming up), make sure the notation is still there. If the plane is too full, the attendants will check your car seat at the gate.

Bottles

Mixing formula on airplanes can get very sloppy. Bring pre-measured water or make up bottles right before you board. For a baby over one year, bring along bottles with 1/3 cup of pre-measured powdered milk inside. Fill bottle to top, shake it, and **voila!**

RECONFIRMING

Call the airline the week before your flight to confirm flight times, make sure notations in your record still exist and find out about food service and whether your plane will have refrigeration. Not all do! Planes without refrigeration do not carry milk.

Negotiating Airports

I love airports. They're busy, they're crazy, and they can be the most challenging part of the trip. Here the masses converge, here humanity at its worst and finest can be found embracing, departing, crying, laughing, rushing, fretting, being bored . . . but I digress.

TIME AND WAITING

Leave lots of time. Arrive with plenty to spare. Better to be bored than frantic. Many airports now have play areas, exhibits, and other fun things to do while you wait. Food is usually bad and expensive—try to bring your own snacks. If you have a long wait for a plane, consider stowing your carry-ons in a coin-operated locker. With only your baby, a wallet, and an extra diaper to hold, you'll be free to wander around and people-watch. Beware the gift shop! It is designed to suck you in and steal your money!

PORTERS AND VALETS

Airports in the U.S. and many other countries usually have porters available to help you carry stuff. They are airport employees, but it is customary to give them a tip. Have a few small bills easily accessible. You don't want to be digging through your bags while your toddler is running away.

CHECKING IN

Get your seats pre-assigned, if possible. Then check your luggage curbside. Even if you have to wait in line at the ticket counter, you'll have an easier time with less stuff to shove along with your feet. Putting identification tags on your bags before you get to the airport will save you time once you're there. If you check a car seat or baby backpack, you'll have to sign a damage waiver, but don't worry, they usually arrive at the other side intact.

CARTS

Most U.S. airports have luggage carts available for around a dollar. Sometimes they're free. Either way, make sure to get one, even if you check your baggage. It will be invaluable for confining your child, for parking your carry-ons, for claiming airport territory, and for zipping from place to place. Most models have a place for little children to sit, similar to a grocery shopping cart.

CONSIDER A STROLLER

Lightweight, fold-up strollers are another approach, even if your kid usually walks. If you have *two* little ones, a double stroller is invaluable. You might look ridiculous, draped with baby gear and slowly maneuvering a wide swath across the crowded airport, but who cares? You'll get there slowly, but you'll get there. Arrive at the gate early. If there is no room in the cabin of the plane to stow the stroller, the (grumbling) airline personnel can check it at the gate and send it downstairs.

MOVING SIDEWALKS

Some allow carts, some don't. They can be dangerous for little hands—be aware!

SHUTTLE BUSES

Hop on. If there are no seats available, look pathetic and desperate. If this doesn't work, ask the driver to ask somebody to move. If none of these tactics work and you absolutely have to stand, hold on and have your child hold on to you. If you have a baby, wear him—in a pack, Snugli, or sling. Stand with your feet wide apart for more support. Brace yourself against a pole—it's more secure than the ceiling straps.

METAL DETECTOR

To get to the gate where you'll meet your plane requires going through the metal detector. You'll have to unload all your stuff from the cart and put it on the moving band so it can be X-rayed. You *may or may not* be able to get your cart back. Ask. Sometimes they'll take it around the side.

THE GATE

Often you'll find fewer amenities here than in the main part of the airport. I usually delay our trip to the gate until shortly before boarding. On the other hand, if you're nervous about time, loaded with stuff, or ready to sit and rest, go to the gate area and claim a bank of seats. Toddlers can watch the planes take off and land. If things get too crowded, you can often find a nearby empty gate where you can still hear announcements and the little ones can run around.

BEFORE BOARDING

If your child is potty-trained, try to have him go *before* you get on the plane. Change diapers here, too. Airport bathrooms are usually easier to negotiate, and often cleaner, than airplane bathrooms. Many airports have nurseries, equipped with changing tables, sinks, towels, and chairs to feed the baby.

On, Off, Up, and Down

You've gotten all the way to the gate! Alas, the journey has yet to begin. Here's the scoop on boarding, deplaning, ascending, descending, and the flight time in between.

BOARDING

Most airlines have a pre-board option for people traveling with small children. Take advantage of it. Settle in, take up space. Get greedy. Grab pillows and blankets and stow your stuff in the luggage bins. Ask for the seats next to you to be left empty as long as possible. Assert yourself. You're traveling with a baby—most people won't want to sit next to you anyway.

STRAPPING IN

If you're not using your car seat, your little one needs to be strapped into a seat belt or held tightly on your lap for take-off and landings. Some international airlines have children's belt extenders—they hook to your seat belt as the child sits on you. I haven't found them in this country. They're worth asking about.

TAKING OFF AND LANDING

Little kids have no natural fear of flying, but they *will* pick up on your tensions. Try to relax. If you're traveling with a toddler or preschooler, explain what is happening.

> Bill says jelly beans do the trick—at least they did for Annie on their recent daddy/daughter trip to L.A. Of course, he's only admitting this **now**.

THE EAR THING

Many parents are concerned about the change in air pressure on take-off and landings, and how it will affect their baby or small child. Contrary to the horror stories you might hear, many pediatricians now believe that there is no relationship between flying and ear infections.

Ascents and descents with an infant should be relatively easy. Encourage them to nurse or, if they're in their car seat, to suck on a bottle or pacifier to keep their ears popped and pain-free. They may feel some discomfort, but it should pass quickly.

The slightly older baby—uncomprehending, uncooperative little dear—may have a slightly harder time, though his cry of dismay at the unaccustomed pressure is nature's way of adjusting. Do whatever you can to get him to swallow.

A small child, over two and communicative, can be worked with. She'll grab her ears or tell you of any discomfort: "Mommy, my ears!" Bring along a sippy cup. Encourage her to yawn. Make silly faces at her, and have her make them back at you. A drop of Vicks vapor rub or eucalyptus oil on a Kleenex held a comfortable distance under your child's nose can also help clear stuffiness. Children over three can chew gum to relieve the pressure.

DRUGS

Benadryl (an antihistamine) unstuffs noses and ears (and has the added benefit of helping kids relax and, potentially, sleep.) Consult your pediatrician for advice and prescriptions. Test the drugs once before you go—they make some kids hyperactive. Exactly what you *don't* want. If your child has a history of motion sickness, talk to your pediatrician about Dramamine.

Whatever the drug, if you'll be on the plane a very long time (over four hours) you may want to weather the take-off and wait awhile before giving the medication. If you do it right away, it will wear off near the end of the trip. You'll be at your most fatigued, and your baby will be wired for the rest of the flight.

If you want your child to relax but you're leery about medicating her, chamomile tea and milk is a natural sedative. Bring a small thermos already made up, but make sure it's not too hot.

> ### Turbulent Times
>
> We flew to Maui on a cold, blustery day when the rivers flooded over their banks. As we waited to board, we admired the fools returning from Hawaii, with their blissed-out expressions and wilting flower leis. Their tan limbs shivered in their shorts and teeny tank tops.
>
> Once aboard, the crew triple-checked everybody's seat belt, the plane accelerated down the runway and took off at a steep angle, cutting sharply up through the storm, and the young flight attendant in front of me surreptitiously crossed herself.
>
> I took deep breaths. I turned to two-year-old Annie to reassure her and was met by a grin. All over the plane, parents grimaced and children giggled as we bounced our way over the Pacific. An hour into the trip the air cleared, the flight attendant smiled, and we were truly on our way.

In-the-Air Survival Skills

Merely getting yourself and your children aboard an airplane can feel like a victory. And it is! Yet there are a few things you should know before you go . . .

DRESS FOR DISASTER

Flying alone with kids, you may have juice dumped on you, and be thrown up or pooped on. The plane may be hours late. Think of it as a job, not a fashion show. Opt for sweats rather

Learning the Hard Way

Jessica knew well about bringing extra outfits for her **kids**, but half an hour into a full day of flying (with a two hour stop-over at Chicago's O'Hare), 18-month-old Alexandra threw up on her. Not just a little, either—Jessica was soaked to the skin with vomit. With no extra clothes except for a sweater, Jessica had no recourse but to remove her shirt, put on her sweater, and spend another eight hours of traveling ignoring both the pungent odors rising from her torso and jeans, and the strange looks from strangers.

than silk. Bring two changes of easy-to-change clothes in a ziplock baggie for each child. Take off everybody's shoes—feet swell—and fly in slippers or thick socks. Make sure to bring sweaters or sweat-shirts—airplane air is *cold! Bring one change of clothes for yourself.* Wet or dirty clothes can be stowed back in their baggie, keeping the rest of your stuff unpolluted.

CHANGING DIAPERS

This is another place where the space in front of the bulkhead seats comes in handy. Usually one of the bathrooms on an airplane has a fold-down changing table. Or look for empty rows of seats. Use the little vomit bags provided in the front seat pocket for dirty disposables and wipes—but don't stow them back inside the pocket. Give them to the attendant or throw them out yourself during your next trip up and down the aisle.

TREATS, TOYS, BRIBERY

Lily once continuously read to Xavier, 3½, on a flight across country. Lily's voice grew hoarse, but Xavier sat quietly the entire trip (quite uncharacteristically for him), and the adjacent passengers got a healthy dose of children's literature.

Don't rely on the airline to supply entertainment—bring lots of things to occupy little hands and mouths. Play-Doh, plastic dinosaurs, lots o' paperback children's books, stickers, coloring books and marking pens, forbidden snacks . . . all of these things can be segregated into separate ziplock baggies and whipped out one by one as the little one gets restless. Make sure you put things away as you go—you'll save yourself an end-of-flight scramble.

Many airlines have complimentary activity packets. Ask the flight attendant. A tape recorder with headphones is a good choice for some children (the plane's headphones may not adjust small enough for a little kid).

Toys that are too tiny or have wheels are *not* good choices. Try to keep things around your seats fairly organized—and save yourself from the mad dash to get everything stowed as the plane descends and the seat-belt light begins to blink for landing.

THE LONG MARCH

Be prepared to walk all the way to Chicago or Tokyo—sometimes pacing the aisle is the only way to calm your kid down. The other passengers are usually charmed.

OTHER KIDS

If there are other babies or small children on the plane, you're in luck! Kids can play together, older ones can admire little ones, parents can spell each other.

FOOD

Don't ever rely on airlines to get your child fed. Meals are *not* provided on every flight. If you are traveling cross-country you may be caught in the twilight zone—two long flights and a layover but, because of flight times, you only get a small breakfast. Bring your own supplies of sandwiches, fruit, and snacks.

Airplane food is notoriously bad. Although it may not be edible, its arrival breaks up the monotony and provides some entertainment value. Special children's meals are sometimes available (at least one airline uses McDonald's Happy Meals). You can call at least a day ahead to request Vegetarian, Kosher, Diabetic, or Seafood meals. One advantage to ordering special meals is that you will often be served first.

When it comes to snacks, try to keep the sugar level down and the energy level up. Small bags of cut-up carrots or celery (watch for choking for the under two set), washed grapes, raisins, Goldfish crackers, home-popped or organic popcorn (doesn't have too much salt), tiny cookies (for treats and bribes), mini-bagels, fruit roll-ups, Cheerios, and cheese cubes are all good choices. Most airlines have switched from peanuts to pretzels for financial reasons—that's O.K., babies and toddlers shouldn't eat peanuts anyway. You might want to review the travel snack information in Chapter 4.

Water! Water! Water!

Airplane air is as dry as the Gobi desert. A lot of the symptoms of jet lag are caused by dehydration. An amazing fact about the human body is that we have a feeble thirst mechanism. By the time you think about taking a drink, your body is already dehydrated. Avoid alcohol; that only makes it worse.

Bill and I always bring a liter of spring water and force ourselves to drink 8 ounces per hour during the course of the flight. We have a separate bottle of water for Annie, and encourage her (frequently) to take sips.

Flying Baby!

On a long flight to Europe, we got lucky. Flying was exciting for seven-month-old Annie, not because of the gorgeous view of Iceland or the free drinks, but because of all the people and attention. Eventually she fell asleep, exhausted from smiling at so many friendly faces. And about the ear thing—we had no problems. Annie nursed during take-offs and landings, except during the final landing when she refused to nurse and sat quietly on my lap, occasionally yawning.

BASSINETS AND SLEEPING BAGS

Bassinets hook onto the wall in the bulkhead section of some airplanes. They are for use only by small babies—and must be removed for take-off and landings. Sleeping bags are useful in the bulkhead section, too. Baby can sleep at your feet while you relax. I suggest asking about and reserving these items in advance.

> On a trip to Seattle, Annie enjoyed the view of the mountains out the window. "Is the pilot driving very fast?" She surprised me by knowing the word for pilot. Two and a half years old. Brilliant? I think so.

THE IMPOSSIBLE CHILD

Your little angel is running up and down the aisles kicking people. Every polite request is met by a high pitched scream of denial. When you try to calm him down with Play-Doh, he throws it against the head of the man in front of you. You've never seen so many tantrums in a two-hour period. Your head is splitting. You suspect that the head of every passenger within four rows of you is splitting. Your kid has turned into a monster.

When a kid is this hyped up, you can try some of your bribes—but they probably won't work. Try not to *lose* it. Take 10 deep breaths, letting each out slowly. Accept that the rest of the people on the plane hate you. So what? They'll probably never see you again. Firmly deal with your child (without screaming). This kind of behavior is not acceptable, no matter how miserable or excited he is.

Take him into the bathroom, kicking or screaming if need be, and keep him there until he is calm. Hold him. Assess the situation. Why is he out of control? He may be miserable *and* excited. Try to remember that crying is the only way your baby has of expressing himself. Is he hungry? Scared? Simply on overload? What can you do to lower his stress?

Take care of his bodily needs. Reassure him. Sometimes just the few minutes in private together will change your child's energy level. Sometimes it won't. Do the best you can— you're not the first parent who's had to deal with behavior like this and you won't be the last. Eventually the flight will be over.

DEALING WITH UNSYMPATHETIC FELLOW FLIERS

There are adults who are intolerant of children—even children who are not acting out. You may even have been one of them once . . . I was. It's their loss. How do you deal with that man across the aisle who's been sending you withering glances while your baby screams? What do you say to the poor woman who's been kicked in the back for the thousandth time by your restless four year old? They look at you like you're the most terrible parent on the planet for allowing her be so out of control.

You may not be able to calm your kid, but you might be able to save your reputation. By translating the situation for the other adults, you'll let them know that you're aware of the situation, and are dealing with it. Verbalize your child's emotions. "I know, it's hard to be strapped in for so long. But the plane is going through a thing called turbulence, and we need to stay in our seats." Or, "I know, I know, you're tired and hungry. Just rest here, Sweetie. Lunch will be here soon." Or even, "Rosie-Posie, you're angry because Mommy got mad at you. But I need you to be more considerate and not kick that man's chair."

"We're There, Honey!"

Yes! You made it! Only a couple more hurdles await . . .

DEPLANING

Resist your impulse to stand up and rush off the plane—you'll just end up standing in the aisle, smashed up against your restless fellow passengers. Stay in your seats as long as you can. Then gracefully depart, first carefully checking around your seats for dropped toys, bottles, and tiny socks.

BAGGAGE CLAIM

You've successfully negotiated the flight. Everybody is tired—but you still have to get your luggage and rent the car! Poor toddlers have been cooped up long enough, now they want to run. The baby is crying in your ear. Gird your loins. This may be the hardest part of the journey.

Rent a little cart again. Stop at the bathroom. While you're waiting for your luggage you may need to get tough and stick the kid in the cart whether or not she likes it. If you aren't in a rush, you can wait for a while before approaching the carousel. The crowds will be thinner, and your luggage will have already been unloaded.

CAR RENTAL

Waiting in car rental lines can be a drag. If you can, arrange ahead of time for your car to be waiting for you. If not, grin and bear it, and save one or two high-protein snacks for the line.

chapter 10

baby-friendly lodging

> *"The great advantage of a hotel is that it's a refuge from home life."*
>
> —George Bernard Shaw

Sleeping is Part of the Adventure

Hotels, motels, hostels, friend's houses, and rental condominiums are more than just a place to park your weary heads; they're part of the adventure. For a little kid, there is magic in the Magic Fingers massager on the motel-room bed, the condominium closets provide secret hiding places, and face it, even for adults, room service is *fun!* This chapter focuses on how to find places to stay that are a blast for little kids, and affordable and easy for you, from fancy digs to down-and-dirty dives. It includes tips on making your stay in your "home away from home" less problematic. You'll find:

- Assessing Your Lodging Needs
- Staying with Friends and Family
- Renting a Room—Research and Reservations

It's the Novelty . . .

The first time my step-kids Aaron and Rachel stayed in a motel (back when Aaron was 5 and Rachel was 2), they couldn't stop bouncing on the bed. For hours it went on—first one, then the other, then both of them, until the inevitable collision occurred and the giggles turned into tears. They had beds at home and they didn't bounce there; what was so exciting?

Bathroom faucets—we take it for granted that they come in different shapes. Kids don't. A new style of window shade! For toddlers and preschoolers, there is little more thrilling than complimentary tiny shampoo bottles, use-once-before-they-dissolve shower caps, and lightweight fold-up travel toothbrush kits.

Combining Your Lodging Types

Nobody said you have to choose one type of lodging and stick to it. For me, the most extreme contrast of lodging types was a trip to New York City, years before wifehood and baby. For the first three nights, I stayed with my Aunt Laurie and Cousin Jesse in the United Nations Plaza hotel, a gleaming metal and glass skyscraper. We indulged ourselves with room service, and enjoyed the dizzying view from the 92nd floor.

Then Laurie and Jesse flew home, and I was on my empty-pocketed own. The taxi driver who picked me up in front

Assessing Your Lodging Needs

Before you jump into making reservations any old place, consider your family's needs. As you read this chapter, consider the following:

- It's cheaper to share a bathroom down the hall—but not a great idea for a child in potty training who, when he has to go, has to go *now!*

- Do you want or need a bathtub?

- Consider the noise factors. Is the hotel noisy? Is your child? Your baby screams all night? "OK, OK, ixnay on the monastery idea."

- What kind of sleeping set-up? Will the place provide the equipment you need?

- What kind of other amenities will you like or need? Will you use the amenities provided? (If you'll never swim, despise room service, and won't use the baby-sitting, a place with a pool, fancy catering, and in-house child care won't do anything for ya.)

- Does it really need to be swanky, or will "functional" do?

Staying with Friends and Family

Staying with friends and family can be the ideal travel set-up, and you certainly can't beat the price. Staying with friends and family, you do risk the relationship. Value the friendship, tread lightly, and here are some things to consider before throwing the phone in the air in glee and shouting, "Yes! Yes! Yes!" when they agree to put you up:

(continued)

of the swanky lobby asked my destination three times before he "got it." I settled into the back seat with my backpack and said loudly again, "The Uptown YMCA, please." That's where I stayed for the next three nights, in the birthplace of the disco song of the same name, hiding in my roach-infested (but very cheap) room as naked men in towels roamed the corridors and TVs blared till dawn.

- Do they have kids (ideally kids in the same age range)? If so, then they'll probably be set up with toys and baby-proofed, and used to the racket and clutter you'll be bringing with you.

- Do they not only *like* kids, but *understand* kids? Is the house kid-friendly? Are they open to making baby-proofing adjustments? ("What a beautiful Tiffany lamp, Aunt Martha. Do you mind if I put it up here in the closet until we're gone? I'd hate Baby Maurice to cause the estate broker any distress . . . .")

- No matter how great a set-up your friends have, and how much they beg you to come, if you have too many high-octane kids, you may feel like you are imposing. They may feel that way, too.

- Are your lifestyles, values, and schedules compatible? (Notice the word "compatible." They don't have to match, but if they diverge widely, you may have a problem.)

- Do they have animals? Are animals an issue for your family (do they frighten, do any of you have allergies)?

Renting a Room—Research and Reservations

As an experienced adventure budget traveler, I hold grim memories of walking up and down the streets of many a city, looking for lodging. As a parent, I've had the experience a couple too many times (well, how do you think I *know* all this stuff?) of *not* reserving, of leaving it up to chance, and then, when the baby suddenly reaches her limit, being forced to find a place to stay *immediately*. A place usually can be found, but inevitably it's at least twice the expected cost. (There was that time in Italy . . . but then again, when do you have the opportunity to stay in a medieval fortress, huh? And it was late, and the baby was tired . . . .)

When traveling with small ones, by all means try to avoid these scenarios. A little advance planning makes a big difference. When contacting potential lodging places (hotels, motels, B & Bs.), these are a few things to ask about:

FACILITIES

- Ask for a full description of facilities. What kinds of rooms are available? Are they set up for children? Does the hotel *like* kids? (It's a good question to ask—they'll rarely admit to a "no," but you may be able to tell from their enthusiasm or lack thereof.)

- If you have more than one grown-up and more than one child, ask about getting two adjoining rooms. Sometimes a two-room suite can provide enough privacy and yet enough togetherness. (In Mexico City, we stayed in a four-bed "suite" that cost little more than a "double" and gave us all the privacy we needed.)

> Don't feel like taking the potty seat, the VCR, the rocking chair, the high chair, and the crib? If you stay at a destination resort, you may want to rent these things. "Baby's Away" rents baby equipment— daily, hourly, weekly, monthly—to visiting parents at over 30 locations. Their number is listed under "Equipment " in the Recommended Readings appendix.

- Ask about the availability of cribs, crib sheets, floor pads, or rollaway beds (if required.) Do they need to be reserved? What size are the "big" beds? Some suites have hide-a-beds for additional flexibility. For us the ideal set-up would include a California king-sized bed—big enough for the *whole* family (no matter what sleeping arrangements we make, Annie ends up in the bed with us anyway . . .).

- Some hotels and motels have "kitchenettes." Do you want to eat breakfast in? Have some late night toast and jam? Not a bad idea with a kid . . .

- Where is the available room located? Unless the view is a draw and the hotel has good elevators, request a ground level room to minimize the "schlep" factor.

MONEY ISSUES

- Ask about rates for kids. Usually they stay free.

- Ask about special rates for AAA members, off-season rates, or other special rates and discounts. (It never hurts to ask.)

- What is their cancellation policy? (Kids *do* get sick . . .)

Find out about payment. Do they take checks? Credit cards? Cash on the barrel head?

SERVICES AND AMENITIES

Ask about special amenities for infants or children (some fancy hotels provide special welcome packages for the toddler set.)

Are they willing/able to help you discover local things to do with kids?

Is there a pool? Spa? What are the hours, and are children allowed? (Sometimes they are not, or the hours they are allowed are restricted.)

IN GENERAL

Reserve as far ahead as you can.

Request written confirmation. And whatever else you forget, remember to *bring the confirmation with you!*

FABULOUS FANCY HOTELS

Look, when you're traveling with little ones, life is hard enough without trying to roughing it, too. There is great emotional value in being pampered—and sometimes you've just gotta go for it. There are trade-offs—when you choose to stay in a fancy rather than a moderate or budget hotel, you are choosing to spend a big percentage of your traveling costs on lodging.

> ### An Advantage of a Fancy Hotel
>
> Sarah was three, and taking a bath in the fancy Los Angeles hotel her mother and father were treating themselves to. They turned their backs, and she pooped in the tub. Life is easy in the fast lane—one phone call to Housekeeping, one moderate tip, one clean tub.

SCINTILLATING, SCUZZY MOTELS

Old roadside motels retain a down'n'dirty, romantic, all-American charm, and though the bed might sag and the bureau may be scarred with ancient cigarette burns, the prices can't be beat. Slightly more upscale and newer motels provide the basics—a bed, a TV, a shower, maybe a pool—and sometimes that's all you need.

KID-DELIGHTING MOTEL FEATURES

- Kids *love* ice machines ("It's free!"), and most motels have them down the corridor.

- Some old beds will, for a quarter in a meter on the side, give you a jiggling "Magic Finger" massage. Treat your kids to *one* a night.

- Modern motels sometimes have super-duper play structures—and somewhere out there is an old fashioned motel with the kind of fun-and-funky playground I remember from when I was a kid.

Once You Arrive . . .

Once you check in, you have a couple of things to do before you dash to catch the last half hour before the Louvre closes, or race to the lake before the wind comes up: You need to make the room livable, and you need to make sure that it's baby-safe.

MAKING IT LIVABLE AND BABY-SAFE

Set the room(s) up so you'll all be comfortable. How are the sleeping arrangements? Does the room have everything you requested or need? Feel free to move furniture around, and if you can't move it yourself, ask for help from the management. If you explain that it is for safety (or comfort) and you promise to return things to their proper positions, they won't squawk about it. (If they do, you might want to gently murmur the word "lawsuit.")

Hotel and motel rooms are usually fairly easy to child-proof. Review the basic Baby-Proofing Checklist in Chapter 2. The suggestions below may give you some additional ideas.

- Have unsafe furniture or delicate objects removed from the room.

- Unless you bring your own toilet lock, it's a good idea to keep the bathroom door closed.

Go for a Swim

It's a driving day? Leave early in the morning, eat breakfast during rush hour, arrive by three in the afternoon, and take a refreshing swim. Motel swimming pools offer the perfect end to a long afternoon in the car.

Once in Port Angeles, Washington, we stayed at a seedy motel with an even seedier swimming pool. Annie, who is **seriously** into won ton soup, must have had a craving, for she invented a game with Bill called Swimming to the Chinese Restaurant. Like a small flea on the back of a dog, she hung onto her daddy's neck as he swam lap after lap, back and forth across the pool. What this had to do with Chinese food, I've never been quite sure, but it didn't really matter—I left them to their delightful game, laid down on the motel bed, and stared into space for a blissful, solitary hour.

Are your child's toilet habits still a little . . . **unpredictable**? Bring water-proof sheets.

- Electrical outlet covers are cheap, light, and small. Carry several with you and plug those outlets.

- Bring a small roll of duct tape for sealing and shutting.

HOTEL BABY-SITTERS

Hotels can often provide or arrange baby-sitting services for their guests. Sometimes these are hotel employees, though usually they are professionals hired through local baby-sitting agencies. (The advantage of agency baby-sitters is that they aren't just the proprietor's fifteen year old niece—they are experienced, and they've been "checked out.")

If you don't like the person the hotel provides, or if the baby-sitter acts like just a "maintenance" person—parking your kids in front of the tube and chatting on the phone or some such nonsense—tell the hotel management at once. They'll change your provider.

Ruminations on Room Service	
Yeah! Room Service!	*Boo. Yuck. Room Service.*
Room Service is fun! It's exciting to hear that knock on the door, see the cart wheeled in, and open the silver lids on the dishes.	Room service is *expensive*. It is ridiculously expensive.
At the end of a long day of travel when you can't bear going out again, room service can save your butt.	Room Service is not always available. Don't ever count on it. Carry emergency supplies.
In a full-service hotel, room service can be an excellent breakfast choice. Kids can take a long time to get ready in the morning, especially in a new environment. By the time they're washed and dressed, they're cranky for lack of food.	Quality can vary from quite good to "If you plug your nose, this is really quite mediocre."

Sometimes you just have to take care of yourself. Sometimes the traveling is too much. In New Delhi, I was sick with bronchitis, and the Indian streets with their people-cows-cars-chickens-trucks-taxis-monkeys were too much for me. My fascination had shifted to an agoraphobia induced by feeling physically crummy. The idea of going out for food filled me with a sense of doom.

We were staying in a middle-class business hotel—cheap by Western standards, expensive by "traveler" standards and this hotel had (oh joy!) room service! Brought to our room, the finest tandoori-and-butter chicken I've ever tasted, accompanied by beautiful buttered nan (bread). I was immediately happy—the world shifted focus, and I knew I'd be all right. Never before had four hotel walls felt so welcoming and warm. Food with no effort. Well worth every rupee (though, like everything in India when you have American dollars, it was **cheap**!).

FOOD DELIVERY

Many restaurants in the United States will be happy to deliver to hotels and motels. For a fallback, there's always pizza or Chinese delivery. In addition, in many major U.S. metropolitan areas, there are also restaurant food-delivery services. These companies usually publish a free listing of the restaurants available and their regular menus.

Craving that special pasta dish from the restaurant across town? Call the food-delivery company, select from one or more restaurants, and they do the hauling. There is usually a minimum charge, a delivery fee ($4-$6 dollars per order), and, if you compare the menus in the brochure and the regular restaurant menus, you'll notice that each item has been slightly marked up. Plus, of course, you should give the delivery person a tip. Many companies will also pick up videos or booze on their way over. ("Party!!!" Not.) If there is no brochure in your room, ask at the front desk or manager's office for details and suggestions.

Beds with Breakfast

In this country, bed and breakfasts are not always the best choices for kids. They are quiet, and precious, and charming, and often small with thin walls. If your kid is high-octane, you might want sturdier walls to bounce off of. If you do decide to go the "quaint and quiet" route . . .

- Make sure to ask the proprietors how they feel about kids before making reservations.

- Many B & B rooms are very small. Where will Junior sleep? Is there room for your porta-crib or for their rollaway bed? Do they have a rollaway bed?

- Be prepared for some serious baby-proofing and knick-knack removal.

- Ask for a room as far away from other rooms as possible.

- Find out what they mean by "breakfast." Coffee and a Danish are not the most nutritious way for a two year old to start her day.

Resorts

At a resort, the lodging isn't *part* of the vacation, the lodging *is* the vacation. Resorts are more than Club Med—there are places to take the mineral waters, places for singles, seniors, kids, and weight loss. There are beach resorts, city resorts, and great old rustic lake resorts where you can rent a row boat, cheap, and the squeaky cots in the cabins date back from 1954. Kid-friendly resorts often offer baby-sitting so the adults can eat a romantic dinner together, or even spend the day alone. Vacationing at a resort is a bit of a commitment. Query carefully before you sign up for a weekend or a week—let them know all about your family, and *listen hard* if they try to discourage you from coming. You should know exactly what you are getting, and so should they.

Family Youth Hostels

You don't have to be a youth to stay in a youth hostel. Youth hostels are an inexpensive way for families to stay all over the world. There are 225 hostels in the United States and Canada, and more than 5,000 hostels worldwide. Hostels worldwide vary tremendously, from a pristine chalet high in the Swiss Alps, to a lonely lighthouse on the Northern California coast, to a huge, gray institutional facility in a German industrial center. Wherever the hostel is located, it is always inexpensive, and there are always opportunities to meet and talk with people of all ages from all over the world.

> On the day after Christmas in Quebec, we spent a snowstorm holed up in a youth hostel, the only guests in a facility that sleeps 200. Outside, the winds blew freezing cold off the Saint Lawrence River, and five feet of snow piled high against the hostel walls. Inside, the warm, radiator-heated air thawed our chilled bones, and we enjoyed the absurdity of choosing between yards and yards of yards of beds.

Youth hostels, while not providing the amenities of a hotel, motel, or bed and breakfast, are usually great fun for kids. They provide a social environment and, quite often, lots of people to gush over Baby.

All hostels have dormitory-style gender-separate accommodations, and many have private rooms for families. (For more information on Youth Hostel membership, see the Resources Appendix)

- *Reserve!*—some hostels fill up three months in advance.
- Hostels provide bare-bones lodging—beds, pillows, and blankets. You bring or rent sheets.
- Some have on-site laundry facilities.
- Family rooms are often available, providing more privacy. There is sometimes a surcharge.

- Youth hostels often provide shared kitchen facilities. (My mother traveled all over Europe a few years ago, cooking a pot of brown rice nightly in the hostel facilities. She called it her "security blanket.")

- Many hostels, especially rural, are closed during the day. For some early-rising families, this is fine—for some it can be an issue. Do you have trouble getting up and out in the morning?

- Be prepared for a "lights out" curfew.

- It's best to travel light when staying in hostels. In some places, security is an issue, but hostels usually provide lockers for valuables and other possessions.

- Kids under 5 are generally free, kids under 12 may receive a discounted rate.

- Special Note: Children under 10 *must* be accompanied by a parent or guardian of the same sex.

House, Apartment, and Condominium Rentals

For many families, short-term house, apartment, or condominium rentals provide the best lodging solutions of all.

Traveling with Condo in the Tropics

Baked and relaxed after her days at the beach, Annie scampered around naked as Bill and I prepared dinner in the kitchen or grilled on the barbecue. Evenings, we watched the sun set between two palm trees on our lanai, dressed only in bathrobes. Annie loved our "Hawaii House" (as she dubbed it) and for months after our return would stop in the middle of playing and, misty-eyed and solemn, ask when we were going back.

CONDOMINIUM RENTALS

For convenience and cost saving, try renting a condominium. The cost per day will fall somewhere between Sleazy Motel and Fancy Hotel, but, ah . . . the convenience! Your own fully-equipped kitchen! A washer and dryer! Extra rooms! (No more hiding out in the hotel bathroom with the flashlight, trying to get some reading done.) In the snowy winter, you can sit . . . or (ahem) whatever . . . in front of a roaring fire with your Sweetie while the baby sleeps in the bedroom. In tropical Hawaii, you can breakfast on papaya and mango on your lanai, listening to the chirping of wild birds and watching whales leap in the ocean below.

- Condominiums are available at many resort destinations. Besides offering discounts and/or packaged activities (ski lift tickets, golfing, snorkeling trips), many condominium complexes have on-site shared barbecues, pools, Jacuzzis, and/or mini-gyms where you can *work* that body. (The Recommending Readings appendix lists a place to start when you're looking for the perfect condominium. Also try the local Chamber of Commerce.)

- Ask about facilities and set-up. Many condominiums are built on multi-levels. Are there balconies? Could a small child fall through the railing? If there are bunk beds, are the ladders detachable?

- Condominiums usually sleep lots of people, and are a good choice for joint family vacations.

- Having a kitchen to prepare at least some of your meals can be a *huge* boon. Eating out with a child three times a day is a challenge. (That's putting it mildly—review the restaurant tips in Chapter 4.) Eating out is also time consuming and *very* expensive. (Multiply the number of days of the trip times three meals plus snacks and you'll feel like your family is the sole support of the region's restaurant industry.) Remember, you can *still* go out to eat . . . and you'll enjoy it more because you're doing it for pleasure rather than just because it's time to refuel *again*.

- Shop around; package deals (air, car, condo) through travel agents may be a better deal than buying separately—or they may not be.

- What's the deal with cleaning? Some places include cleaning in the price, some tack on an additional charge, some rely on you to scrub it down. Find out in advance.

- Some places provide sheets and towels, some provide them for a fee. Depending upon your travel mode, you may want to bring your own from home. (For little ones, familiar bedding can ease the stress of being in a strange place.)

- Condominiums are often privately owned, and decor, style, color, and furnishings vary widely. *Some* are quite tasteful. Condominiums usually provide dishes and cooking utensils, though the quality can vary here, too—from top-of-the-line microwaves to burnt-bottomed pots and pans and knives that struggle to cut the butter. You'll usually find an assortment of non-perishable food basics like salt, pepper, and spices, and often the cabinets will have oil, popcorn, chocolate pudding, or other items that previous guests have donated. When you check out, don't leave any perishables, and either replace the macaroni & cheese and the cans o' alphabet soup you borrowed, or donate a few non-perishables of your own.

FURNISHED HOUSE AND APARTMENT RENTAL

Condominiums are available primarily in resort areas, but in many places around the world you can achieve the same benefits by renting a furnished house or apartment. Besides the comfort and savings (house or apartment rental is usually *much* cheaper than a hotel), you'll

Braving the Elements, Inside and Out

Things don't always **exactly** turn out as planned, but that's where adventure usually begins. We planned a weekend of sunny snow play with our friends Ailsa and Stephen and their girls Shoshi and Ellie. But at the last moment, their girls were sick and the weather forecasters were predicting the worst storm of the season (chains required, sand bags available, "Batten down the hatches, Matey.") So we went alone. "Pack in a lot of food," the rental manager told us as we picked up the keys. "You may not get out tomorrow."

The condominium was built on four levels and could sleep eight to ten people, and we were only three. Annie and Bill played in the snow until the storm began in earnest. Then, Annie ran up and down the carpeted stairs, establishing territories in each bedroom. She established the School for Hard Plastic Animals in a walk-in closet, and a bed became the hospital (her stuffed Kitty was **very** sick after falling over the balcony). I spaced out on bad novels and took a bath. "Oooh! Super Nintendo!" Bill said, and except for groaning each time he lost another "Mario," said little after that . . . until the electricity went off.

That's when we realized that the condominium was all-electric—stove, heat, water heater, coffee pot. When we tried to light the fireplace, the condo filled with smoke, and the smoke detector went off and wouldn't stop (**it** wasn't electric) until we opened all the windows and doors. The storm turned to blizzard.

get a feel for the culture that you can only get by living there.

In Europe (I'm talking Paris, London, Rome, Madrid), this type of lodging, known as "self-catering," is very popular. Self-catering is a great idea for family reunions (you can rent a castle in Italy! The more the merrier—and the cheaper!) Houses and apartments are usually rented in one-week increments, though in Provence or Tuscany you may need to commit to a two week stay. (Oh, poor baby. You *have* to stay two weeks in Tuscany? Shut up before I drool on you.)

- International house and apartment rentals can be set up through family travel agencies (once again, see the Recommended Readings).

- There are numerous agencies in England that provide "self-catering." Check out the listings in the *London Times* and *The Guardian*. (These newspapers may be available at a local independent bookstore or newsstand.)

- Furnished apartments are also available in this country, if an area is at all touristed. Contact an area's Chamber of Commerce for the names of local real estate agencies.

Home Swaps

A home swap is, simply, swapping your home with another family for a certain amount of time. You get the apartment in Bombay, they get the apartment in New York, everybody has a great time, and the washing machine is available day and night.

The advantages? Save yourself a lot of money, live like the locals, and make sure your home stays secure and your house plants watered while you are away. With small children and babies, establishing a known "turf" can make all the difference in the world. The disadvantages? Strangers are living in your house. You are not there to protect it. They may have misrepresented themselves or their home. You have to do laundry and clean up after yourselves, and while *you're* cleaning, they might be doing a *really* sloppy job (this may sound like a small thing, but varying standards of cleanliness is actually the primary complaint that house swappers express).

Can you imagine it? More to the point, ask yourself if you would consider it relaxing to save the vast amounts of money you'll need to find decent lodging, and live in a home that is already set up with all the necessary gear. You can cook and live the local lifestyle. For some people this sounds like a dream. For others, a vacation is a time to avoid cooking and cleaning; they would worry too much about accidentally damaging things and, worst of all, they would spend their time stressing out about what was happening back in their own home.

(continued)

Once we opened the flue, we built a roaring fire and shut the windows. The electricity came on just long enough to make dinner, went off, then came on again in the morning just long enough to make coffee. It wasn't what we planned, but the snow was beautiful, we were far from the hassles of home life, and we were having fun together. On the morning we left, I shoveled three feet of snow off the 20 steps down, cleared a passageway along a 10-foot path, then dug the car out of the garage. I felt strong, I felt resourceful—living in the San Francisco Bay Area where it doesn't snow, this was actually my idea of a good time!

Home swapping is probably not for worrywarts; it relies on good will and communication, and setting it up can sometimes be complex. It's an intimate relationship. You need to find somebody whose home is roughly equal to yours, who has somewhat similar values, who lives someplace you want to visit and is interested in visiting your place, and who, after copious communication (mostly through fax, mail, and e-mail) you believe you can trust.

In the ideal home-swap situation, you'll have a bit of overlap and be able to meet your exchange family in one locale or the other. It is sometimes a good idea, too, to have a friend or family member meet the family that will be staying in your house and show them how things work—that pesky furnace, that toilet handle that needs to be jiggled, the timer setting on the sprinkler system. It's always good to have a friend or family member available in case of emergencies.

If you're planning on a home swap, it's best to begin early. Many home swaps are arranged up to a year in advance. (For information on how to set up a home swap, see the Recommended Readings.)

Advantages of House Swapping	*Disadvantages of House Swapping*
Live like the locals. Shop in the local markets and cook local food!	Who came on vacation to do daily chores? Plus, you have to leave the house cleaner than you found it.
Avoid the local Laundromat. Wash clothes while you relax. Save a bundle of money. Can't beat the price—it's free!	Money is no object and you *hate* washing clothes—the hotel or resort will do the wash for you.
More bucks to spend on souvenirs!	If things don't pan out on the other end, you may up spending that "saved" money on home repairs.
Sometimes the swap family will provide introductions to friends—and you will meet wonderful people you'd have never otherwise met.	Sometimes the swap family will provide introductions to friends—and you will meet horrible people you'd have never otherwise met.
When the Hallinans (3 kids) home swapped in England, they accidentally broke a teapot so they replaced it with a nicer one. They came home to discover that their exchange family had accidentally broken three wine glasses and replaced them with far more beautiful (and expensive) ones	Things can get damaged. They might (and this is a true story, albeit third hand) clog the toilet and flood the house with sewage water. You have to be OK with the idea that this might happen while you trip the light fantastic in Cannes, London, or Bucharest. Remember you hold pretty strong cards—you hold their house hostage, too!
With all the communication back and forth, you may develop a true international friendship, and a family to exchange with for years on end . . .	It does take a while to set up . . .
It's about trust.	It's about trust.

Assorted Odd Lodging

Sometimes you'll have to resort to something unorthodox—and sometimes that'll be your most memorable stay! Keep an open mind, and you may end up someplace unique, and maybe cheap.

CHEAP WAYS TO STAY IN ANY COLLEGE TOWN

Staying somewhere for a month or so during the summer? Any town with a college will have dormitories and apartments available off-season, and usually they will rent or sublet them on a monthly basis. You'll need to set this up a few months in advance. Call the university housing office and follow the phone tree until you reach the right person. University "conference services" often rent dorm rooms on a nightly basis—much cheaper than a hotel.

MONASTERIES AND CONVENTS IN EUROPE

Actually, you *can* stay at that monastery or convent, even without taking a vow of silence. People who have done so in Europe swear by the experience—it's a chance to stay in a historic and beautiful setting, with meals often included and young children often welcomed. Monasteries and convents often have minimum and maximum stays, or other restrictions.

GUEST HOUSES

They're known as "guest houses" in Thailand, "losman" in Indonesia, and other names around the world. These are basically small, family-run inns in developing nations, providing shelter to 'round-the-world-with-a-backpack, on-a-shoestring travelers, often in the family home. They are often the *best* way of getting insight into a culture, if you are staying only a short time. Prices are inexpensive and lodgings range from rudimentary to quite nice. Many are listed in the Lonely Planet guidebooks—many others you'll find by listening to touts in train stations, or by word-of-mouth from other travelers. As with other kinds of lodging, some are appropriate—even quite wonderful—for kids, and some are not.

You Mean You Want to Sleep Here?

Of course, hotels, motels, condos, castles, and guest houses are for more than storing your stuff while you wander around town, take pictures, and buy souvenirs. Eventually night falls. It's time to sleep. *"Sleep?"*

EXPECT A LITTLE MELTDOWN

Evenings on the road can be hard when you've been cooped up in a car or sightseeing among strangers all day. Expect a little baby meltdown. The hotel, motel, condo, or B & B is a

We always know when we've pushed a little too hard or far because our normally charming and delightful child suddenly turns into a small, demonic dervish. She won't listen, she screams, she hits, she laughs when scolded. What keeps us from despairing completely ("I'm a terrible parent, I've raised a monster!") or from losing it completely, is the fact that she is so obviously exhausted, tired, wired, maybe hungry. A firm hug, a small scold, and **time alone with one of us** seems to be the cure.

private place—there are no strangers *here*, this is time for just you and your kid, who really just needs some reassurance, no matter how *awful* she is acting.

- Rather than scold, try to comfort.

- Create a quiet time—try reading a book cuddled together.

- Try to focus on the child; this is *not* the time to get fed up and park him in front of the TV. He's giving you a very distinct message— "I need you, Daddy, and I need you now!"

MAINTAINING BEDTIME ROUTINES

Maintaining your normal bedtime routine is important. All the excitement of being on the road and in a new place can keep kids from falling asleep easily.

- Duplicate your home routine as much as possible. If you read before bed, make sure to bring some soothing favorites from home.

- Darken the room so he is less aware of how foreign the surroundings are from his room at home. (If he's afraid of the dark, pack along "Mr. Night Light" and plug it in near the bed.)

- Familiar sheets and blankets are useful—if you have enough room to bring them along. This is the time to haul out the "stowaway" lovey toys for cuddling.

- Your baby or child might regress to a less-mature state. This is normal (though sometimes a pain in the patootie for the parents.) Be kind—she is feeling insecure.

- A newly potty-trained child might feel better in a night-time pull-up.

- A baby might wake more frequently for nursing. Let her—the reassurance will help her sleep better *tomorrow* night.

- In desperation, we've been known to stick Annie in the bed with us, and watch something banal and boring on TV until she drops off and we can transfer her to "her" bed.

WHAT TO DO ONCE THE BABY SLEEPS

OK, he's down for the night. You're stuck in the hotel room. Now what? No matter how much you may want to *flee*, do *not* leave Baby Boris alone.

- If there is more than one adult, you can take turns painting the town red. Or not.

- Hang out in the motel bathroom—Annie wakes up if the room is too light, so I bring the Powerbook and write, sitting on the floor in front of the toilet, using the seat as a desk.

- Read your guidebooks. Plan tomorrow's itinerary. ("Go slow!")

- Read, meditate, or do your stretching exercises. This is "down" time. Remember, this is your vacation. Take a break, baby.

- Watch pay-per-view TV at low volume.

- Turn in early yourself.

Hotel-Room Horrors Quiz

Are you up for a challenge? OK, screw up your courage and get ready to hear—and resolve—the following gruesome hotel-room scenarios.
(Answers at end of chapter)

Scenario A *You hit town. It's late. You've been in afternoon traffic for three hours. The baby has been screaming for the last two. It's a town with motels near the train station, all geared to serve the train traffic—that's you. Your train leaves at 8:00am and you have to be there an hour before. An hour of cruising up and down the main drag follows. The baby wears himself out screaming and falls asleep—his third nap of the day, and he usually only takes one. Many motels sport No Vacancy signs. At the ones that don't, you stop the car, your companion hops out, enters the office, and is told that things are, indeed, full up. Finally you find a motel. It's a dive, but it's home for the night. You drive in, pull up, and settle in.*

How could you have improved this scenario?

Scenario B *It's 11:45pm, you're in a quaint and quiet bed and breakfast inn and your kid (or worse, kids) are still bouncing. Wild. They refuse to sleep, your throat is hoarse from yelling, you hate your spouse, your spouse hates you, and the neighbors are about to get you evicted. How do you deal with it? You cannot A) Let them scream and run (for your sake as well as the neighbors—you're exhausted and you have that 8:00am ferry to catch!) Wild, evil fantasies enter your head. However, neither can you B) Take up child abuse (besides the obvious immorality of it, this is a very quaint and very quiet bed and breakfast). You cannot C) Lock them in their room and head to the kitchen for a well-deserved cup of herb tea or to the bathroom for a bubble soak—because the kids don't have a separate room, you don't have tea, and the bathroom is right in the middle of the fray. You cannot leave. There is nowhere to go. It's late, you're tired, and in your nighties.*

Any ideas?

> **Scenario C**   *It's Paris, Paris,* Paris *at last! You reach the budget hotel, but you cannot find a parking space. Your traveling partner runs to the* banque *to change your greenbacks into francs to pay for dinner; you double-park the rental car and carry the baby and a suitcase upstairs to the small concierge's office, where a large green parrot stares from a cage and a kindly lady scoops the baby out of your arms and says, "I watch. Pas de problem, no problem. You get ze luggage, I hold zis bebe." You agree. Snookums doesn't look unhappy, and the concierge looks so kind, and has so much authority in her voice. Twenty minutes later, hassled out of your mind from fighting Parisian traffic (and worrying about your baby), you return to a screeching parrot, a screaming child, a frustrated looking concierge. Your travel partner isn't back with the money yet. Baby stares at you with large, bloodshot eyes and hiccups loudly—you know she's been crying for at least 10 minutes.*

How could you have avoided this?

ANSWERS TO HOTEL-ROOM HORRORS QUIZ

There are few real answers when you are in the middle of horrendous (and true-life, I confess) scenarios such as these three above. Much of the solution is in the prevention.

Scenario A   O.K., things aren't going as planned *at all*. Time for a little attitude adjustment. Time for an adjustment of plans. Stop driving. Commute traffic is bad news. Call ahead to the train town and make a motel reservation. (Get motel names from the phone book, if you are close enough, or the Chamber of Commerce, if open). You might also revise your plans, find a motel in the area where you are stuck in traffic, turn in early, and drive to the train station at dawn. (I'm not going to pick on you for not having a motel reservation in the first place.)

Say you stick out the screaming baby and tied-up traffic and hit town, as in the scenario, only to find yourself cruising the main drag. This is a time to split up—one adult takes the baby to a park or cafe, the other gets major brownie points for doing the driving and motel-locating. There's no reason for a tired, cranky baby to put up with an hour-long motel search, too. And by letting the baby scream his way into his third nap, you're setting up a nightmarish night.

Scenario B   Well, maybe B & B's are not the best idea for the next few years. But did you try the bathtub? Water has tremendous powers to entertain and soothe and—most of all—to change the mood. We all have 20-20 vision in hindsight, but once things are calmer, analyze why the kids went ballistic. Did they get over-tired during the day? Was there a lack of stimulation? What foods were involved?

Scenario C   Yeah, I know you're excited by Paris, but you blew it, Cherie. You risked having the car towed and you risked baby's life and limb. You shouldn't have let your partner go to the bank. The hotel would have changed enough money for the evening—and even if the exchange rate was higher than the bank, it would have been worth it. *Never* leave the baby with a stranger. It's not just a matter of safety (the concierge *was* a nice lady), it's a matter of baby being comfortable. You could have left the baby in the car, and taken turns shuttling the luggage upstairs (with one person guarding baby and car at the same time.) The parrot should have given you a shiver of anticipation—you can never tell how an animal will react to a child, and visa versa. And in Paris or any other major city, traffic is always unpredictable, and it *always* takes a while to park.

chapter 11

outdoor adventures

> *It was a wild wild wood. Wild flowers grew all over the ground and wild winds blew through the air.*
>
> —Margaret Wise Brown

Inviting Wonder

Children belong outdoors. I live in a city where the night sky has no stars, where I must drive to hear the crash of an ocean wave. Yet it is vital to me that my daughter feel a connection to—and a reverence for—the natural world. That she can put her hand in spring water and know that water is more than fluid from a tap. That she walk, even occasionally, on ground that isn't sidewalk and cement. That she know the moon. That the natural world is natural to her.

There are too many telephones, cars, and walls in our lives. Bring your toddler to the beach, to the mountains, into the woods; watch as she changes, mellows, responds to the elements. And for you too—a couple of days in nature and something inside releases. Gone is the city's frantic energy, the "Come-on-baby-we're-late" pace of busy life. This chapter is about visiting the Outdoors. It covers:

Once in Maui we rose at four a.m. to drive 37 miles from sea level to the 10,000-foot summit of Haleakala, the ancient volcano. Our goal: a breathtaking sunrise over the crater. The moon shone full, etching Maui in silver, black and white. At the summit, the eerie landscape was barely visible through the waning darkness. Frost covered the ground. A mini-bus belched tourists in shorts who hopped from foot to sunburnt foot, wrapping themselves in beach towels in a futile attempt to warm up. Despite her 16 layers of clothing, Annie's nose turned beet red. "It'll be beautiful, honey," I promised, teeth chattering next to her icy ear.

The sky turned pink. "Almost time!" somebody yelled. "Here we go," I told Annie. The expectant crowd leaned in. And just then the fog socked us in, a hard rain began, and, freezing, foiled, and frustrated, we all ran for our cars.

Awe of Nature

How many miles had we traveled to get to this Hawaiian beach? Yet Annie took one look at the gently lapping ocean, broke into frightened hysterics, and refused to have anything to do with it. We talked to her. We tried to see it from her perspective. Awe of nature is a good thing, I told myself. The bravest of us all fear the sea.

Finally, Bill and I had to be **flexible**. We dug a huge hole for Annie to sit and dig in, and took turns running to the waves. By day two, she was giggling with us in the surf—she just needed a chance to process the new scenery.

- Day Trip to Nature
- Beaching It
- Small Boats and Safety
- The Snow
- Camping
- Backpacking
- When Nature Calls in Nature
- Avoiding Outdoor Disaster

Day Trip to Nature

Tired of the runaround? At or away from home, you can do nature as a day trip. City dwellers can find solitude in regional parks, urban streams, and botanical gardens. Venture a little farther—a day hike, a walk in the woods, a day at the beach, a trip up a volcano—the change of pace will do everybody good. These day trips feel like vacations, even if they're only a few miles from home. You'll return feeling that combination of refreshed and exhausted that only a day in nature can provide.

Beaching It

There is magic where water and land come together. For me, the word "beach" elicits memories of walks along the Northern California coast, Annie's face buried in my chest against the wind, of wading with her at Lido, Venice, far across the Adriatic from war-torn Yugoslavia, and of lazy days of white sand and warm waters in Hawaii. There is something magical about digging holes in sand with a child, searching for shells, and collecting green, brown, orange, blue jewels of ocean-smoothed glass. There is something about a long hot day on a lake beach that defines summer. There is something lulling about the sound of foghorns as you fall asleep after a long day of ocean-gazing.

BEACH TOYS

You can do very nicely with nothing but what the beach provides, but a single bucket and a shovel are fine things. Old yogurt containers are exactly the right shape for castle turrets. A few largish, hard-plastic animals are fun for toddlers—make sure that they're not too important to the child (they may get lost in the sand or the sea).

TIDAL AWARENESS

Children are rarely immune to the mysteries and power of the sea. The tides rise and fall twice daily, and if you'll be beach hiking, its a good idea to know where in the tidal cycle you are. Walking along the beach at low tide, the sands are full of natural treasures, and you can get to magnificent hidden places—but be careful that when the tide comes in, you don't find yourself stranded! Check the tide tables before doing extensive hiking.

Removing Sand from a Toddler's Bottom

When it comes to sand, no place is sacred. The best solution is to march quickly, little one tightly in arms, into the showers available at most public beaches. Enjoy a scream and a giggle in the refreshing (read: cold) water, and let some run down the inside of her suit. Then strip and wrap inside a big beach towel, and either carry her in the towel or re-diaper her, sand and all, and hightail it back to your lodgings. A short warm bath will rinse it all out. The offending sand will swirl down the drain, leaving you with a clean child—and maybe some guilt about the building's plumbing.

BEACH RECOVERY

When it's time to leave, do some sand removal before climbing into the car. Shake out shoes, if you've been wearing them. Sit your kid in the car with her feet dangling out, and gently brush off as much as possible. Sand is abrasive, and can hurt tender skin if you're too rough.

Small Boats and Safety

There is little more thrilling than a boat ride on a smooth-as-glass lake or bay. Yet on small boats, safety is everything. Mary Mapes McConnell's book, *Outdoor Adventures with Kids* has a vital chapter on choosing an appropriate life vest for children. Finding a safe PFD (personal flotation device) will require a little research, but when you consider the frightening statistics you'll realize there are no shortcuts for this vital piece of equipment:

 Eleven children drown in the United States every day.

 Nine out of ten drownings occur in inland waters.

Josh and the Power Boat

Every summer, our extended family spends a week at a cabin on Pinecrest Lake, in the Sierra, North of Yosemite National Park. The cabin is accessible only by motor boat, or by 40 minute hike. On a warm day, in calm waters, ten-year-old Josh was allowed to help steer the boat across the lake. Annie and I sat on the dock and watched the lesson.

Here's the scene from my perspective: one empty lake and one solemn boy, flanked by three watchful adults ready to wrest the wheel from his hands at any hint of danger. Here's the scene from Annie's perspective: Josh—who isn't too old to play "doodle bug," "hide-and-seek," and Legos with her—is in **charge**, actually **steering** the boat across the lake!

She looked at me, eyes big with hero worship. "Mommy, when I'm four, can I drive the boat?"

- Most drowning victims own but are not wearing their life vests.

- Some PFDs float a child on her stomach rather than on her back.

A life jacket (PFD) should be designed like a vest. Make sure it's comfortable, fits well, and doesn't ride up. It should also be fitted with quick release crotch straps. **Most importantly:** The vest must be designed so that the majority of the flotation material is in the chest area—look for asymmetrical flotation that will float the child onto her back, keeping her head and face above water, within six seconds.

The Snow

On a sunny day, there is nothing as beautiful and fun as a romp in drifts of fresh, mountain snow. On a blizzardy day, snow is best admired from the comfort of a warm room.

- You don't need fancy sleds, skis, or saucers (which can be dangerous for little kids, anyway). Beach and sand toys make great snow toys. Playing, throwing, digging, rolling, sliding, and building snowmen, snow women, snow bunnies, and snow giraffes can keep toddlers giggling.

- Resist the desire to stay out too long. Playing in the snow is tiring, and cold. Keep it to less than an hour—return to the drifts after hot chocolate, or at least a rest in the warmth of the car.

- Be aware of the dangers of snow glare. Baby and child sunglasses are vital.

- Once out of the snow, check to see if Bubbala's socks are wet. If so, dry those little footsies and change socks.

SNOW CLOTHING BASICS

Leave lots of room in the suitcase for clothing. Sweaters are bulky, you'll want to layer, and you'll need to have many outfits available for when Wee Willy gets wet. Keep warm, but if you're from a non-snowy climate and venturing into the cold for an occasional weekend, there is no need to spend a fortune on fancy-schmancy snow gear. The five extremities—head, two hands, and two feet—should be well covered.

Layer your child (see layering information, later in this chapter).

- In cold weather, long underwear is a must. Some experts suggest winter underwear should be constructed of several layers of fabric.

- Hat that covers the ears (and not the eyes). Most heat is lost through the head.

- Waterproof mittens and a warm scarf.

- Waterproof shoes or boots. Oversized rain boots with two pairs of socks will work.

- Waterproof or water-resistant pants, or "snow bib" to go over insulation pants. (Check used baby and children's clothing stores—these are frequently outgrown before being worn out.)

- For extra protection, a standard, flexible raincoat or parka to go over all.

What a Difference a Year Makes . . .

When Annie was three, we drove into the mountains for our first snow adventure since she was 18 months old, too little to remember the fluffy white stuff. To our surprise, she was too scared to touch it at first—she wouldn't step in it, she clung to our necks like Velcro. It was 24 hours before she relaxed—and then she couldn't stop snow-angeling and giggling. A year later, it was a completely different story. Annie was like a racehorse at the gate, a champion boxer at the bell, a . . . you get the picture. Every bit of her said, "Let me at it!"

Camping

Just a three-hour drive from our house in the city hides our favorite national forest, 100 square miles of rarely visited mountains, creeks, and wilderness, uncrossed by paved roads. In the forest, days can go by without contact with other people or cars. Here, my city child can listen to the birds; pick wild fruit; swim in clean, rushing water; and sleep under the stars. Here she can learn the dangers of the forest—fire pits, splinters, sunburn, rattlesnakes, poison oak. Annie thrives here. She bounces in the tent, watches caterpillars, watches butterflies, and begins to understand the relationship between the two. She laughs at hopping frogs and points out small fish in the creek and birds in the trees. She sleeps well, lulled by the murmur of the nearby water.

Each summer we venture in, fording flooded streams and navigating miles of rutted forest service roads in our four-wheel drive vehicle. The trip is well worth it, for hidden within the scrub oak and cedar pine, bitter watercress stands in the bubbling granite-lined creeks, tiny

You don't have to start big—your backyard may be the perfect place to pitch a tent or lay down the sleeping bags. Bring out the barbecue and roast hot dogs and marshmallows for dinner. (No! Let the answering machine get that phone!) Listen to the crickets, and sleep soundly in the cool night air.

strawberries hide underfoot, and black raspberries grow plump in the summer heat. High on the mountain, cold water springs fresh from the split root of a fir tree. The green meadows are dotted with flowers, and wildlife is everywhere: lizards, bears, deer, turtles, water snakes, frogs. Circling above the campsite, a single lazy hawk by day, bats by night.

TRAILER CAMPING AND MOTOR HOMES

Many families use their trailers to get *out* into the outdoor world and still have the convenience of having it all with them. Trailers make weekend getaways easy—just grab kids, clothes, and food, and hit the road! The little ones can run in the woods, fish, and swim in natural water, yet still have the security of a "home." Resist the impulse to take the TV, the boom box, the cell phone (except for emergencies. Promise?) The United States is covered with trailer parks and campgrounds. Contact your local AAA office for more information.

WHERE TO FIND WILDERNESS

In the United States, we are fortunate to have access to beautiful and accessible national, state, and regional park systems. Choose your adventure and then venture in—to the rain forests of northern Washington, the Florida Everglades, the high mesas of the Southwest. Explore low deserts, rugged mountains, gentle redwood forests. State and regional parks are inexpensive and family-friendly. Plan a trip to Yosemite, camping easily on the valley floor. Backpack into the true wilderness, where sometimes days pass between sightings of other people, and the only thing that reminds you civilization still exists is the trail of an airplane, miles above, scratching a white trail in the blue sky.

DISTANCE FROM CIVILIZATION

General Rule: When camping, include at least one adult per preschool child.

Car camping runs the gamut from KOA campgrounds with hot showers and plugs for blow dryers in the bathrooms to back-country sites with rudimentary clearings, an established fire pit, an outhouse not too far away, and no water except what you lug along or purify yourself from the local creek. Backpacking, you'll often have no established campsite at all.

When choosing a wilderness destination or campsite, remember the equation: **distance from city + lack of amenities = true wilderness.** Establish your priorities. How far are you willing to travel? What kinds of amenities do you want or need? How far from medical help are you willing to go?

When you have kids of different ages, you should gear your trip for the lowest common denominator—the youngest one. That doesn't mean you can't do a wilderness trip—it just means set reasonable goals and *go slow.*

Call your pediatrician and tell her about your plans. If your child has a chronic medical condition, find out what she recommends, and if you should limit your activities.

Take a trip to the library, local, independent bookstore, or camping supply store and browse the camping books for inspiration and location.

During your stay at the campground, before you enter the forest, your main source of information is the ranger. Whenever possible, call the ranger station or camp office to find out about poison oak or ivy, nettles, thistles, mosquitoes, snakes, and so on *before* you pack up for a trip in the wilds. When you get there, check in at the station.

EQUIPMENT FOR CAMPING

Cut up that credit card—you *don't* need to buy out the camping store! If you've never camped before, get supply advice (and maybe a few loaners) from experienced friends, visit an outdoor equipment store and browse (this is a really fun thing to do with kids!), and visit a Sierra Club bookstore or your public library. There are many excellent books on camping that will give you wonderful equipment suggestions (see the Recommended Readings). Go light—you need less than you think, and you can make do with little. Chapter 8 has the basic packing list—here are some notes and amendments:

Always carry a good, comprehensive first-aid book with you. Even if nothing happens—and probably nothing *will* happen—it will be worth its weight in reassurance. Most accidents and incidents are *not* serious, but even casual bumps and scrapes can cause anxiety if you're away from medical care. A good first-aid book will give you the detailed information you need, at the time that you need it.

Bring a good first-aid kit. No need to buy a special "camping" kit, you can customize your own (I've got some ideas under **M** in the Alphappendix).

Take a backpack to carry your child. Toddlers don't always want to walk, and your hikes may turn to snail-paced strolls as the little one examines every fallen leaf, twig, bug, rock, mossy patch, and gray lizard.

An extra tarp can create a play area, and an extra old blanket or two provides warmth on a cold night (or spread it on the extra tarp for good napping).

Bring extra boxes of diaper wipes, even if your child is toilet-trained. You'll need approximately one box for every four days you'll be camping. Kids get dirty in the

The Three-Layer Approach to Outdoor Clothing

How should you dress your kids? You'll be outside all day: it's cold and drizzly in the mornings, it's hot at noon, and the mosquitoes come out at dusk. Try thin layers that can be shed for heat or put back on for cold or bad weather or to protect from bug bites. Here's how to layer effectively for rugged outdoor adventuring:

The Inner Layer—This layer should stay dry from outside moisture, keep baby or child warm, and wick perspiration away from the skin.

The Insulation Layer—This layer should continue wicking moisture from the skin, and provide insulation. Wool, down, and synthetic fleece retain their warmth even when wet. The new, lightweight, synthetic fleeces dry quickly and are soft as, well, **fleece**.

The Outer Layer—Gore-Tex shells, parkas, raincoats. This is the waterproof, snow-resistant layer. Some raincoats are stiff and hard to walk in. Try to find a flexible fabric that covers the body, and the head.

woods—and they should—so you'll need to swab down their hands and feet before they climb into the tent with you. (Diaper wipes come in handy for the adults, too. Get the unscented type unless you *like* appreciating mountain air through a cloud of chemical freshness—or smelling like a clean baby's butt.)

Don't forget the special lovey toys for *inside* the tent. Keep them hidden until bedtime. The familiar friends will be a welcome touch of home for sleepy children wanting comfort in a strange environment.

If you have room in the car, pack a tot seat to hook on the picnic table.

Bring a few containers (old plastic yogurt cups, egg cartons) to collect small objects for inspection at the campsite. (But remember, leave nothing but footprints.)

A day pack for dragging diapers—not your good "around town" one; bring one that can get dirty, 'cause it will.

Plastic bags, assorted sizes. For everything.

A sleeping bag for the child. Baby bags are quickly outgrown—consider getting your child a regular one.

Snack food, high energy and non-perishable.

Special cups that don't spill, the kind with covers. Spilled juice attracts insects.

Sturdy, easy-to-clean toys; not too small, and not too many. Let them learn to play with Nature's toys—sticks, rocks, and shells. Bring glue and cardboard to make nature collages from leaves and pine cones and moss.

SLEEPING ARRANGEMENTS

To tent, or not to tent? Tents are not *strictly* necessary, though they are a good idea for small kids. Tents confine, reassure, and prevent insect and animal bites. They also provide shelter from morning dew and rain. Consider borrowing or renting one for your first few trips until you figure out what you need. Large family tents are relatively inexpensive to buy, and each year's model is easier to set up.

Bill never used a tent until I came into his life with my little green pup tent (which we now bring along as a special "Annie Play Area"). Bill camped under the stars with his older kids every year, from the time Aaron was three weeks old. Occasionally he hung a tarp over a tree limb to protect them from dew, and the kids always slept between the adults for safety.

- Nights are even chillier in the woods without the confining warmth of a tent. Socks should be thick, pajamas should be warm, and sleeping bags should be warmer. If it's really chilly, consider a stocking cap.

- There is nothing more magical than waking in the night under a black sky full of stars, or in the morning as the sun rises.

CAMPING CLOTHING

- Generally, bring ugly clothes you hate, and stay away from pastel colors; after five minutes in the woods they'll be wet, muddy, or covered with berries and roasted marshmallow debris.

- Bright colors, while rather *ugly*, make your child easy to spot if you lose him.

- Sturdy shoes are a *must*. This is no time for sandals or jellies.

- Jeans and overalls can be worn until filthy (remember, this is *natural* dirt).

- Bring long sleeves and long-pants to help protect Hunny Bunny's delicate skin from sun, mosquito bites, ticks, and poison oak.

Tents

Sheila, Peter, and their **very** active 18-month-old daughter Julie loved to car camp. Julie was (and is) a very active, curious child—into, and out of, everything. How would they keep her safe? Solution: a family tent with two rooms. The family slept in the inner room, Julie between her parents. Sheila and Pete figured that with two sets of zippers between Julie and the outside (plus climbing over at least one parent), they could relax enough to sleep.

Active Child Watch

When they go camping, Sheila and Pete are careful to **explicitly** assign "Julie Duty" at all times. Pete might say, "I've got Julie." Until Sheila and Pete verbally agree that Sheila is the one in charge, Pete is the **man**. By clearly communicating, Sheila and Pete are avoiding potential disaster and the awful conversation no parents ever want to have:
"I thought you had her . . ."
"I thought **you** had her!"

No Safety Gates in the Wilderness

"It's **hot**" I told her. "No, no, very **hot**." As my only darling daughter examined the campfire's glowing coals with fascination, I reminded myself that children have survived open fires since the dawn of humanity. In some pre-industrial cultures, mothers watch their crawling babies approach the fire pit and say nothing. "They have to learn for themselves," they say. I tried to be pre-industrial. I held my breath as Annie investigated. Then, as she came within four feet of the scarring, searing embers, I swept her up in my arms, terrified.

Attention Carnivores

If you eat meat, wrap it raw in meal-size portions and freeze it before you leave home. Wrap it again in tightly taped newspaper. Placed next to a block of ice, it will slowly thaw and remain O.K. for two to four days. (In a good ice chest, block ice lasts about four days. Past that, no perishables.)

CAMPFIRES

There is nothing more heartwarming than sitting around the campfire in the evening, singing together, telling stories about the Glow People who live in the embers. If well-supervised, even a young child can learn about fire safety—how to collect kindling, and build, light, and watch over a fire. Make it into a ritual—teach her the rules. A campfire touches something deep in all humans, no matter how young.

CAMPING CUISINE

Camping stimulates the appetite. What you'll eat camping depends on your family and child's eating habits and pleasures, but the simplest menu tastes twice as good in the great outdoors. Growing up, my family brought jars of flour and sugar, spices, bags of potatoes, and more on our camping trips. Bill and I love to cook but we aren't always so ambitious—though we rarely open cans of food at home, we depend on them when we go car camping. We want to relax too, you know. Plan ahead, and bring a lot (unused cans can go in your Emergency box).

We bring a cooler with one or two blocks of ice (it lasts longer than cube ice). Half-and-half for coffee stays fresh for at least two days if kept next to the ice. Eggs and butter will keep even longer. Drain the melted water every day, and store in the shade while you're out at the water hole.

Powdered milk for the kiddo is a good, non-perishable alternative—be careful of the water (read **W** in the Alphappendix for more on water safety).

Canned beans are always good (for the first few hours after dinner, at least) and kids usually love them. Canned tuna makes a great lunch. (Pair with crispy green pepper!)

Fresh fruits and vegetables last for days and days—if kept cool. Vegetables taste delicious steamed over the fire. Corn on the cob is a hit with the younger set.

- Rice is hard to do, even over a camp stove. Stick with boiled potatoes, pasta, or bread.

- Bring olive oil, vinegar, butter, salt, pepper, garlic cloves, spices, and onions. Sautéed onions spice up anything. Don't mention them, and kids will usually eat without complaint.

- Roasted marshmallows and s'mores (roasted marshmallows smashed with a chocolate bar between two graham crackers) are better in memory than in their sticky reality. They're a family tradition, though, and who can argue with a good tradition?

- For the child who eats only various versions of pasta, you're in luck—open-air spaghetti tastes great!

WASHING DISHES

If you're cooking over a fire, put on a pot of water to heat before you sit down to eat. Campgrounds often have spigots of cold running water. Scrape the dishes and rinse in cold water. Add a little biodegradable soap to the hot water, and give the dishes a quick go over. Rinse in the cold.

CHILDPROOFING A CAMPSITE

A campsite will never be childproof. The first hours before your child understands her boundaries will challenge you. Be watchful of where you put the stove, fuel, matches, axes, knives, lanterns, first aid kit and other items which might be dangerous. For parents, the woods become a world of NOs.

- Minimize the dangers by keeping knives, axes, stoves, lanterns, and so on as far away from temptation as possible. (You might want to keep them locked in the car, except when in use.)

- Define the campground danger areas in terms your child is familiar with: "This is the stove, this is the fireplace. They get *hot*." Then watch your child *like a hawk*!

Washing Dishes in a Stream

If you wash dishes in a stream, scrape them well away from the water. Squat near the stream. Make sure another adult is watching the child. Only use biodegradable soap (and not too much)—and don't worry about getting the dishes too clean. The sponge will get scummy, the dishes will be greasy, but come on, this is **camping**! Lay each completed dish or utensil well away from the water, or you risk having your possessions float away. Dry them with a dishcloth to polish off residual grease and scum.

GARBAGE

Leave it cleaner than you found it. Campsites are rarely as well maintained as they could be, and there's nothing worse than finding a beautiful site that somebody has trashed. After our camp gear is set up, we move around, noses to ground, and collect garbage—old pop tops, bottle caps, broken glass. For preschoolers, make it into a game. Who can find the most garbage? (Not good for kids still in the pop-it-in-your-mouth stage.) Paper can be burned in the campfire, but make sure everything you put in a campfire burns. Never burn disposable diapers. Don't leave garbage in the fire pit. At the end of a camping trip we're like Santa Claus, packing a "ho-ho-ho" lot of garbage out.

WASHING CLOTHES

For short camping and backpacking trips, you can avoid doing laundry by bringing enough clothes, and planning on being a little dirty. For longer trips, handwashing may be inevitable, but splashing in the water can be a fun, family affair (but keep the kids away from the poopy diapers).

- Wash clothes well away from streams.
- Bring clothesline with you.
- Always use biodegradable soap.
- Toddlers can help wring out clothing.
- If you'll be washing diapers, bring a lightweight plastic bucket.

CAMPING, JUST CAMPING IN THE RAIN

Rain can be great fun! A light rain clears the air and flattens the dust. Children delight in clomping in their rainboots, squishing through mud, watching worms squirm. Kids are waterproof (and so are you). If the weather is warm enough, there is no need to stay inside just because of a little precipitation. Toddlers can play in the rain, get soaked, and be fine—as long as dry clothes are available for quick changes. Getting rain-drenched is *not* a great idea for a baby who isn't moving around enough to keep from getting chilled.

A cold, heavy rain, on the other hand, can dampen any outdoor adventure. Getting too wet in cold rain puts kids (and parents) at the risk of hypothermia. Use rain gear, seek protection, and change into dry clothing. Cozy up in the tent or car and read to the sounds of the pattering precipitation. If it's too soggy, you might want to head for an alternative place.

A family tent is a cozy hideaway in the rain. Well protected, you can snuggle down and read together, tell stories, and nibble on snacks.

- Never use a heater or kerosene lamp inside a tent.

- As long as you're dry, you're less likely to be miserable.

- In some older tent models, if you touch the sides, the rain will come in. Your mission, should you choose to accept it, is to keep your kid from bouncing off the tent walls.

- Drag the extra tarp that you used as a play area for your baby over the picnic table with all its gear.

Backpacking

Hiking in the woods with a baby on your back, you are both with your child yet alone in blissful solitude. Baby, high on her perch on your back enjoys the elements and the gentle rocking movements of your walking, and she looks around peacefully or dozes, comforted by your warmth.

- Unless you are a very experienced backpacker, start small with a few day hikes.

- If you plan on taking a hike or a real backpacking trip with Baby on your back, practice wearing the pack around town, around the house, and maybe a few long evening walks in the neighborhood. That's also a good time to break in new hiking shoes.

> **Backpacking Ratios:** The more people per baby the better—an excellent ratio is 4 adults per 1 child.

- Before you take off for a few *days*, do a day hike with a fully loaded pack.

- The joke of trimming a toothbrush to get it thinner and lighter is not a joke—every ounce counts.

- Plan carefully—get a topographical map and plan to go slowly.

- Your child is not a parasitic growth on your back. No matter how young, he's a participant. Keep him in mind.

- If you're backpacking with a walking/hiking child, make sure the little one is willing and able to hike, and that you're in good shape, too.

- If your little ones are walking and carrying their own packs (some four year olds are up for this, some not), make sure that their pack weighs no more than 20 percent of their body weight. Be prepared to heft both kid and pack if necessary.

- If it starts to rain, hike with a waterproof tarp as a little shelf over Baby.

When Nature Calls in Nature

Easier to care for a baby outside? Some say so. You'll probably use a few less diapers a day than you would at home. If you swim in a creek, baby can be bottomless (with lots of sunscreen on that little tush). For long camping trips and backpacking journeys, use cloth diapers and hand-wash them daily. Baby waste is biodegradable, but make sure you wash *well* away from streams to avoid the spread of disease. Drying diapers in the sun both bleaches and sterilizes them. For shorter trips, you can use disposable diapers and lug them out (Aha—another use for jumbo plastic bags!)

POTTY TRAINING AND THE CAMPSITE OUTHOUSE

Some well-appointed campsites have bathrooms with flush toilets, but at many your only option is the outhouse, or porta-potty. These facilities can be frightening for little ones who are just getting comfortable on a standard toilet—they stink, and it's a *loooooooong*, dark way down. I confess, I'm a little nervous about Annie using an outhouse, too. I don't know how potty training occurred when all facilities were in out-buildings. Maybe children were tougher then. Maybe outhouses were simply a rough introduction to Life-with-a-Capital-L. Here are some options:

- Hold the child while she goes. Reassure her (and yourself) that she won't fall in.

- Pack along a potty seat. This is a drag, because you'll have to clean it under rustic conditions.

- Revert to diapers—also a drag because you'll have to wash them or lug the trash out.

- Have the child be like a bear and go in the woods (see instructions coming up). This isn't a good solution in well-populated areas, and it's best not to bury human waste unless you have no choice.

Wildlife

Animals, large and small, live in the wilderness. Teach your children how to gently collect bugs, snails, and slugs—put them in a jar with holes in the lid and examine them briefly before releasing them back to their "homes." Watch for birds—jays, gulls, chickadees, hawks, robins. See the little chipmunk hiding in that tree?

Teach your children to observe but not disturb wild animals. Most animal and snake bites occur because the animal feels threatened and tries to defend itself. Kids like to touch things. As a parent, your job is to know the potential dangers, and supervise your child.

> ## Being Like a Bear
>
> Here's the official way to do it: Dig a hole with a stick at least six inches deep and at least 150 feet away from water, then bury the waste thoroughly, covering the spot with topsoil and leaves. Burn the toilet paper or put it in a ziplock baggie and pack it out. Wash your hands well, or rub with a wipe, a stub of soap, and another wipe.

Rule Number One: *Don't feed the animals.* It's bad for them, and potentially bad for you. If you are in bear country, tree your food. Contact the ranger station for information about local wildlife and how to deal with the food situation.

Rule Number Two: *Don't **ever** pet the animals.* (My friend Tilly saw a visitor in Yellowstone actually sit his child on the back of a wild buffalo.) No matter how cute or sweet they look, wild animals are wild. They may bite or charge, and they carry diseases. If you or your child are bitten by a wild animal, you may need rabies shots.

Avoiding Outdoor Disaster

Yes, the wilds are wild, but by taking a few precautions, troubles can be minimized or avoided.

THE SUN

Protecting yourself and your baby from the ravages of the sun requires a three-pronged approach: sunscreen, sunglasses, and protective clothing. Remember that a fair-skinned child will burn more quickly and more severely than a child with more skin pigment, but anybody can develop skin cancer: The skin of *all* kids should be protected from the sun.

SUNSCREEN

Thirty minutes before your child is exposed to the sun, apply a hypo-allergenic sunblock of at least #15 spf with both UVA and UVB protection. If she'll be swimming, go for the waterproof stuff. If you can, avoid PABA, fragrance and mineral oil. Lipbalm with #15 spf is also available. Reapply sunscreen every two to three hours, or after swimming, sweating, or toweling. When camping, the white lotion will blend nicely with the brown dirt covering your child's body to form a protective camouflage. If your child's skin is very fair, apply the white goop—zinc oxide or titanium dioxide—on her nose, ears, and lips.

Sunscreen is not recommended for babies under six months—his skin is very sensitive and burns easily. Keep him out of direct sun between 10am and 3pm, and dress him in lightweight clothing that covers his full body. Babies should never be deliberately exposed to the sun.

Surf's Up!

Beach sun is bold sun. The sun reflects off the water and sand, making sun protection even more vital. Try a beach umbrella and hang out and nap in the shade. Slather your child in sunscreen half an hour before you hit the beach to allow it to fully soak in and dry. The sight of a toddler completely coated in sticky sand is a sad, sad sight.

SUNGLASSES

"Cool, baby!" Those sunglasses are for more than the hip and happenin' look. Because of the thinning ozone layer, sunglasses should be a part of every baby's outdoor gear. Inexpensive baby sunglasses (and straps to hold them on) are available in many sizes and styles. Use 'em.

PROTECTIVE CLOTHING

Combine thin clothing with sunscreen, and your child should be fine. In very sunny climates, or between 10am and 3pm when the sun is strongest, combine sunscreen with a more textured weave.

Hats Broad-brimmed hats shade heads, faces, and necks. Hats are particularly important for bald babies. It may be a battle to keep a hat on a baby or toddler, but the more accustomed they are to hats, the more they'll learn to deal with it. (If you wear your hat, baby might wear his too!)

Sunburn can be very serious. If your child has a mild burn, coat the burn with aloe vera gel. Try cool compresses or a cool bath with baking soda. Cover with something really soft and stay out of the sun. Use Ibuprofen for pain relief. Administer plenty of liquids. Seek medical attention for blisters.

Long Sleeves and Legs Lightweight cotton blouses and shirts make sense to protect delicate limbs, especially those fresh from the ravages of cold winter weather. Lightweight cotton pants offer comfort from breeze and sun.

SNAKEBITES

Snakes are scary, but though over 7,000 people are bitten every year by poisonous snakes, only a dozen die each year. There are only four kinds of poisonous snakes in the U.S.: the coral snake, the copperhead, the water moccasin, and the rattlesnake. See the Alphappendix under **C** (for Critters) for more information on snakes. (You'll also find information there on little crawling and flying things—mosquitoes, spiders, and so on.)

POISON OAK, IVY, AND SUMAC

Gnarly contact dermatitis results from these allergenic plants. If you know you've touched a poisonous plant, you may be able to stave off the reaction if you rinse well with cold water and detergent or wipe the skin with alcohol within five minutes. Baking soda, cold compresses, and calamine lotion may relieve mild symptoms. Hydrocortisone cream also helps. Keep fingernails cut short, and contact your doctor if the case is severe.

SAFE DRINKING WATER

Giardia, a microorganism that can cause severe intestinal health problems, is a major problem in wilderness areas. (Interesting note: Giardia is also a common problem in child-care centers.) Never drink untreated water from a creek, lake, river, pristine mountain spring, waterfall, and so on. Some campsites have running water, and signs should be posted if it is unsafe. For our car-camping trips, we bring a couple five-gallon containers of spring water. For information on making your drinking water safe, see **W** in the Alphappendix.

Never Poke Your Fingers into "Gopher" Holes

One morning in the forest I glanced down beneath the camp picnic table to see a four-foot-long rattlesnake, with 12 rattles, gently sleeping inches from my feet. Annie's feet never touched the ground in that campsite again. Trying not to impose my own prejudices on my child's wildlife experience, I held her in my arms and backed away slowly, saying, "See the big snake, Annie? Look, isn't it **big**?"

We retreated to the safety of the car, doors locked, while Bill, protective testosterone raging, transferred the entire camp to another, less snake-friendly campsite in 10 minutes, stopping only to take a picture for posterity and to lecture the innocent serpent. I waited until Annie's attention was diverted before turning my back to silently scream, remembering her little fingers exploring small "gopher" holes in the ground the day before. Gopher holes? Squirrel holes? **Snake holes! "Aaahhh!"**

chapter 12
traveling solo with children

> *I have a little shadow that goes in and out with me,*
> *And what can be the use of him is more than I can see.*
>
> —Robert Louis Stevenson

Alone with the Monster

Secret adventures, special uninterrupted time together, a chance to carve out a separate relationship away from the daily hullabaloo—these are rare opportunities in our rush, rush, rush lives. Yes, there are big benefits to traveling alone with your small child. (Plus it can be fun!)

Yet (and now we enter the Dark Side), the idea of traveling solo with babies or small children seems to bring out intense fear and trepidation in many parents. Being a single parent, even briefly, brings its own concerns. Traveling solo with a kid or kids can be daunting. But hey, don't get all housebound, or anything. This chapter brings you face-to-face with traveling alone with the lovely little monster. We'll look at:

 The Zen of the Traveling Parent

 Tools for Successful Solo Travel

- Airports and Airplanes Alone with Little Alfie
- Doing the Driving Trip Alone
- Family Reunions Alone
- Hotel Rooms Alone
- Dealing with Anxieties and Fears
- For the Parent Staying Home

Just to Clarify . . .

I use the term "solo" to mean anybody traveling alone with a child, regardless of their marital or partnership status at home.

The Zen of the Traveling Parent

Traveling solo with baby? Pack up your endurance, store up your sense of humor. You may need both. There may be times when the baby is screaming, the plane is delayed for six hours, your rental car gets a flat tire, the hotel loses your reservation, and your twins suddenly develop the stomach flu and throw up all over your last change of clothing.

This type of travel *is* challenging by nature. You have no other adults to help you. Nobody to spell you when you're tired and cranky. You are the bottom line. It helps if you *expect* it to be hard. Little kids don't usually understand when things aren't working out. They take their cues from you; they feel your tension. Hard moments become harder when you overreact. Take 10 deep breaths and try to step back from it all. Give *in* to the experience. Get Zen about it. Laughter is sometimes the best and only response.

Down the Cliff, Over the Fence, Around the Mud Puddle . . .

Actual traveling and transitional times tend to be the hardest. Think of them as obstacle courses to be navigated. Lower your expectations. If you can get there with everybody reasonably intact, you're doing great.

Tools for Successful Solo Travel

The secrets to successful solo travel with little ones are *lowered expectations, flexibility, delight in small things,* and *tight organization.*

EXPECT THE WORST, EXPERIENCE THE BEST

By expecting and planning for difficult situations, you'll probably be delighted by the surprise of a wonderful trip.

BEND LIKE A BLADE OF GRASS IN THE WIND

First, let's do the '70s chant—"Cosmic. Trippy-and-a-half, man. Groovy, cool, I can relate. Sausalito Sunset. Zoid." Now, let's take it to heart. No really—you have to take it as slow as you can, allow *tons* of time for everything in the world to go wrong, and let your baby be your barometer.

TIGHTEN YOUR ORGANIZATION

Before you leave, try to anticipate problem areas. There are certain things you can do to lower your stress and help ensure smooth seas:

> ### Taking Just One
>
> If you have kids plural, you might consider taking a trip with just one of them. You'll enjoy special time with your child that may be hard to come by at home, and avoid situations caused by sibling rivalry. Take the older one—let Melanie know she's still special. Or take the younger one—give Danny the rare experience of being alone with Mommy or Daddy. The one who stays home also gets special solo time with a parent, and both kids might find, to their surprise, that they even **miss** their sibling.

- Try to minimize what you bring. The less you have to lug and balance, the better. Can you pick everything up at once, and the baby, too?

- Choose destinations where you will feel comfortable. (Perhaps a visit to friends or relatives—you *do* want to show off that gorgeous kid!) And if you can splurge a little on comfort, now is the time to do it.

- Consider traveling with a friend, perhaps another parent.

- ID your kids. Waterproof bracelets and dog tags are available (I've got a source for them listed in the Recommended Readings).

- Stay where you might meet other adults or parents traveling solo with kids. Consider youth hostels where you'll share common dining and living areas with other travelers. (This is not a suggestion for finding romance—you probably won't look your best with that frazzled expression and cookie crumbs adorning your hair.) A little adult conversation is a good thing.

- Know that you may need to enlist help from passersby. (This can be especially hard for solo dads.)

- Plan to eat early, before kids get hungry and desperation sets in; you'll save yourself some heartache—and maybe even cash (see "Saving Money," coming up).

- Take resource materials (maps, guidebooks). This can save time and stress, and give you something to do during those long, lonely hotel nights.

Some people think traveling solo is **easier** than traveling with a partner. Leslie, who has done a number of trips alone with her two year old and three month old, prefers to go without her husband, who tends to get more stressed than she does. Leslie does it by being totally organized, and giving herself pep talks when the going gets rough: "This is not going to be easy, don't expect it to be easy, you can manage, you can do it . . . "

We've got one of those suitcases with wheels and a pull-strap. Bill forgoes the cart and lets Annie ride on the suitcase like a horse as he pulls it along the airport floor. But she's four now, and a "big girl." And he and I, like all co-parents, sometimes have different approaches. ("Hey, Honey, I'm not saying you're wrong . . . ")

Our three-year-old friend Gus flew from California to Michigan and (blissfully for his soloing mom), fell asleep before take-off and slept the entire flight. As they disembarked, Gus looked around puzzled and asked, "Why are we back in the airport again?"

SAVING MONEY

There are practical benefits to solo travel with little kids. Fewer adults means less money spent. If your child is under two, most transportation is free.

- Consider sharing travel and room expenses with other single or solo parents.

- Breakfast is often the least expensive meal in restaurants, so plan that as your main meal. Eat lightly from your own food when you get up, then if you time it right, you can eat your breakfast right before lunch time.

- Hoorah for lunch specials! Eating your main meal in the middle of the day is better for the digestive system anyway, I've been told.

- Many restaurants offer Early-Bird dinner specials.

- Do Juniorette and you eat more than one meal, but not enough for two? Consider all-you-can-eat buffets. Kids often eat free or for only a few dollars. The casual atmosphere is ideal for toddlers and preschoolers, and everybody, even the pickiest eater can usually find *something* to eat.

- For cheap lodging, consider state or national park campsites (go back and look at Chapter 11). When traveling solo, never camp unless there are two or more other cars there.

NO BREAKS FOR THE WEARY — COMBATING FATIGUE

- You're thinking for two (or three, or four) so don't skimp on your own sleep. Nap when the little one naps (or just lie down and close your eyes). Avoid the temptation to drive on in the blissful silence. You need to stay fresh.

- Remember, you're not crazy, you're jet-lagged.

- Take a break! Hire a hotel baby-sitter, visit relatives, take a rest. You deserve time to yourself. Relax!

Airports and Airplanes Alone with Little Alfie

The tips below are *especially* important if you're doing it solo. For basic airport/airline information, read Chapter 9.

- If your child naps, plan flights around nap time.

- Leave lots of time to get to the airport. *Lots of time.* An extra *hour* even. I mean it. It's really, really important.

- Before you get to the airport, stash a few *easily accessible* $1 bills for valets and porters, and for renting your little cart.

- Cut a deal with your toddler. Jonah can either hold your hand or sit in the stroller or cart. He cannot run around or walk by himself. It is too dangerous. If Jonah is a very good boy, he can have _____ (insert small bribe here).

- Carry your tickets, money, and important documents on your body. Strap your camera around your neck. Your bags should contain nothing irreplaceable; there may be times when Emily breaks free and bounds across the airport. She's your first priority—you must feel O.K. about leaving things for a second, and possibly losing something to a thief.

- Once in flight, give up on the idea of magazines and movies—unless the little booger falls asleep.

- Stay hydrated. I'm a firm believer in drinking lots of water on flights, but traveling solo with Annie means I simply

Schlepping Solo Across Airports

Help! The first leg of your two-leg flight is arriving late. You're still in the air; you've been circling for 30 minutes. Your connecting flight is leaving in 10, and the gate is half an airport away. The baby and toddler are hungry, you're going to have to balance two diaper bags plus your carry-ons, and you anticipate having to sprint through the airport to make your next flight. What can you do?

- Sweetly explain your plight to the flight attendant (who, with luck, doesn't hate you already). Ask if they can call ahead for an electric cart to assist you (they do it for people who have physical disabilities). With any luck you'll find yourself gliding high above the fray in a little electric cart that goes "Beep! Beep! Beep!" and scatters travelers like chickens.

- You can also ask an airline-gate person to call your departing flight's gate to tell them you're on your way, and to please hold the plane for you. Then grab the kids and the carry-ons, and **run**.

- Ask for help. This may be a good time to rely on the kindness of strangers. Get them to carry your **stuff**. You carry your child.

- If you miss your connection, first laugh at the absurdity of life. Then feed your kids a snack. **Then** start raising a ruckus to get on the next available flight. If you missed the plane and it's not your fault, the

(continued)

airline might: a) Give you a voucher for free or reduced travel next time, b) Get you on another airline's flight, or c) Put you up in a hotel until another flight is available. If they give you an option that is unacceptable, gently press a little harder. They may accommodate you, and it never hurts to ask. (Sit your gooey-faced little pookie on the ticket counter while you negotiate—charmed or repelled, the staff will steam into action!).

can't lug an extra bottle of water with me. I use it as an excuse for exercise and defeating boredom—Annie and I make *frequent* trips up and down the aisle for water.

FLYING SOLO WITH TWO OR MORE

When you're flying with more than one, you may have a built-in ally—your older child! Treat Big Brother or Big Sister as a fellow adventurer who you can't manage without, and they'll often come through. A three-year-old can hand you Baby's bottle, a four-year-old can sing to the baby while you readjust your load.

Entertaining little ones at different stages in development can also be hard.

- Enlist the flight staff as allies. This means being extra courteous.

- Ask for meals to be served early.

- Don't order hot beverages on the plane. They may end up on a lap.

- Rely heavily on bribes and treats (but keep sugar treats to a minimum or it may back fire on you!). Pack enough doo-dads so that you can surprise each child every half-hour or so.

- Accept that you can't always contain them; sometimes you'll need to let them run.

- Forget about what other people think.

Doing the Driving Trip Alone

Traveling solo, you won't be able to hand off food and drink when the whining gets intense. You won't be able to soothe a screaming baby as you cruise down the highway at 60 mph. You'll have to pull over frequently. You'll have to take it slow. (These tips are in addition to the information provided in Chapter 6.)

- Here's where that flexibility comes in handy. If you're driving alone with a nursing baby, plan to stop frequently for nursing breaks.

- Mark 45 minute increments on the map ahead of time. When you get to the marked places, *STOP!*

- Don't drive during rush hour.

- Try not to travel late in the day when kids get cranky.

- Travel a few hours into the night while they are sleeping.

- Make reservations ahead of time, and have your daily travel goal in mind. This is not the time to cruise up and down city streets at dusk looking for the Vacancy signs.

- Always bring along food and water (Chapter 4 has snack suggestions).

- Don't push your limits. If you or your kids are tired and cranky, take a little break. Stop and sing a song. Splurge on an ice-cream cone. When people get tense, bad moods get amplified. Do something silly to break the tension.

- It is *always* further than it looks on the map.

Family Reunions Alone

Any trip "back home" to the bosom of your extended family can be both wonderful and emotionally draining. A family reunion can be a great choice for the solo parent—you'll get a break from duty from loving relatives who can't wait to spend time with your little darling.

- Know that you're doing your child a wonderful favor by exposing him or her to historical links. Family bonds are cemented by shared times.

- Though you may feel at home, your baby may get nervous. Imagine what it's like: "All these screaming strangers keep *grabbing* me!" Familiarize your child with who they'll meet ahead of time. Look at photos of relatives on the plane, or pin them to the back of the seat so baby can see them as you drive.

- The rules of your extended family may be different than your rules at home, and if you assert *your* rules, you might open up old family tensions. Yikes. You may have to fend off unwanted, unneeded parenting advice. That's hard to do when you're the only one marching to a certain beat. Remember: As the parent, *you* are the authority. You owe it to your kids to maintain some consistency.

- At the same time, this is a good opportunity to teach your children that different people do things in different ways. Be flexible where you can. You might say, "At home we all eat together at the big table, but when we're at Aunt Stacey's, the kids eat at the little table and the grown-ups eat at the big table. At home we'll eat together again."

Be aware that you might inadvertently slide back into old patterns of behavior that you thought you'd grown out of. Without a partner or spouse to keep you centered on who you are now, maintaining your adult identity can sometimes be difficult. This temporary personality alteration might confuse and upset your kids. ("Who *is* that weird woman who looks like Mom?") Make special time for just you and your child(ren). They need the security of knowing that you are still the same old Mom or Dad. You probably need that security, too.

Testimonial

Gizelle and her two-year-old daughter Arielle took a special vacation together, just the two of them, to San Diego. Yes, there were complications—getting across the airport was hard, it rained, and Gizelle got the flu. Despite all this, Gizelle insists, "I'd do it again! I wanted to go so badly I didn't let my fears get in the way, and it was wonderful. I loved being there with my little girl—she's so cute and funny! Arielle was like my little date for five days. She was entertained just by being out, and she picked up on my mood—everything was exciting to her. One day she sang from 3:00 to bedtime. Six months later, Arielle still remembers and talks about the trip."

Safer Among Strangers

"You take your baby overseas?" Isn't that dangerous?" Crime statistics worldwide show that most places in the world are safer than the United States. And, everywhere, most crimes occur between acquaintances. You may be safer "out there" than you are at home.

Hotel Rooms Alone

Read Chapter 10 for general advice. Below are some "solo" specifics.

SAFETY

Always make doubly sure that the room is safe for the baby (review the "proofing" information in Chapters 2 and 10). Have the management remove anything you feel is dangerous.

HOTELS AND DINING ALONE

You've settled your stuff in, now it's time to go out for dinner. Your baby or toddler is tired from the long travel day, and will enjoy the chance to check out the new environment. You'll probably enjoy an early evening stroll. But sometimes it is really *too* much to go out. If everybody is exhausted, cranky, and unwilling, take the night off and explore other options. Traveling solo, you can't send somebody to the store while you stay with your children. Kids must eat when they're hungry, and you should too. Now's when you dig into your supplies (and have a *big* breakfast tomorrow), or order from room service or a restaurant or delivery service. (Chapter 10 has more information.)

SLEEPING ARRANGEMENTS

Since you're the only adult, there should be plenty of room in the bed. Annie and I happily share. Many people don't like their kids to sleep with them. Get a hotel room with two double beds, ask for a crib, cot, or roll-away, or create a bed on the floor.

BEDTIME RITUALS

As exciting as travel is, you and your child may become lonesome for the ones left at home. Bedtime rituals are even more important if the kids are away from—and missing—the usual loving caretaker. If you're going to be gone more than few days, the half-hour before bedtime is a good time to play tape recordings sent by Mom or Dad, read or write letters and postcards, or make phone calls.

LONELY NIGHTS

Bring along things to occupy your time after the baby falls asleep. Unless you hire a hotel baby-sitter (there's more on this in Chapter 10), you won't be doing the big boogie at the disco down the street. Plan tomorrow's itinerary, watch a movie, read a book. Or catch up on your sleep. You have a big day ahead of you.

Dealing with Anxieties and Fears

It's perfectly normal to feel anxious about being alone with the kids on the road. Anxiety alerts us to the need for caution and preparation. Plan, prepare, and take the normal precautions (avoid deserted alleys, lock your hotel room at night, don't volunteer too much information to strangers—you know the drill). But don't be so frightened that you shut yourself off from adventure. Some people find themselves so fearful that they experience extreme anxiety and fear, or avoid the experience altogether. If you're considering traveling solo with children but feel overwhelmed by the idea, go back to Chapter 2 for a pep-talk, and try the following:

How Close Is Too Close?

I was alone with Annie on the streets of Venice one evening. We were standing outside a restaurant when a young woman came down the narrow cobblestone street. She approached us and lifted Annie out of my surprised arms, murmuring endearments, **"Che bella! Bellissima!"** I simply stood there, unable to move. Should I grab my baby back? The woman didn't seem to mean any harm. This culture has a different sense of personal boundaries, my thoughts raced. Will I insult the woman if I remove Annie from her arms?

After a moment, the woman handed my baby back. After another moment, she had disappeared down the dark street. Though the woman had been kind, I was shaken and upset. Without another adult with me—one I knew and trusted—I had found myself unable to judge the danger level or appropriateness of the situation. All I knew was that I had felt intensely uncomfortable.

Since then I try to pay more attention to my personal comfort level, and to Annie's. Now when strangers come too close for my comfort—when they tweak her cheek, touch her hair, or try to hold her—I imagine that I'm a mother lioness protecting my cub.

"Thanks for being so friendly, but you know, that's her body, and I would prefer that you respect her privacy," I say. Sometimes I try to spare their feelings: "Uh . . . you probably don't want to touch her, she's still contagious." Sometimes I just react: **"No!!! Put her down!"**

Even when they might not understand my words, they understand my tone of

(continued)

voice and back away. And if people get huffy ("Well! I was **just** being friendly!"), I remind myself of the majesty of the lioness, growling at strangers as she gently places her velvet paw on her baby's head, claws sheathed.

Try verbalizing your fears or writing them down. It's like opening the closet door at night for your toddler—in bright light, the monsters often disappear.

Assess your fears. Are you worried about personal safety, or about your ability to handle difficult or scary situations?

What are some potentially scary situations? What would you do if they occurred?

Now might be a good time to talk to other parents who have traveled solo with kids. What were their experiences? What was the worst thing that happened? What was the best? What surprised them? Let somebody you trust help you assess the real dangers. They're probably fewer than you imagine.

LEARNING STRENGTH

Being a single parent even for a day can be an exercise in self-assertion. You are your kids' ally, their buffer against the real world. Nowhere can this be more evident—or necessary—than when you are outside your controlled home environment. If asserting yourself is hard for you, practice ahead of time. Nicely contradict somebody in public. Tell yourself you don't care *what* other people think.

For the Parent Staying Home

I watched them disappear through the sliding glass doors of the airport—tall Bill and tiny Annie, with her castle-shaped backpack, off on her adventure with her Daddy. The airport guard smiled, but firmly waved me back into my car. I drove on. Life, for a parent staying home alone, can feel mixed. I'd been looking forward to the time alone, but I felt a little lost, and a little jealous—of both of them on their upcoming adventure, and of Bill for getting to watch Annie discover new things in the big city of Los Angeles.

Then time . . . four days of uninterrupted *time* . . . stretched before me, and my heart beat faster with the possibilities. I got work done. I gabbed on the phone. I read a book and took a two-hour bath. I got a lot, *a lot,* of blissful, solid, uninterrupted *sleep* (and I can tell you that sleep is highly underrated in this society). But I missed my Annie.

When Annie was two months old, a separation of more than two hours felt agonizing to me. At four years, I get occasional pangs of longing, as well as occasional pangs of guilt for not feeling *more* longing. It's important that Annie and Bill have special experiences together, and it's worth the wait to see the look on Annie's face as she comes racing down the airport ramp yelling, "Mommy! Mommy! Mommy!", delight, excitement, and love jumping from her face.

chapter

13

baby business

> *"If I see something good, I will fax it to you. All right Annie?"*
>
> —Emma, age 3 ¹/₂

The Fax, the Phone, the Pacifier

Enough of the fun stuff: the day trips, the castles in Italy, the woods. This is the millennium, man. Kiss the kid good-bye, dry your tears, and get back to work. But wait, you forgot something important! You forgot the baby!

Part of incorporating "le kid" into everyday life means bringing him into your work life, as well. More and more people are doing it; trying to merge all the diverse elements of their lives into one cohesive, happy whole. Doing business with Baby means sometimes you take Baby with you on the road, sometimes you and Baby try to "work it out" at home, and sometimes Baby goes to the office. This chapter discusses all those possibilities. It includes:

- Working on the Road with the Little Poopsie
- Child Care for the Business Trip or Home
- The Office at Home

- The Office Baby
- Finding and Keeping your Balance

Working on the Road with the Little Poopsie

Besides the guilt I feel, I get *lonely* on the road—the long hotel nights, the impersonal coffee shops; each town seems the same to me, the movies and the factory remind me that I'd like to be ho-omeward bound . . . . Oops, sorry Art, sorry Paul. Start again, Ericka.

> *"I like being with David, and he likes being with me, and when there's too long of a separation, we both miss each other terribly. Bringing him with me has its hassles, but leaving him home, with the accompanying worry and planning, has its hassles, too. When I'm not with him, I worry. Then I have trouble focusing on my work."*
>
> —Lee Black

So, you need to do some business out-of-town. Here are some reasons to bring Baby along:

- You just *want* to. No, you're not *weird* for wanting your child near you; she wants to be with you, too. If you bring her with you, you won't miss each other. Until much later in your child's life (when she will spend her time trying to break away), you are your child's universe. Whither thou goest, she wants to go.

- Be trendy! More and more parents are doing business with a baby. Time was when, female or male, you were considered a lightweight if you brought your kid with you. The times they are a changin' . . . . Sorry, Bob.

- Though you won't be spending your actual work hours with Small Sam, you may have *more* time with him than you would at home. He'll be happy, and you'll be happy. (Doesn't a nice cuddle with your baby sound like the perfect cure for the hotel blues?)

- You'll avoid those rough "Daddy's leaving" and "Daddy's home again" transitions, and your child's separation anxiety will be reduced.

- Your own "worry-quotient" will drop—you'll know exactly how she's doing, because you'll *be* there.

- If you travel regularly to the same places, your child will get familiar with the routine. Babies who travel a lot do it more easily than those who do it occasionally.

- Child-care logistics can be tricky—but child-care logistics are *always* tricky, on-the-road or not. Don't stress out; we'll discuss child care at home and on the road a little later in this chapter.

PLANNING THE BUSINESS TRIP

When you plan your schedule, try to limit your activities more than you would if you were by yourself. If your organization is doing the planning, try to negotiate a slower pace. Consider incorporating a vacation day into the mix—you're doing double duty—as parent and as worker. Ideally, you want *them* (the people with whom you're doing business) to be specific about the schedule, and you want the ability to be flexible within those parameters. (I *said* ideally!)

SPECIAL PACKING REQUIREMENTS

Sensible or not, you really shouldn't wear your stained sweats on the plane. You are on a *business* trip. Also, try to leave the silk and cashmere at home (or change once well away from baby burp and sticky, jammy hands). Your challenge is to find special clothes that look professional, feel comfy, and are easily cleaned. I strongly recommend rayon—hang it in the bathroom while you shower and the wrinkles should steam out. Unlike other business travelers (poor dears; calm on the outside, pining for their children on the inside), you have double requirements clothes-wise, and with all the baby gear, you probably can't get away with just a carry-on bag.

WORKING ON THE PLANE

Probably not. Unless baby sleeps. Apple juice and laptops are an unfortunate combo.

NO "DRINKS WITH THE GUYS" AFTER THE BOARD MEETING

Unless you're on the kind of trip where the "real" business occurs after hours on the golf course, you should probably keep your trip a little more "all-business" than you would if you were alone. (Life is long. You'll be back to Chicago another year—you can hear blues at the Blue Note then.)

"Mama's on a Business Call, Sweetpea"

Scenario: The first round of meetings went quite well, you **think**. You have to prep for tomorrow's round after Baby Heather goes to sleep, but she's a little agitated—the travel, the strange place, the baby-sitter . . . . The phone rings. It's the Big Client calling to go over those figures. Suddenly the baby goes ballistic! Screams! What can you do?

Solution: Unless Heather is screaming from pain (in which case you say, "I have an emergency, I'll call you back," and hang up), maintain your calm tone and Plug That Hole. A baby with a full mouth cannot scream. Use a bottle, a banana, a cracker. If you're nursing, whip up your shirt and offer your breast. A nursing baby will usually nurse when offered the opportunity, and this is no time to worry about feeding schedules.

If nursing is not an option and bananas, bottles, or pacifiers are not working, calmly explain that you are very sorry, but you'll need to call back in 10 minutes. The key here is the calm, professional voice that says, "I'm so together that nothing can faze me." Get the number (don't trust yourself to remember!), hang up, and deal with the situation. You've bought 10 minutes, and 10 minutes is a **long time** in babyhood. You can deal with almost anything in 10 minutes.

Try to remain serene—if you're freaking out that you may have blown the most important deal of the century, you'll never change your child's mood, let alone her diaper. Comfort, caress, kiss. Set baby up with enough distractions to

Child Care for the Business Trip or Home

Who will take care of the baby during work hours? Perhaps the ideal situation is for the whole family to go—you work, and your loved ones play. This is not always economically or logistically feasible—perhaps you're a single parent, perhaps your partner can't take time off. When you bring baby on the road for business, you have several options.

- Hotel baby-sitters (we talked about those in Chapter 10).
- Conference child care
- BYO child care

CONFERENCE CHILD CARE

This only applies if you're going to a conference—and not all conferences provide this option. Conference child care is usually provided on-site for parents who bring their children. Before you jet off with Junior, get information about *who* is doing the care, *what* ages they will accept, *where* the care facility will be, *how* many kids they will take, and *when* the child-care center will be open. How long can you leave your baby? Two hours? All day? Then ask yourself, "How long do I *want* to leave my baby?" Have a back-up plan, and get information about hotel baby-sitting before you go. That way, if you get there and get a bad vibe about the place, you can remedy the situation and not miss that important paper on "The Sexual Secretions of Lower Invertebrates."

BRING THE BABY-SITTER

If you have the bucks, it may be worth it to bring child care with you. The care-giver doesn't have to be your full-time or even regular baby-sitter (though that would be ideal). Are any young adults in your life eager to get somewhere and willing to work in exchange for transportation? Back when I was 19 and my cousin Jesse was four months old, my Aunt Laurie had to give a couple of speeches on the other coast. The people who hired her ponied up the plane fare for a baby-sitter—*me!*—and I got a free trip to Boston and New York, spent some time with my delicious nephew, and stayed on by myself for a week of adventure and fun before flying home. (O.K., I'm busted. Remember back in the Introduction when I said I'd never held an infant before Annie was born? I exaggerated. So sue me.)

NANNIES AND AU PAIRS

Hiring a full-time care-taker for your child—for home and/or the road—can be agonizing. That's because it matters so much! It can be scary, too. Nanny horror stories abound (Remember that movie about the psycho baby-sitter, *The Hand that Rocks the Cradle*? Actually, I never saw it. Who needs nightmares?) Less often, we hear the very common success stories of friendship, bonded families, and the joys of bringing a new person to respect and love in your lives.

> (continued)
>
> carry you through the call and, precisely 10 minutes later (demonstrating how organized and professional you are to the client—they can't see your formula-drenched clothes), call back. Apologize briefly (without details) and continue to sell, sell, sell!

> Nancy, who worked part-time at home, hired a teenage "mother's helper," somebody slightly less than a baby-sitter, to come in the afternoons (with Mommy present) and play with her son, do odd chores, and remove the baby from the room **immediately** if the phone rang. This young man also accompanied her on a number of almost-local business trips. They all drove together in the car, and Nancy was able to nurse Jasper right before and after seeing clients.

INTERVIEWING FOR A NANNY—FOR TRAVEL OR OTHERWISE

For my friend Ailsa who has a three year old, a four year old, a career, and a husband who works *very* full time, the nanny is an essential piece in the logistical puzzle of her family's busy life. When hiring a nanny, she suggests that you:

- Interview with your head *and* with your heart. References are vital, as is your gut feeling about whether or not you like somebody, and whether you think they will be good for your baby.

- Decide in advance how many hours and how much you're willing to pay (ask other parents to determine the going rates in your community)

- Contact agencies. You give them your parameters, they set up the appointments. Agencies are more expensive than hiring independently, but they also will be in charge of taxes, be responsible for your satisfaction, and will check out employees' records.

Who Are You Looking For?

Some say, "Look for somebody who parents like you do." But if you're a new parent, you may not **know** your own parenting style. Others suggest choosing a child-care provider to **augment** your care; somebody who can offer qualities or skills that you cannot. Here's a mental checklist. Does your potential nanny pass?

- Is he responsive to the child? Experienced?

- Can she both nurture and foster autonomy?

- How does he handle conflict? Are you comfortable with his approach? Will he listen to your requests regarding conflict and "discipline?"

- Does she hold religious or cultural beliefs that run counter to yours in terms of day-to-day care? In other words, her religion and culture are her own, but if she'll be teaching your child activities or habits that make you uncomfortable, then it probably isn't a good fit.

Advertise independently in local newspapers, religious papers, neighborhood newsletters. Try putting up signs in kids stores, preschools, bookstores, or other appropriate places (try the Child Development office at the local college or university).

Speak with the potential nanny on the phone. If you like her (or him), set up an interview time and get her references.

Call references *before* meeting with the potential nanny. In a 45-minute, face-to-face interview, it's hard to get all the information you need to trust that person with your child.

References can give you facts (when did the person work for them, for how long) and also answer vital questions: Are they usually punctual? Are they messy? Do they sit in front of the TV all day? What language do they speak (there are pros and cons to bilingualism)? How do they display their temper—were there any odd or uncomfortable incidents? How do they handle criticism? Are they flexible? Do they need to do everything their way? (Of course, using this criterion, Mary Poppins, who did things *her* way and never explained, would *not* be a good nanny candidate).

References can also alert you to potential trouble areas and help you prepare your questions.

If it doesn't feel right after talking to the previous employers, cancel the face-to-face appointment before you've both wasted too much time.

If the references are glowing (and the facts the potential nanny gave you check out), continue the process. Watch how the person relates to your children, and how the children respond to the potential nanny. The interview is the time to assess the potential match.

Ask the nanny to baby-sit for a couple of hours. See how it goes, how your kids do, and how the nanny feels. Will she or he like working for you? Does it *feel* right to you?

NANNY TAXES

Part of the process of hiring your nanny, full-time baby-sitter or au pair is setting up the pay thing. You'll probably contract for a certain range of hours per week, and you'll arrange how you're going to pay them—in cash or by check, and whether or not you're going to be withholding taxes for them.

Since you'll be taking taxes out for them (come on, it's the law and you don't want to blow your chance at elected office over something so small), you need to call the IRS (I've included the number in the Recommended Readings). Give yourself a pedicure while they keep you on hold. When you reach them, they will set you up as an employer and provide you with a wage book with instructions and a schedule of taxes.

The Office at Home

More and more people telecommute or free-lance from home, and home offices have gone from being a rarity to a norm.

THE FANTASY

As a scribe-for-hire, I've worked at least partially at home since 1990. It took me years to learn how to ignore the piles of unfolded laundry and dirty dishes during work hours (or at least save them for a "coffee" break), but I eventually learned to focus, do my work, and mentally put on a whole new hat when it's work time.

"This will be a piece of cake," I thought when I got blissfully pregnant. "How lucky it is that I'm a writer—I can write when the baby is asleep or in a playpen next to my desk!" I had images of a sunny room (never mind that my office is a little dank); a bubbly, cooing baby batting at toys near me; and great prose streaming from my fingertips into the computer. Yes, I planned to mother and do great art *at the same time*. Well, I told you I hadn't spent much time around babies . . . .

In Support of the Au Pair . . .

Many moons ago, I was an au pair in an old chateau in France. The chateau was gorgeous and the grounds phenomenal—chestnut trees arcing over the long drive, hedgehogs scuttling, a long misty view from my window over pheasant-filled fields down to the Loire River . . . . Sounds romantic, huh? Hah. More like slave labor. Taking care of three kids (ages three, six, and seven, polishing the silver, ironing Monsieur's underwear . . . . What good is Paradise if you're on your knees scrubbing out the bathtub, crabby kids hanging on your back, while Madame takes a leisurely nap? How can you enjoy the French lifestyle when the nearest small city is 14 kilometers away and your only transportation is a bicycle?

My purpose telling this story (other than **revenge,** should they ever read this—down, Ericka, down!) is to put in a word for the au pairs of this world. Please, I beg you, do not abuse them. Do not take advantage. Yes, they are living in your house, traveling with you, getting the opportunity to visit Baltimore and Hawaii. Yes, they are part of your "family." But they need a life, too. If they are kind and accommodating and love your children, and you are tired and stressed, it is easy to forget that they really **do need that day off—no exceptions!** Polish your own silver and iron your own skivvies. Stay focused. Light housekeeping does not include windows. An au pair is there for the kids. (End of rant.)

First Day at Roots and Wings

It was the ideal day-care solution: three blocks away, in a loving, well-recommended family home with Maribeth, a great child-care provider. The night before Annie's first day, I had a vivid nightmare of seeing Maribeth drunk, eight months pregnant, and crying. I awoke with a start. I got Annie out of bed, got her dressed, and, trying not to let her see how traumatized I was, drove down the block.

Maribeth was so nice (and neither drunk, pregnant, nor weeping). I sat in the kitchen, steeling myself to leave my one-and-only child. The aroma of toasting muffins and fresh-cut peaches filled the air. I had a deep urge to stay all day, to sit down on one of the tiny stools and join the kids for honey muffins and hard-boiled eggs, to play with paint and books and animals, to snuggle down on a little pad at naptime. But it was time to go. Annie—ready for her own adventures—kissed and dismissed me, and I wandered out into the sunlight, teary, empty, and bereft.

Children of the Nineties

Two year olds Stella and Andrew were making mudpies in the sandbox at their preschool and Andrew got sloppy and wet. Stella ran into the classroom, "Teacher Debbie, can you e-mail Andrew's mommy and tell her to bring some new clothes?"

THE REALITY

The reality is that I *need* child care to be able to work more than occasionally. Parenting is work—it is intensive, disruptive, and not conducive to the quiet, uninterrupted stretches of time I need. The other reality is that, even with top-notch child care, there may be times when I need to work *and* take care of my baby. Sometimes the universe cooperates and I can, indeed, parent and work at the same time. At other times . . . "@*#&!$@!#!!!" (Your experience will also depend on the type of work you do. You might be able to nurse a baby and type with one hand—it is harder nurse a baby and conduct a psychotherapy session, or do a massage, or video-conference a board meeting.)

HOME OFFICE SURVIVAL TIPS

- Expect—no, *allow for*—extreme flexibility. If you are telecommuting, it helps to have a flexible boss.

- Don't count on the nine-to-five thing. You may find that your best work happens between three and five a.m. when the house is finally quiet. Or, you might work best in two-hour chunks scattered throughout the day.

- Try to establish a schedule, no matter how odd. It will be better for the baby—she'll get a general sense of when you're working and when you're not, and it will be better for you. Part of the challenge of working at home is legitimizing your work day. Scheduling regular work time helps. This might mean taking a lunch break at the same time everyday, or quitting at the same time.

- Keep in mind that a toddler needs more attention than a baby.

DAY CARE WHILE YOU SLAVE AT HOME

Let's face it—good parenting is a full-time job. You cannot concurrently work two full-time jobs and do a good job at either. While you will need an *individual* care giver for your business trips, if you are working at home, you can explore other options—swapping with other parents, family home day care, infant centers, and preschool.

WORKING WITH BABY IN THE ROOM

Well, you can try. It may be an exercise in frustration, particularly if you're trying to do a task that requires extended concentration. Keep in mind that the child's needs will always be more real and more pressing than the report you *have* to finish—and that is appropriate. A small child needs attention, and he is not "bad" for asking for it.

> Even now that Annie is four and an old pro at having work-at-home parents, we still have moments of "challenge." Just a few minutes ago, Bill was on the phone with a university president, I was on the other phone interviewing a child-care expert, and Annie started yelling from the bathroom, "Mommy! Daddy! I'm done going poo! Come wipe me!"

- Much of your baby-tote travel gear—the Snugli, the backpack—will be essential for working in the house or office, though be careful when you swing around with a backpack on your back (those things are *wide*).

- If you're trying to take care of a baby and work at the same time, you might find yourself standing up with baby strapped to your body much of the time. If you're using a sling, make sure you switch sides often or you'll end up feeling as lopsided as Quasimoto.

- If you work at a keyboard, set up your desk so that it is ergonomically comfortable and safe for your body. This is especially important if your baby will spend some or all of the day on your body. In some areas, an ergonomic expert can come to your office, assess your working area, and make suggestions for raising or lowering your chair, positioning your keyboard if you work on a computer, and so on.

- A preschooler can sometimes sit near you and do activities with parental input from time to time—but don't count on it.

- Pediatricians, child-development experts, and movement therapists are all very concerned about the damage that results from putting babies in swings, "jump-ups," walkers, crawlers, or other devices that put a child in a position or allow her to make movements she is unable to make on her own. Though they may free your hands for working, these are not recommended solutions. (Walkers are particularly unsafe because babies can move at speeds they're not ready for and accidents can happen very quickly.)

You can try a playpen for limited periods. Part of its success will depend on the temperament of your particular baby—some babies and small children simply require more constant physical contact than others. Even if your child seems "independent," never leave them in a playpen for more than 20 minutes at a time (unless, of course, the little angel is asleep).

Children *need* to move their bodies for proper physical, neurological, and emotion development, and keeping them physically restricted is inappropriate and wrong.

For the mobile baby, try baby-proofing your office. Yes, that includes dealing with all those computer cords.

EMOTIONAL CHALLENGES OF A HOME OFFICE

Once she is past babyhood, working in a home office with Kiddo in the house becomes both easier and more challenging. On the plus side, she can play with a baby-sitter or another parent and you won't feel the same driving urge to run and cuddle her each time she cries. The challenge comes from Kiddo herself. She just can't understand that sometimes Mommy or Daddy needs to be left alone. "But I need to be with you . . . I'll be very quiet . . . I won't bother you, Mommy!" The little eyes run with tears, the baby-sitter stands feebly at the door waiting to see what you'll do, and you feel like an ogre. Yet you must work. You can explain and explain how lucky Kiddo is, not to have a parent gone all day every day, but a three or four year old cannot comprehend. All she knows is that she needs Mommy or Daddy *now.*

Step One: Don't be angry at your child; she's just being honest about her desires.

Step Two: Have a private talk with the baby-sitter. It is his or her job to make sure that you are undisturbed.

Step Three: Provide as much physical distance as possible—a door that locks, another part of the abode.

Step Four: Be clear that sometimes your kid *does* need you, and need you immediately. Your task is to figure out when it can be avoided, and when it is real.

THE HOME OFFICE—TOOLS OF THE TRADE

A home office can be a separate room, with a private entrance and a lock on the door, or a cabinet where you keep your stuff and . . . the kitchen table. Of course, the more privacy the better, with the added incentive that you won't be able to deduct your "office" from you taxes unless it really *is* a separate room used only for office purposes.

BE AWARE OF THE ISOLATION FACTOR

Working at home with a baby or little kid can be a double-whammy: People who work from home complain about feeling isolated, and parents alone with their children all day complain about feeling isolated. Imagine this: You have a major project due and the baby has colic. You haven't talked to a grown up, let alone a colleague, for what seems like days, and you are getting *very* depressed. Well, who wouldn't?

 Can you do some of your work in the park? In a cafe? In a restaurant?

Take your baby to work one day a week (we'll go into that in a minute).

Get some exercise on your "lunch break." Take baby to the gym (many gyms have child-watch facilities—remember that section in Chapter 7?), or strap him on your back and take a vigorous walk.

Cordless Phones—More Than an Office "Must"

Cordless phones are a must. We're not completely happy with existing cordless-phone technology (whenever somebody talking on a cellular phone drives by, we lose our connection) but I **swear** by their capacities. How else could I dash from room to room following a toddler in destruction mode and schedule appointments at the same time?

Come to think of it, this is far more than a business tip. Hanging out with a baby all day can be isolating, and chatting on the phone while performing mundane duties in various rooms can make the hours go quicker. When Annie was an infant, my phone calls with friends or my sister sometimes lasted through a couple of baby naps, sinks full of dishes, and loads of laundry. Attention to a baby is vital—attention to yourself, and to life outside the home cocoon, is vital, too.

TAKING BABY ON AN OFFICE VISIT

If you're working off-site from your home office, you may need to get into work occasionally, for meetings, to keep "in touch," or to alleviate your isolation. Part of the problem is that out-of-sight (or off-of-site) is often out-of-mind, and unless you make an occasional appearance, you may find yourself completely out of the loop. (This applies only to people who *have* jobs. Freelancers like me need to find other ways to communicate with others in their field: conferences, meetings, writers' support groups.)

If the site is safe (no babies at the nuclear power plant, please), drop by. Make up an excuse, if necessary. Beware: The reality shift may be disconcerting. You're spending your time at home, dealing with very primal, beautiful, and deep issues of new life and development, and they're still in their cubicles, sneaking forbidden games of Minesweeper on their computers in between dishing the dirt on the clients and whining about the workload. Walking back into the worksite may feel weird (everything in *your* life has changed, everything there is just the same), but it can also feel grounding. "Ah—*there* I am, the "me" I was before I had a baby!"

BE ALL BUSINESS

Make an effort to talk about work, not Junior. The anti-child contingent will appreciate that your brain hasn't turned into creamed banana, and the baby-lovers and other parents will respect your seriousness and loyalty to the job. (Yes, a little cooing and beaming is allowed.)

The Office Baby

Depending upon the level of support you receive from your co-workers and management, working on-site with a baby, while certainly not appropriate for all situations, is sometimes possible. When my niece Emma was born, Jessica took a few months off of her arts administration job and then returned full-time—with Emma. Her office filled with diaper pails, toys, and baby totes. Life wasn't easy—but until Emma began crawling like crazy and there was an opening in a day-care center a few blocks from Jess' office, bringing Emma with her was the best solution for all. When Alexandra was born, she too came to work with Jessica until she began to crawl.

Having babies in the workplace is still a new phenomenon in our society—you'll be a pioneer, so be considerate and conscientious about smoothing the way. The tips I've provided for working with a baby in the room still apply, but here are a few more suggestions:

- Rearrange your office furniture so that the area where the baby plays or sleeps is out of sight. Babies are messy, and you're there as a worker, not a professional parent—your co-workers shouldn't have to look at baby-clutter. Make sure all toys are stored at the end of the day and that the office looks like an office.

- Baby-proof the office just as you would your home or hotel room.

- A baby, no matter how teeny, *needs* your attention. You may end up feeling like both jobs—the paid one and parenthood—are suffering. Plan for a lighter work load for the first six months.

- The baby doesn't just enter your office, she enters the entire building. She (and you) will be better received if you invite the rest of the building into your baby's life. Bring her around for visits when she's in a particularly giggly, cuddly mood, or invite people to drop in—"Whenever you need a baby fix." Baby is your ally among those who might feel some resentment. It's hard not to like a baby. They might not like *you*, but who can resist that little yummy tummy?

- It helps to have a baby-friendly co-worker who is willing—and able—to whisk Little Porky away for a few moments when the Big Boss calls, the client drops by, or when you have to sound *very* professional on the phone and having baby-babble in the background doesn't help.

If you're bringing your baby to a meeting, it's common courtesy to let people know ahead of time.

Be considerate of the janitorial service that cleans the office at night. They are paid to empty trash cans full of paper and paper clips, not baby waste. Jessica brought her own trash bags and removed them daily.

If you're in an office where you need to look presentable, your baby should, too. Appearances do matter, and you want your baby to be welcomed. Don't leave her in stained, smelly clothing.

Jessica swears by food treats. A box of organic O's cereal can go a long way.

Keep a tape player and some lullabies or other soothing tapes handy. Turn on the music when the baby cries—even if it doesn't calm her down, the sound of soft music may mute the crying and keep your co-workers from getting too irritated.

Know that your pace *will* be slowed. Talk with your boss ahead of time about how you'll handle the job on days when your child is having a really hard time. Plan on your work taking longer and your production being lower.

Once your baby is mobile, keeping him at the office may no longer be feasible. How about agitating for on-site day care? Many corporations are going this route—you can visit at the center on your "coffee," "bathroom," and "lunch" breaks, and having baby on-site usually leads to more output, less absenteeism, and a generally happier staff.

Doing Business with a Baby

When Annie was 20 months old, I brought her with me to a job interview. The short flight was painless—Annie slept. I collected the rental car with ease. With Annie strapped in the rented car seat, I negotiated the long drive to the home of Dr. V, an esteemed man who had written a 3,000-page autobiography he needed whittled down to something publishable. I hoped to be the whittler.

Dr. V lived in a fabulous house with fine furnishings and a great art collection. We sat in his sumptuous living room. Annie played at our feet. The impressive man was charmed—he frequently interrupted himself to play peek-a-boo with her. Again and again he handed her priceless objets d'art to play with, murmuring, "It is nothing, it is only a thing. If it breaks, it breaks. It only matters that this little darling have a good time." Again and again I carefully pried my daughter's fingers from Faberge eggs and pre-historic relics.

The interview was not going well. "This project will take a special person with wisdom, grace, life experience, and sensibilities that match my own," Dr. V pronounced. I nodded, trying to look wise, graceful, experienced, and sensible. At about this point, loud sounds emitted from the bottom half of Annie's body, and she began to cry. Dr. V.'s nose twitched. "I think you maybe need to make a little change?"

"Oh. Oh!" I said. "Excuse me, I have to get the diaper bag." As I said this, I had a horrible vision—the diaper bag left propped up against the car rental kiosk.

Finding and Keeping Your Balance

If you do business with a baby around, you're one of many parents trying to balance their lives and get it all done. Baby business requires the same three skills that parenting and travel do—*flexibility*, *humor*, and *a sense of adventure*. Here's the deal—if you learn to do it effectively, you'll be able to do anything, go anywhere, be a star! (Cue the music, Joe: "If I can make it there, I'll make it anywhere . . . ") Here are two survival tips:

- Get thee to the gym or the dance class. Take a brisk walk in the warm, spring air. Physical expenditure of energy will give you *more* energy, not less.

- Strongly encourage your best friend to get to know your baby better—and encourage them out the door and all the way to the playground for an hour. Grab a book, some chocolate, and fill a bathtub with hot, bubbly water. Now sit in it.

NOTE TO THE OVERWHELMED:

If your life includes working for money (and the majority of our lives do), you're probably running a constant game of catch-up, living too many lives. Try to slow down, rearrange your financial priorities, rent a smaller apartment, arrange for a job share, ask for birthday gifts of child care, splurge on a massage, or take a mini-vacation. Remember that this is an *era*. It will change. Coffee will go out of fashion, warm milk and meditation will come back in. It will! Too many people are complaining too much of the time.

(continued)

"I'll watch the precious baby," said Dr. V.

"No, no. I'll change her in the car," I smiled nervously. Holding Annie, I backed ungracefully out of the house, hoping I was mistaken. I could tell already it was a disaster. Annie had been constipated for a few days—now she clearly wasn't. I balanced her against my shoulder as I opened the car door. I quickly looked through my stuff. No luck—no diaper bag, no diapers, no wipes, no extras in the carry-on or purse.

This was no time for panic, I clearly needed supplies. "O.K. Sweetie, into the car seat," I said, plopping her right on her leaky diaper. I raced a mile and a half to a supermarket, unstrapped and grabbed Annie, ran into the store, grabbed a package of diapers and a box of wipes, waited impatiently while the checkout clerk corrected an over-ride, ran with Annie back to the car, changed her, clicked her back into her car seat, and roared back up the hill. I composed myself carefully and checked the time. I'd been gone 22 minutes.

Hoping that it had been so long since Dr. V had been around babies that he didn't know how long it took to change a diaper, I sauntered back in. Gracious Dr. V continued where he'd left off. I looked down at my white blouse, and casually pulled my blazer over a small brown stain.

Ah, Life. All of us mess up some-times—diapers and diaper bags are replaceable—and at least I didn't leave the baby at the airport! As for Dr. V, well, I guess our sensibilities didn't match.

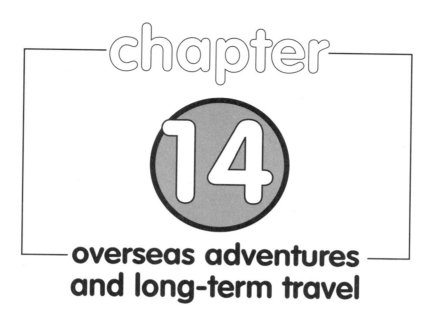

chapter
14
overseas adventures and long-term travel

> *"The greatest lesson children learn through adventure travel is the one they learn effortlessly—an understanding of the world they live in."*
>
> —Nan Jeffrey

> *"Wherever you go, there you are."*
>
> —The Adventures of Buckaroo Banzai

Expand Your Horizons

Will you wait forever to see the majestic Andes, to safari in Kenya, to taste tropical fruit on a tropical island with white sands and blue waters? Listen to the wind. Stand on the shore of the Pacific Ocean and gaze out—the vast clamor of China awaits you, the spice bazaars of

Java call. Adventuring overseas is not about being wild or irresponsible, it's about learning, growing, experiencing, and incorporating your children into your life. It's *about* responsibility. If you believe the world is one planet, teach that to your kid—by example, by experience. Bringing your baby along will open the cultures of the world to the entire family. And it's not as hard as you may think. This chapter includes:

- Baby as an Ambassador for Peace
- Tolerance
- Toddling Around the World
- Staying Safe and Defeating Fear
- Basic Overseas Maneuvering
- On-the-Road Experiences
- Finding the Familiar
- Transportation in Developing Nations
- Long-Term Stays Abroad

Baby as an Ambassador for Peace

All of humanity loves a baby. In a small town in the backwoods of the small Indonesian island of Sumba, Bill met a French couple with a two year old who had been on the road for almost two years—through Europe, Thailand, Australia, and now Indonesia. Wherever they went, other travelers would come and go in a few days, but they would stay a few weeks or a month, settling in, learning the community. When Bill got to Sumba, the family had already been there several weeks. Evenings, they'd go to a small restaurant where the proprietors' children loved little Veronique and whisked her away to play while the couple ate in peace. In time, the French travelers were invited to the restaurant proprietor's home, and the two families—one French, one Sumbanese—became quite close. This was a common experience for the couple—this slow-moving budget travel, this true opening up of a culture, aided by shared love of the child they escorted.

I want to put in a few words for traveling overseas on a budget, for slowing down and avoiding tourist locales, for being, in a word, a *traveler* instead of a *tourist*. A tourist is a contained unit, a short-term visitor, carefully protected by tours and hotels. In general, the tourist only meets people in the tourist industry. The traveler aims to get away from the "beaten path," to meet the natives, to experience the culture, and, in doing so, to share a bit of the traveler's own culture with the culture being visited. The traveler does not sit in air-conditioned tour buses, watching the sights silently through tinted windows, as if in an aquarium. The traveler has an impact, because the traveler has the contact.

BENEFITS FOR YOU AND YOUR FAMILY

Adventure travel, traveling long-term, and living abroad are ways of expanding your horizons as a human being. Bringing a small child along only deepens the experience. Traveling with a baby lets the traveler experience different ways of living. The baby enjoys and benefits from the consistency of having her parent(s) with her all the time. The toddler or preschooler begins to learn about the world and all its possibilities.

> "Travel with kids is different. Much more people-centered than activity-based. You have to change your expectations of what you can accomplish in a day and alter the pace. The rewards are definitely worth the effort. You see the country through very different eyes than the regular backpacker. People who would never normally engage with a Western traveler are much more open to you—particularly women and families. You gain greater respect as a family and attract a warmer, more intimate, welcome."
>
> —John Eyles, world traveler and father of Ava, age 5, and Salila, age 2

Tolerance

Travel in developing nations requires a certain relaxed attitude. So there are ants in the sugar? Pick them out. Electricity only between 6 and 10pm? Time for bed. The bed is lumpy? Adjust your body. Children tend to be more flexible than adults—*you* are the one who will be freaked out by the ants, the toddler will quickly learn how to remove them, and unless you act upset, she will be completely casual about it.

Tolerance of other people and their cultures is similar. Baby has the advantage. No child is born a racist. Human behaviors and attitudes—including hate—are learned, and there are countless ways to live a human life. It is easy to criticize another nation simply because they don't do things the way we do at home, but what you may find odd or distasteful your child, who hasn't had time to learn your prejudices, will simply take in stride. The world needs tolerance, and being exposed to differences from an early age will help create a kinder, more tolerant adult. And you may learn from your child's open-minded example.

WHOSE TOLERANCE? DEALING WITH CULTURAL REACTIONS TO YOU

Things are smoother with children along. It sounds simple, but the logic is this—wherever you go there are people, and people are basically helpful and kind. People all over the world have children, and people all over the world love children.

Toddling Around the World

Many hard-core "travelers" gallivant aimlessly from country to country, taking a job here, an excursion there, topping each other's stories of hellish bus rides through India and landslides in Bhutan. With a family it is inappropriate to be so boundary-less or budget-minded. You *can* go for the upgrade and skip the rock-bottom traveling, while still using public transport instead of tour buses. If you spend a little more time and a very little more money, if you open yourself to the world and savor it slowly, the experience will last a lifetime.

> Read, read, read up on your destinations before you go. The Lonely Planet guide-books are a great resource for on-a-shoestring travelers. Hang out at your local youth hostel, and listen to the foreign travelers compare notes on their travels. Invite a hosteler home for dinner. Chances are they'll return the favor when you're in **their** country! Ah, dinner in a Tuscan village!

Staying Safe and Defeating Fear

Ericka says, "Preparation *is* reassurance." Trepidation about travel, especially adventure travel is normal (so is excitement). Information and preparation can quell most of your fears—fear of inadequate medical care, language barriers, malaria, jet lag—but some of your normal nervousness will not dissipate until you actually get out in the world. For gaining confidence and information, check out the Alph-appendix. I also highly recommend Nan Jeffrey's Book, *Adventuring with Children,* and Maureen Wheeler's on-a-shoestring guide, *Travel with Children.* Don't be afraid to start small. Plan to take a month in Bali—where the tourist amenities are well-established—before moving on to the jungles of Sumatra in search of the wild tiger.

Basic Overseas Maneuvering

When you're traveling with a baby or tot, you *must* have all your papers in order. It's easy to get casual and forget (after a year on the road, our friend Linda was so relaxed that she forgot to get a visa for India and was stuck on the Nepali border for two days before bribing an official to let her through—but she was traveling solo—border guards are far more stringent about people traveling with kids).

GETTING A PASSPORT

If you're a U.S. citizen, you'll need a passport to travel in all foreign countries except Mexico, Canada, and a few selected Caribbean islands. You can obtain your passport from the State Department or through your local post office. Adult passports, good for 10 years, cost $65.

Passports for children cost $40 and are good for five years. Allow four to five weeks for processing. In an *emergency* (and you'll have to justify yourself), passports may be issued within a few days from a passport agency (located in larger U.S. cities). To get a passport you will need:

> You're in for a treat when you take your baby overseas. To many people of other nations, the United States is not considered a very child-friendly place. This doesn't imply that we are **un**-friendly, simply that many other countries are **more** tuned in to and accepting of children as a part of daily life.

- Two passport photos, 2×2. (There are a variety of requirements for passport photos, including "no hats allowed," so it's best to have a professional passport photographer do them—check your phone book. Always get extra—you'll need them for visa applications.)

- Passport application (available at the post office, call for details)

- Picture identification (this is for you—you will vouch for your child)

- A certified birth-certificate for you and for baby

GETTING VISAS

A visa is a permission slip stamped into your passport. Many countries require tourist, work, or student visas, and visas often take time to process, so start early. It's usually best to apply from home. (However, if you're in Thailand, for instance, and you suddenly decide to go to Nepal, you can get your visa in Bangkok through a travel agency. It's a little scary because you have to leave your passport for a few days while it's being processed, and it's not a great feeling to be without your passport overseas). Visas require passport-sized photos, so always carry extras.

OTHER PERMISSIONS AND PAPERWORK

- In a number of countries (including our neighbor, Mexico), if you are traveling alone with a child, you must have written permission from the other parent before you can enter the country. (What if you are a single parent? Different countries have different policies; always check with the consulate or embassy *before* you go, to find out how much red tape you'll have to wade through.)

- Many countries require proof of immunizations.

- If your name is different from your child's, it's worthwhile to carry paperwork that reflects that fact. Since my last name is different from Annie's, I carry copies of her birth certificate as well as her passport, even if we are just going to Canada.

BODILY FUNCTIONS, OVERSEAS

Well, it's diapers again (with a baby it's always diapers). We're back to the great debate—remember Chapter 3? Here are some additional thoughts for overseas adventuring:

Disposable Diapers and the Metric System

When I was a kid, we had to learn metrics in school because the U.S. was about to join the rest of the world in that measuring standard. They lied, and I **still** can't remember how many centimeters make an inch. Buying disposable diapers overseas makes me wish I'd paid more attention to Mrs. Stamper, and less to Leon Johnson making faces at me from across the room. Here's the metric conversion— 1 Kilo = 2.2 pounds. (That means that if you have a 22 pound baby, you're talking 10 kilos.) For more on-the-road diapering details, check back to Chapter 3.

- Supplies of "your kind" of disposables may be unreliable overseas. When you find a brand you like, fill a duffel bag. Once empty, fill it with souvenirs.

- An infant under six months will need about 15 cloth diapers per day (carry a three-day supply). An older baby will require fewer. Bring a half-dozen diaper covers and/or plastic pants and safety pins.

- Disposal of disposable diapers can be a problem in areas where trash is burned. The gel in gel diapers releases hazardous fumes when burned. Always bring garbage bags in case you need to lug them out. In the Himalayas, for instance, where garbage is burned or dumped into landfill, you'll be polluting the air with dangerous fumes or leaving non-biodegradable material in the most beautiful mountains in the world. Stick to cloth (which you can rinse and dry as you hike), or triple-bag the waste and hire an extra porter.

- Pre-folded cotton diapers take longer to dry—stick with the regular ones. Many places provide inexpensive washing services. Always let them know that your laundry includes diapers. Rinse out feces ahead of time, and store damp, dirty diapers in a well-sealed plastic bag.

- Disposables wick away moisture better than cloth and can prevent a prickly heat rash (also known as *milaria*—not to be confused with malaria.) A more earth-friendly (and tush-friendly) option for avoiding diaper rash is using cotton and leaving baby bare-bummed for as much of the day as possible. Review the information on rashes in Chapter 3.

WHAT TO EXPECT: SQUAT TOILETS AND NO PAPER

You know that extra roll of toilet paper I suggested you always bring in Chapter 8? In Asia, bring more. Very few places supply paper at all (some supply a bucket of water and a scoop). Toilet paper is commonly available for large sums in tourist areas (and comes in three styles—bumpy, raspy, or waxy.)

Many places have "squat" toilets instead of the sit-down style we're used to. For those of you who have never used a squat toilet, there is usually a platform (or concrete footprints) for squatting over a hole. While there is medical evidence that this style of toilet is physically better for your body (and more hygienic), it can be hard for a little child to learn how to effectively perch, and kids are sometimes terrified of falling in. Stand or squat facing your child and hold their hands. Always supervise little ones.

IMMUNIZATION AND DISEASE PREVENTION

Many countries, including those in Europe, require no immunizations. Once you select your destination(s), contact your local Public Health Department, the Center for Disease Control, or your pediatrician to find out about immunizations and disease prevention of diseases such as typhoid, hepatitis, malaria, yellow fever, and cholera. Look at the Alphappendix, under **M** for Medical, and **R** for

> Carry your own packet of sterile hypodermic needles and syringe when traveling in developing nations. You will have to get a prescription (and a doctor's permission slip) for them. Many diseases, including AIDS, may be transmitted through unsterilized equipment. If you or your child needs an injection, it's best to be prepared.

"the Runs." Also coming up in the Alphappendix, you'll find sections for water and food safety. Check it out—**W** for Water safety, **F** for Food safety. Maureen Wheeler's book *Travel with Children* also has a good breakdown of health risks and preventative measures for overseas adventure travel.

- Sterilize bottles and cups frequently by boiling them for 15 to 20 minutes.

- Drink lots of water in tropical climates (did ya check out **W** in the Alphappendix yet? You'll get there.)

- If you'll be in a tropical climates, remember to protect those little bodies (and your own) from the sun with long shirts, hats, and sunscreen. The sun-protection recommendations in Chapter 11 (that's the outdoors chapter) apply to overseas adventure travel, as well.

- In malaria country, bring flying-insect spray to spray sleeping areas before bedtime. More details about malaria are under **M** in the Alphappendix.

- Before you go: Know your child's blood type.

On-the-Road Experiences

Here's the "core" of "hard-core" traveling. Most kids are amazingly flexible—you'll be surprised at how easy it can be . . .

> Bring a child's sleeping bag. Hotels (especially the budget kind) and guest houses are not always equipped for children. Go the "extra dollar" and get a little more floor space so the baby can crawl—you won't often want him crawling on the ground outside, and those little limbs need exercise.

ESTABLISHING HOME BASE WHEN ALL YOU'VE GOT IS A SUITCASE

"Where do we live, Mommy?" When you are traveling overseas for a long time, your child's sense of "home" may change. Family—by definition—is familiar, but when you are shifting locations frequently, little else may be. For a child, *you* are your child's home.

Travel with familiar items—a blanket that Shawn always sleeps with, Katie's special lovey toy. Bring pictures of people, places, and things from home. Photograph your house, your neighborhood, your local store. These pictures will comfort your toddler, and fascinate the people of the cultures you'll meet.

BRINGING YOUR RHYTHM WITH YOU, OR DEVELOPING IT THERE

Develop a rhythm to your aimless lifestyle, and everybody will do well. How about this? Leisurely breakfasts, mid-morning playtime, afternoon adventures, evenings of hanging out, and traveling no more than every fourth or fifth day. If you let it, your family will fall naturally into a routine—and sometimes you'll remember the routine (like our daily Balinese breakfast of sweet black rice, bananas, and papaya) long after the individual events fade from memory.

LUGGING IT

No doubt about it: With a baby, you'll have to bring more gear than you would if you were on your own. We like to do what I call "satellite" travel—park most of your stuff at a hotel or guest house (they'll charge a small fee), load a backpack of necessary items, and adventure light for a few days. This means you don't lug your winter jackets (which you'll need next month in the Alps) all the way through the Greek Isles.

LANGUAGE ISSUES

English has become the international language of travel and commerce. It always helps to speak the local tongue, but it really isn't necessary (how many of us can quickly pick up Serbo-Croatian, Mandarin, Javanese, Tamil, and Nepali?) Traveling with a toddler or preschooler, you're in luck—kids pick up a language called "Pidgin Child" very quickly. Learn the words for "Thank you," "Hello," and "Beautiful." Always, everywhere, good will, hand signals, and smiles go a very long way.

A SMALL CHILD'S EXPERIENCE

Little kids don't have the same social barriers adults do—they easily make friends wherever they go. Kids on the road also don't need as many toys as the bored toddler at home—they're getting stimulation from exterior sources. Kids improvise—a twig becomes a magic wand, a sarong draped over a chair becomes a secret cave. Bring art supplies, a ball, some animal figures, and maybe some small musical instruments—you'll pick up more along the way.

INCORPORATING YOUR CHILD INTO THE GLOBAL VILLAGE

Who will you find when your family hits the road? Not only the locals. All over the world there is an informal fellowship of Western expatriates and travelers who have paved the way for you—from Germany, France, Canada, Russia, Holland, Israel, Brazil, Japan, Mexico, Australia, Greece, Britain, Egypt, Surinam, the United States, and everywhere else. You'll meet them while journeying from place to place on the trains, boats, and busses. You'll meet the same ones, a week later, in a budget hotel at the other side of the jungle.

The stereotypical long-term traveler stands out in any crowd—ethnic pants weathered from handwashing, hair a bit shaggy, passport stuffed with extensions—but look again—these are not just aimless hippies longing for a return to the '60s. These are accomplished souls: bankers, artists, psychotherapists, merchants, writers, dentists, students—out for a couple of months or a year to take a closer look at the world. And yes, there are more babies and little kids than you can imagine.

The travelers are your lifeline, your source of information as to the best guest house in Cuzco, the finest pediatrician in New Delhi, the best place to buy bottled water and toilet paper in the next town. One day you'll find yourself at a table waiting for fresh green mussels with people from four nations in a slow-serving restaurant on a Thai island. You'll play backgammon and talk about Democracy, dysentery, and Celine Dion. The baby will play in the sand at your feet, and you'll suddenly realize that you're comfortable anywhere in the world; that you've joined the world's community.

Finding the Familiar

There are things your family will miss from home. Skippy peanut butter. Roast beef. In Southeast Asia, we craved cheese. The acrid tang of a good dried parmesan and melting, oozing Gruyere over sourdough bread. Ripe Camembert. Expatriates and travelers compare notes and obsessions: "Chocolate," the American says. "Oh, don't talk about chocolate," says the Austrian. Then after a pause he chimes in, "Have you ever had . . . Toblerone?" The group sighs with remembered pleasure.

A Taste of Home

My own obsession with Pepperidge Farm goldfish crackers began long ago when, most of the way through a year in Asia, Bill and I spent three aching weeks in

(continued)

India. There I was—sick and tired, in the bus station in the city of Jaipur, surrounded by beggars with no fingers hounding us for money ("Baksheesh, Madam, baksheesh") and by heartbreakingly beautiful children with no parents in sight.

Then, through the misery and hordes I spied a Western woman holding a large bucket of Pepperidge Farm goldfish. The yellow bucket shone across the station like a beacon. The smiling fish called to me. I homed in, moving as if in a dream, approaching and politely introducing myself to the British woman who, it turned out, was on her way to help Mother Theresa in Calcutta.

"Would you like a couple of these?" she finally asked me, taking pity, no doubt sensing my x-ray eyes trying to penetrate the container as we talked. Only years of socialization at the hands of my polite parents kept me from snatching more than a handful, though I wished desperately that my hand would suddenly grow much, much larger.

They tasted delicious. Something about the comforting, slightly salty crunch of the tiny crackers loosed something inside me and brought tears to my eyes, and I think it was then that I gave up, and decided to leave India, go back to Thailand, and begin the long journey home.

For the average American kid in the '90s, goldfish crackers are just part of childhood, but who knows to what length these toddlers might go when, years later, they are faced with their comfort food calling to them from across a scary, sad, place like the Jaipur, India bus station . . . .

Your picky three-year-old may take a while to adjust to his new diet. *Let* him eat plain rice, and supplement with vitamins. He'll soon catch on. If you'll be spending numerous months overseas, you may want to arrange to have the occasional care package of "familiar" food sent. In larger cities you may be able to find much of what you crave, though you'll probably *pay* for that familiarity. Don't worry—when you get home, you'll have a preschooler sobbing for mangosteen or Gado Gado.

Transportation in Developing Nations

Most of the transportation basics we explored in Chapter 6 apply overseas, too, but there are a few odd permutations.

BUSES

In some countries, buses are the only way to get from point A to point B, though there are times when going a few miles will feel like going from A to Z to B, what with the bus breakdowns and the uncomfortable positions your body is forced to take when they cram in double the seating capacity—and then bring on the livestock. With a little one, you may get more room, or you may not. On the other hand, little kids don't often have the same need for personal space as adult Westerners, and may enjoy the sensuous quality of all that body contact. They may also enjoy (or at least not be offended by) the sometimes pungent smells. And finally, they're smaller and more flexible and find it far easier to squish.

> *"Traveling around Costa Rica is a little rugged. Many of the buses are old Bluebird school buses, most of the roads unpaved and windy, and most of the bus windows stuck open to enhance the heavy smells of diesel dust and too many people on a bus. The exception is the ride to the Caribbean Coast from San Jose. These buses are all Mercedes with plush seats, air conditioning, reading lights, and some with bathrooms! You know conditions are a little austere when a bathroom brings such joy!"*
>
> —Annie McManus

BANANA BOATS, ELEPHANT RIDES, YAK'S BACKS

Large plastic garbage bags are vital for keeping backpacks dry on small boat trips.

When you're adventuring, you'll have lots of opportunities to experience alternative forms of travel. Always assess the safety element—there are no guarantees in life, but some "exotic" forms of transport are actually safer than some "regular" forms of transport (like motorcycles and cars).

TREKKING

For experienced travelers or a family that likes to backpack, trekking—which is like backpacking without the camping part—is a terrific adventure.

- If you've never backpacked with a baby or toddler before, *start small!* In the Himalayas, there are many beautiful and gratifying two- and three-day treks.

- Consider hiring a separate porter to carry child-supplies—and the toddler when she gets tired of hiking.

- Always consider the distance from medical treatment. You'll be walking slowly, but can a running porter get there in half a day or less?

- If there's more than one adult on this journey, consider splitting up for a week or so. One adult takes the baby to a resort area and hangs out while the other treks. Then switch—it's the other adult's turn for wild adventure. Perhaps a camel ride through Rajhisthan?

Long-Term Stays Abroad

The best way to learn a culture is to live there and explore at your leisure. Living in a foreign place with a small child, you'll have great opportunities to meet your neighbors—Baby provides the best opening there is.

CREATING A HOME BASE

If you'll be staying somewhere more than a month, consider renting a house or apartment. Renting is much cheaper than hotels, and you'll be able to establish a sense of familiarity and security for the kids (and yourself). You may not be able to rent a place before you arrive— arrange for a hotel or find a guest house to tide you over, then spend a few days getting oriented and deciding where you would like to live. At that point, you can contact a local real estate business (check the tourist office for referrals). Here are some things to keep in mind when renting:

- How close is it to public transportation? To the market? To the expatriate community hang-outs?

- Check out the bathrooms in any rental units. Are they shared? Pay a little more for private bathing (except possibly in Japan where the public sentos are a treat.)

- Is it furnished? Do a thorough check of all utilities and furniture, and make sure you and the rental agency agree on the condition of any appliances and furniture.

STAYING IN TOUCH WITH HOME

It's now possible to call, e-mail, fax, or send letters from almost anywhere in the world, and only slightly more complex to receive them. For preschoolers, staying in touch with loved ones at home is essential—it helps keep them happy and contented on the road. It's nice for adults to hear from home, too.

alphappendix
troubleshooting A to Z

A Troubleshooting Alphabet

Travel with a weeny one is not without its complications. But most hassles turn out to be minor hullabaloo over nothing, and the complications that do manifest are the stuff of life, the adventures that will *bond* your family. (After all, you need something to retell again and again in your old age; something with which to embarrass your kids and fascinate your grand-kids.) This Alphappendix has assorted odds and ends about emergencies and hassles—how to avoid trouble, and how to deal with trouble once it arrives.

A

ANIMALS AND ALLERGIES

A is for domestic animals. Big animals like dogs and horses, small animals like rabbits and cats. Big animals can frighten small children, and some are dangerous—animals when threatened can bite.

An over-enthusiastic dog can scare a small child by jumping up and licking him. Then, if the child runs, the dog might think he is playing, and chase along behind. If the child falls to the ground, screaming and cowering in fear, the dog might think he is ready for a wrestle, and jump on, tail wagging furiously. (This happened to my niece Emma—she's been frightened of dogs ever since.) Teach your child to stand still instead of screaming and running; never stare a strange dog in the eye; and, if she is knocked down or falls, curl into a ball, covering her head with her hands.

Some kids are fearless—they may be more challenging than a naturally cautious child. Animals, when threatened or frightened, will bite. If you are unfamiliar with an animal—keep your child well away. Teach your child not to touch or pet strange animals without your permission, even if the owner says, "Oh, Bowser *loves* kids!" Yeah. For breakfast.

If your child is bitten by an animal, seek medical attention immediately. Make sure you know and can locate the biting animal—it may save you and Junior from a trip home and rabies shots.

A is also for allergies and asthma (and its accompanying medication, Albuterol). Many kids are allergic to animals—ask about possible exposure to Persian kitties at the bed and breakfast before you reserve, and certainly ask that distant cousin in Fresno who would *love* to put you up. Is Amanda allergic to feathers? Check the beds and request that they "dump the down." If your child is allergy-prone, carry any medicines with you—even if it isn't allergy season at home, who knows what strange plant might set a sensitive child's nose and lungs a-quiver?

B

BABY BOTTOMS

B is for baby bottoms, and the on-the-road, out-of-house diaper emergencies that can befall them (and you). When you're out of the house, away from Command Central (the diaper changing table) lots can happen, much of it funny—in retrospect. Here are some tips on dealing with common Diaper Emergencies.

Problem	*Solution*
You use cotton diapers and your only diaper cover or plastic pant is hopelessly soiled.	Try a triple diaper. A double diaper will merely keep the leakage from running down his leg—a triple diaper will keep his clothes from being

Problem	Solution
	drenched. Leaky Larry will be bottom heavy but it *will* help keep him from crawling out of reach.
You're out of diaper wipes.	Use alternatives such as moistened paper towels, carefully wielded wads of bathroom tissue, or a clean, damp cloth diaper. Resign yourself to a baby bath in the *near* future. **Warning:** *Never* tear up disposable diapers—they contain powerful chemicals that can damage your baby's skin and lungs.
You use safety pins on cloth diapers, and a pin breaks.	Try paper clips. You can try folding and tucking. Folding and tucking requires frequent re-folding and re-tucking.
No wipes, no water.	Be aware of possible contamination. Say you're in the car, you're out of wipes, you've changed a poopy diaper with the roll of toilet paper you keep in the glove compartment for emergencies. Now, treat your hands as though they are now a teeming mass of bacteria (they are!) and don't touch anybody until you can wash. Once you thoroughly clean up, wipe your steering wheel.
No diapers. You've left the diaper bag at home.	Hit the store. This is no time to be squeamish about disposable diapers.
Out of diapers, it's midnight, and you can't get to a store.	Many fervent believers in cloth keep an emergency packet of disposables on hand. If you don't, it's time to be creative! Got any old towels? Create a loin cloth. Or let baby air out on an old, soft, washable something. What if you're in a rental car or Uncle Jack's borrowed Jag with the all-white interior? Are you really *that* attached to your shirt?

C

CRANKY, CRABBY, CHILDREN AND CRITTERS

C is for cranky, crabby, crummy, and crass—which your kids will probably be, from time to time. While every trip has its down points, no vacation day will be more perfect than a normal day at home. You don't expect perfection (from your kids or yourself) at home, it isn't logical to expect perfection on the road.

- To help prevent a Case of the Cranks, *slow down!* (I really mean it this time.) Give your kid a chance to adjust.

- Try to keep it light. Go for the surprises—dip into your emergency stash of special "somethings" (and I don't just mean food—try stickers, Band-Aids, a miniature kaleidoscope). Sing that special song you only sing when things go wrong. You don't have one? Try "Trouble" by Cat Stevens, or for more sugary uplift, "Tomorrow" from the musical *Annie*.

C is also for Critters—Mosquitoes, Ticks, Bees, Wasps, Spiders and Snakes . . . After reading this section, you may feel like sealing yourself and your child in a protective bubble for the rest of your natural lives. Resist the impulse—for the vast majority of people, for the vast majority of time, insects are a small nuisance, easily dealt with.

- The best treatment for insect bites is *prevention*—light-colored long sleeves and long-pants garments (don't forget socks), and insect repellent on all exposed skin. Insect repellent is not recommended for small babies.

- In this country, *mosquito bites* are largely a nuisance (see **M** for Malaria information), though they can become infected if scratched with dirty little hands. Keep fingernails short and treat bites with antihistamine cream or calamine lotion. Over-the-counter hydrocortisone creams reduce swelling, but avoid using them on the face.

- Most *tick bites* are harmless, but some ticks can carry Rocky Mountain Spotted Fever or Lyme Disease. If you're in an area with ticks, you should wear long sleeves, pants, and *socks*. Tuck your pants legs in. Tick repellent can safely be applied to clothing. Check your child's entire body nightly, especially in the hair—ticks aren't always easy to see or feel.

- If you find a tick, don't panic—and *don't* rip it out. Review the instructions for tick removal in your first-aid book. Firmly grasp the tick as close to the base as possible and gently pull straight upward with steady, even pressure. Make sure to save the insect for analysis. Watch the bite area for 4-6 weeks. If a circular rash or red-ness develops, contact your physician immediately.

 Avoid *bee stings* by not looking or smelling like a flower (leave the perfume at home). Don't swat at a bee or run away—retreat slowly if necessary. Bee stings hurt. If your child is stung, reassure her; the pain is frightening, but only 1 percent of all children (and 4 percent of all adults) are allergic to bee venom. Remove the stinger by scraping with a long fingernail, apply an ice pack (if available). Give an oral antihistamine. Mud soothes, as does a baking soda and water paste, or calamine lotion. Observe the victim for 30 minutes for allergic reactions (see your first-aid book).

For *wasp* or *hornet stings*, Dr. Spock recommends rubbing a drop of vinegar into the spot.

Make a habit of shaking out shoes before putting them on to dislodge any little insect friends (spiders, scorpions) who might be hiding inside. *Spider bites* are nasty, and the venom of Black Widows and Brown Recluse spiders can be deadly. Capture the spider if possible, clean the area with alcohol, and seek immediate medical attention. *Scorpions* are rare in this country.

Though *snakebites* are rare, prepare for disaster by reading up on snakebite proce-dures before you hit the woods or wilds. Don't get too close to a snake—back away slowly so it won't feel threatened. Remember that Coral snakes are very colorful, with stripes of red, yellow, and black. Rattlesnakes are very slow and not aggres-sive; contrary to myth, they don't have to rattle or coil before they strike.

D

TRAVELING WITH KIDS WHO HAVE DISABILITIES

D is for kids with disabilities. Of course you can travel with them! Any limitations will be specific, because every disability is different. *You*, especially, need to be prepared and plan ahead. Several organizations are geared specifically towards travelers with disabilities (see "Disability " in the Recommended Readings). And be aware that you may be dealing with cultural reactions to disability, not just physical limitations. If your child is old enough to be aware of the reactions of others, it might be a good idea to prepare her, to the best of her understanding (given her age) about what she might expect. "Some people are not very nice, Honey. Sometimes people might laugh or stare at you. We don't pay attention to people like that. They are not very smart or nice." (Also see **U**, Unwanted Attention.)

E

EMBASSIES AND CONSULATES

E is for embassy. When you're overseas, it's a good idea to know where your embassy or consulate is. Here is what your embassy and consulate will probably *not* do: Bail you out if you're arrested for drugs, lend or give you money if you come up broke, fly you or your family home if you are ill. Here's how the embassy and consulate *can* help you out: register your absentee ballot; extend your passport; give you valuable information about visas, travel advisories ("There's a revolution on the Northern border—please avoid"), medical care, and long-term schooling. If you're in a trouble-zone (and just why *are* you there with Baby Enrico, I ask you?) it's a good idea to check in with the consulate or embassy. Just in case.

F

FIRST DAYS, AND FOOD SAFETY

F is for the first day of a trip. The first day on the road, plan for disaster. Inevitably, everything that can possibly go wrong on a first day, will. You'll be fighting the flu. The kids will come down with colds (and will *not* be gracious about it), the plane will be delayed, your luggage will be lost, you'll be stranded on the dock when the ferry pulls out early, the taxi driver will cheat you, and you'll risk herniating yourself trying to lift your daughter's luggage. There may be bed bugs, bad food, or rain (there will *usually* be rain.) A word to the frustrated, the disappointed, the distressed: Hang in there. Keep this in mind—the first day of a trip is not, is *rarely* an omen of things to come.

    F is also for food safety. Food-safety issues can affect everybody—whether at home or on the way to Katmandu, Timbuktu, or Kalamazoo. Here are some guidelines for avoiding that nasty bacteria waiting to make you and your baby ill.

> Always wash your hands before eating. It's not pleasant to think about, but most contamination comes from ourselves. Pay attention to where and what you eat and make sure *you* don't introduce disease. Busy toddlers get into everything ("Wow! There's something shiny on the sidewalk—right next to that pile of dog poop!") Wash their hands frequently. (Dip into your diaper wipes, carry a little plastic baggie with a stub of soap.)

> Food safety is of particular concern for infants. Their systems are vulnerable. Make sure formula is not contaminated. Powdered formula is better than concentrate

(which spoils quickly), as long as the water is safe. Check out **W** (below) for more on water safety.

Be especially careful about any child with chronic conditions (including frequent ear infections), or any child who has suffered a gastrointestinal insult (like a serious bout with diarrhea). If your child is healthy, food safety is mostly common sense.

Many food-borne pathogens are carried in the high-protein foods—milk, meat, eggs, beans, and so on.

Make sure all juice and milk is *pasteurized*. E Coli and other nasties can live in unpasteurized juices. Tuberculosis can be passed through unpasteurized milk. In many countries, stick with powdered, condensed, or sterilized milk, or skip it. Your child needs milk, but only if you trust the source. Milk which has been vigorously boiled should be safe if drunk promptly. Better a few days with no milk than amoebas, diarrhea, vomiting . . . .

Make sure meat is cooked through, and that the juices run clear. Skip the Steak Tartare experience.

Picnic foods are a known danger. No lukewarm mayonnaise, out-all-day chicken, or sitting-in-the-car-too-long deviled eggs. Bring a cooler, or follow the **2 hour rule**—no more than 2 hours out of the refrigerator for meat, poultry, or eggs. Use your common sense—this depends upon the weather. Bacteria reproduce faster in a hot climate.

Discard food if you fear it might be contaminated or too old. Better safe than groaning in agony.

Best foods to bring on the road: Canned food, dried food, bread stuff, starches, fresh fruits and vegetables (peel them unless the water is safe to drink.) Think of it like preparing for an earthquake, tornado, or big storm. Jarred baby food is great, but make sure the safety button pops up when you open it.

In general, commercially prepared food tends to be safer than home-prepared food. (It may not *taste* better, though some of it is pretty yummy.)

On the road, look for busy restaurants. Restaurants don't stay popular if they poison their clientele, plus, busy means quick food turnover—food has less of a chance to spoil.

In an "iffy" situation, cook it, boil it, or peel it—or don't eat it.

G

GOING HOME

G is for Going Home Again. Whew, you made it there and back safely. Welcome Home! Watch out! It's amazing how fast the relaxing benefits of two weeks at the beach can disappear. Unlock the door and life crashes in. The basement has flooded. There are 17 messages on the phone machine, and 23 e-mail messages. The mail is overflowing the mail box. The bag of garbage that you forgot to take out when the Airport Shuttle honked three minutes early is still by the kitchen door—and the ants have found it, and they've had a party while you were away.

You think *you're* overwhelmed—look at the baby. Poor dear is experiencing a flood of emotions—not all of them bad: he remembers this place, he likes it, he's *tired*, wow, he missed it and he didn't even know it! Here are some stuffed animal friends! He's happy, he's exhausted, he can relax, he can release, he can giggle, he can scream!

> **Step One:** Sit down. Don't deal with the mail, the e-mail, the garbage, the baggage, the flood, the calls from the office. Don't even *call* the office. *Sit!* Take at least 15 minutes (set the kitchen timer if you have to.)
>
> **Step Two:** Breathe. Focus on the baby. Hug the baby. Take a few moments to play.
>
> **Step Three:** Try to ignore the mess and take time to revisit your vacation in your mind. After the first flood of anxiety, you'll usually find that the benefits of those two weeks (or two months) have *not* disappeared.
>
> **Step Four:** Now *deal* with it!

(Also see **Z**, Time ZONES and Jet Lag.)

H

HUMOR

H is for Humor—your best weapon against travel Hassles. Traveling with a baby is inherently Hysterical. You're still the same person you were before parenthood, but now you have this little Hunk of living flesh that goes with you. Traveling with children, funny things Happen. All of this is Humbling, and puts you deeply in touch with your Humanity.

I

"IRRESPONSIBLE BEHAVIOR" AND INFANT SEATS

I is for Irresponsible Behavior and Infant Seats. There may be emergencies when you have to break the law. Say it's raining in Manhattan, and you *have* to catch a cab. You aren't carrying a car seat. Say you're in Sri Lanka, and the rental car has no seat belts. No seat belts means no way to attach the car seat.

Sometimes you have to just *go for it*. Try to remain calm—panic won't help. If necessary, remember your own childhood, bouncing in the station wagon as your parents drove across country. I remember my cousins Rebekah and Toby zooming around town *standing up* in front of my Uncle Rob on his motor scooter. What you're doing is not safe, but you and your child will probably survive. That said—(and I shake my finger at you) don't make a habit of it.

IF YOU'RE A RIDER

- Put the seatbelt around you (not the baby) and hold the baby or toddler tightly on your lap (using your strictest grown-up voice to make clear the importance of this) no matter how much she wiggles and screams. For toddlers who understand, you can stress that they are riding "like a grown-up."

- Hope that the journey is short.

- Be strict with the driver, too. Say, "I want you to drive safely and slow. I'm concerned about my child."

IF YOU RENT A CAR IN A FOREIGN COUNTRY

If you rent a car by phone or fax ahead of time, make sure to ask about seat belts, and specify that you *must* have them. (Try to get it in writing—not that it will hold up in any court). It's worth being ridiculed for asking: "Of *course* we have seat belts, what kind of savages do you think we are?" or "Seatbelts? *Hah!* What do you think this is? America?")

In some countries the rental cars may not have seat belts. In this case, you won't be able to attach an infant or toddler car seat. There is no easy solution. I went through the phone tree at the U.S. Department of Transportation and talked to three experts. Some people (not the experts, who were baffled at the question) suggest bringing your own seatbelts, hiring a garage to remove the seat, and bolting in a set of seat belts. This is beyond most of us. Others suggest wedging the infant seat behind the passenger seat on the floor. I suggest taking the train. Do *not* put a child in an unattached infant or toddler seat. This is *treacherous and potentially fatal.* Better to hold the child than let an unrestrained infant or car seat bounce around. **Special Note:** Never buckle two kids in one seat belt—it increases the chance of serious injury.

J

JERKS, AND HOW TO DEAL WITH THEM

J is for Jerk. People all over the world have ideas about parenting—and many total strangers aren't afraid to voice their opinions. Unsolicited advice can be annoying particularly because *you* know your child and your situation. Sometimes parenting differences are cultural. Be sensitive to cultural differences, but have confidence that you are the best parent for your child, and politely ignore, explain, or defend.

K

KID TIME

K is for Kids, and their own sense of time and space. Henry David Thoreau wrote: "The man who goes alone can start today; but he who travels with another must wait until that other is ready." He could have been talking about recalcitrant toddlers.

Kids have their own agenda. Kids have their own interests. Wisdom—the ability to see the big picture—comes only with age. You'll find this is true out in the world with your child: Toddlers see the world in minutiae—you're admiring Half Dome and they're playing with a leaf. Try to find a marriage between their interests, sense of time, and your own.

L

LOST CHILDREN

L is for Lost Children. The idea of losing a child gives parents nightmares, and terrifies children, too. The majority of the time, lost children don't stay lost very long. Abductions by strangers are extremely rare. Nevertheless, even a brief separation can feel traumatic for all concerned.

Here are some ideas for getting and keeping your children found.

- Stress the importance of staying with Daddy, Mommy, or Aunt Sherry—and tell your kids to look for the RED SHIRT, PURPLE HAT, (WHATEVER YOU'RE WEARING). (Annie knows to look for Daddy—Bill's tall, so he stands out in most crowds.)

◊ Dress your *child* in bright colors.

◊ Make sure your child knows her full name, and if possible, the name of the place the family is staying. ("De Cwown Hotew.") Her full address won't help if you're traveling in Southern Zaire.

◊ Tag 'em. See the Recommended Readings under "Other Resources" for information on inexpensive, disposable ID wrist bands. You can have a separate band for each destination.

◊ Teach your child to ask for help from "officials," (police authorities, shop clerks, security guards) or other parents, rather than strangers.

◊ Learn to whistle. My dad used to call us with one long high and two low whistles—a whistle he originally developed for Sweet Harry, his old horse.

IF YOUR CHILD *DOES* GET LOST

Don't panic! Try to think logically, and *then* alert everybody. Was he casting goo-goo eyes at the horsy ride at the supermarket? Might he have wandered that way? At big, organized events (county fairs, theme parks), announcements can sometimes be broadcast. Some stores provide this service, too.

Once you find your child, you will probably feel angry and may yell at your wayward kid. This is normal—the worry is replaced by relief, yet those tense emotions have nowhere to go. Being aware of this tendency can keep you from screaming, hitting, or otherwise punishing already frightened little Fanny. P.L.C.S. (Post Lost Child Syndrome) will pass faster if you let your child cry, be clingy, and tell the story over and over again. As for you, don't vent on your child, but *vent!* Yes, it *was* scary! If the scare was severe (more than 15 minutes), be prepared for Fanny to have nightmares, or to otherwise regress a bit.

M

MEDICAL EMERGENCIES AND FIRST AID

M is for Medical, Minor and Major. Most illnesses are Minor. You get sick at home, and you'll get sick on the road, too. Your family may even experience *less* illness if you experience the day-care, "Pass it around again, Sam" syndrome at home. (Don't forget "The Runs." Check out letter **R** below.)

FIRST AID

Every parent should know their way around a first-aid kit. If you are doing adventure travel, you'll find it helpful for *other* people's kids, too—a Band-Aid in Belize, a splint in Srinigar. You are not a doctor though (unless you are), so never give any strange child unprescribed medicine. Create your own kit, and consider including items from the following lists:

BASIC FAMILY FIRST-AID TRAVEL KIT

First-aid guide(s) including information on wilderness first aid • Ace bandages • Acetaminophen and/or Ibuprofen—for both baby and you Adhesive tape • Antibacterial cream or ointment • Antihistamine liquid • Antiseptic towlettes • Anti-yeast cream • Band-Aids large and small, gauze bandages, butterfly bandages • Benedryl or other anti-itch cream • Calamine lotion • Cotton balls • Diaper-rash ointment • Eye pads and eye wash • Hydrocortisone 1% • Hydrogen peroxide • Ipecac (don't use without speaking with a doctor or poison control center) • Measuring spoon, dropper, or syringe for oral medications • Motion sickness medicine • Prescription medications • Small scissors • Splints • Surgical tape • Teething stuff (if teething is an issue) • Thermometer • Tweezers

CAMPING/OUTDOOR/WILDERNESS FIRST-AID KIT

All of the above, but add:

Broad-spectrum antibiotics (erythromycin, sulfa, penicillin) • Baking soda to apply to stings • Calamine lotion or aloe vera gel • Codeine pain medication • Injectible epinephrine (for bee sting or other insect bite allergies—this is a prescription drug but may save lives.) • Insect repellent (5-10% DEET for infants through preschoolers, 25% for you) • Moleskin for blisters • Needles and safety pins • Snake-bite and tick-removal kits • Suction bulb • Sunscreen (#15 spf, waterproof, with both UVA and UVB protection) • Waterproof matches and compass (not strictly first aid, but vital) • Water filter, iodine water treatment kit, or water purification tablets

ADVENTURE TRAVEL FIRST-AID ADDITIONS

Items from both lists above plus:

Hypodermic needles, sterile syringe, and a note from your doctor explaining why you have them (for injections in foreign countries) • Oral rehydration powder • PeptoBismol (chewable tablets) • Sterile hospital gloves and IV drip (for those going to truly risky places)

EMERGENCY COURSES

Consider taking a course in emergency infant or child care *before* you go. Courses should cover practical tips and preventive measures including cardiac resuscitation basics, burns, poison control, and choking. Hospitals and the Red Cross often offer free or inexpensive classes, often in the evening. Parenting organizations are another resource. A group of families can often hire a certified instructor (check local parenting publications for resources). Hiring in a group has the added bonus of helping you build a parenting network/community.

HOSPITALS AND HEALTH SERVICES EVERYWHERE

- Your best overseas resource for a doctor or a hospital is the consulate or embassy. Hotels and tourist bureaus can also be a source of information.

- Many doctors speak English. Try to find one, so you don't have to worry about your sick kid *and* figure out how to say "chicken pox" in French. IAMAT provides a world directory of English-speaking, Western-trained doctors. Contact information is listed in the Recommended Readings appendix under "Overseas Travel Resources."

- For up-to-date care and equipment, get to a major metropolitan area.

- Hook up with the expat community and find out who *they* recommend.

- Fancy hotels can also recommend medical personnel.

- You are always a plane ride from home—in extreme emergency, you may not be able to leave, but somebody can always come in.

- Medical care in other countries is usually good—sometimes better, and often cheaper, than ours.

Malaria

Malaria is spread by the anopheles mosquito common in certain areas of the world. It can cause recurrent fevers, sweats, chills, headaches, delirium, and other unpleasantness. Malaria is curable. But if not treated, malaria can lead to anemia, kidney failure, coma, or death. The malaria-carrying mosquito bites from dusk to dawn, so take preventative measures: Wear light-colored long-sleeves and pants, sleep under netting, and use bug repellent containing DEET. Spray your sleeping quarters with flying-insect spray. Mosquito coils—which burn like smelly incense—are also available in Southeast Asia, but some people may be allergic to the smoke. You and your baby should be on prophylactic medication—yes, protection against certain types of malaria **can** be given to your baby (the Center for Disease Control in Atlanta has all the details—get their address, phone number, and Web site from the Recommended Readings under "Overseas Travel Resources"). You have to start your medication two weeks before you enter Malaria Country, and you'll have to continue for four weeks after you return. Seek medical attention if symptoms develop.

N

WHERE NOT TO TAKE BABY

N is for No-No, Not *There,* and No Children Allowed. Is it your dream to scale K2 with a dagger in your teeth? Are you dying to push your survival skills to the limit? Re-evaluate—adventure doesn't necessarily mean endurance—there will be time for endurance travel later. There are places where small children don't belong. Be sensible. Risk death, boredom, and moral destruction when you are by yourself. Be understanding of Baby, be considerate of other adults, be safe.

O

OPTIMISM AND OPTOMETRY

O is for Optimism, both the need for it when traveling with a little One, and the Optimism that you'll gain from your experiences. Things can get complicated on the road—you'll need to hang on to your intrinsic belief that "things will work out." Try to remember that most of the time the hullabaloo is just that—a lot of hullabaloo over not much at all. If you can keep your balance when the train has broken down or the hotel has lost your reservations, you'll enjoy your trip far more.

As for *gaining* Optimism—it's a funny thing. Long-term travelers—the ones who've been on the road for years, in the danger zones, the jungles, mountains, deserts, the harshest conditions on earth—often have the *most* confidence in the potentials and kindnesses of human beings, and who have the best sense of the future to come. Perhaps travel will bring you this optimism, too.

O is also for Optometry. If you or your child wear glasses or contacts, bring along an extra set or a copy of your prescription. One time Josh accidentally knocked Aunt Julie's glasses into the lake at Pinecrest and she spent a precious day driving into the Valley and waiting hours for the "one-hour" optometrist to make her a new pair. In Thailand we had knock-off prescription RayBan sunglasses made from our prescriptions—at about one-eighth of the cost. They sure were useful on that pineapple boat to the islands!

P

TRAVELING PREGNANT

P is for Traveling Pregnant. Let your body be your guide—some women feel perfectly fine and enjoy being pregnant on the road, some find it difficult and unpleasant. It depends on what you're doing—mountain climbing, or lying on a beach in Cancun. The best time to travel pregnant may be during the second trimester—not too early and not too late. During the first trimester, you may experience morning sickness and fatigue. In the last trimester, you'll want to stay close to good medical care. You shouldn't do any physically strenuous travel after about the fifth month.

 Before traveling while pregnant, check with your doctor for restrictions and advice.

Before traveling while pregnant, check with your doctor for restrictions and advice.

You can fly safely through your sixth month, and then you'll need a doctor's note. Many airlines won't carry a woman in her third trimester. Call your airline for guidelines and restrictions.

When selecting a destination, consider the food. Choose a place with food you like, because when you're pregnant, you're gonna get *very* hungry. If pregnant, I would avoid Italy—the smell of garlic was utterly repugnant to me when pregnant. Maybe spicy food makes you heave—in that case, stay away from Thailand.

Drink plenty of fluids. It's easy to get dehydrated.

If you feel queasy, avoid boats or long car travel which only makes it worse. Try anti-nausea wrist bands, available in maternity shops. These operate on accupressure principals, and are "all-natural."

If you travel to countries that require immunizations, get them before getting pregnant (ideally) and, if pregnant, avoid "live" vaccines. Talk to your OB/GYN about malaria—it can pass from mother to fetus. Pregnant women may get a more serious case of malaria. Some prophylactic drugs are O.K.

You're going to be tired. Travel with a little kid (or kids) is fatiguing anyway, and you're adding the normal fatigue of pregnancy. Be nice to yourself. Your best option is short travel times, parking yourself in a great location, and leisurely having fun.

Q

QUARRELS AND FIGHTS IN PUBLIC

Q is for Quarreling. Fighting in public, screaming at your kid or your partner, *losing it.* Nobody is perfect. There are times when you will air your dirty diapers in public. You *will* make a fool of yourself. You're human. When you travel, you'll get deeply in touch with that fact.

R

"THE RUNS" ON THE ROAD

R is for "The Runs" and how to avoid and treat diarrhea on the road. Stomach upsets are the most common traveler complaint (30 to 50 percent of travelers on a two-week trip experience symptoms). The main danger of simple diarrhea (I'm not talking major amoebas, here) is dehydration, especially for babies and little kids. Weak tea with a little sugar, soda water with sugar, or "flat" diluted soft drinks help rehydrate a child. In a tropical climate with a reputation for the runs, carry an oral rehydration mixture. Rehydration powder (also known as ORS) is available at the drugstore and consists of electrolytes and sugar that you mix with water. You can make your own by mixing 1 quart of water with 1/2 teaspoon salt and 3 Tablespoons of sugar. (Read **W**, and make sure the water is safe!)

- PeptoBismol is usually safe for all ages—though talk to your pediatrician for dosages, counterindications, and limitations (yes, there are some).

- Lomotil, Imodium, and other drugs that "stop up" the action are not good choices for children.

- Seek medical advice for stomach upset that lasts more than a couple days. You may need treatment for diarrhea with blood and mucous, if it is accompanied by fever and lethargy or vomiting, or if there is extreme discomfort and bloating.

S

SEA SICKNESS, CAR SICKNESS

S is for Motion Sickness. A lot of kids get nauseous in cars or on boats. Winding, bumpy roads; heat; and gas and diesel fumes can upset the stomach of a child sensitive to motion sickness. It's not only kids—adults get motion sickness, too.

Avoiding and Dealing with Car and Sea Sickness

- Keep the air fresh. Crack the window, and no smoking in the car. (You should *never* smoke in the car with a kid!) Sometimes diesel fumes can bring on illness, so don't open the window if the air is fumey. Air conditioning can sometimes help.

- Have child look out the car window, preferably the front (kids can get sick by looking through the side windows). You can keep them focused by playing "I Spy" games and preventing them from focusing on close stuff like books or coloring. If the kid is really queasy, move her to the front seat. If she is *really* queasy, pull over.

🍼 Avoid carbonated drinks and milk, which can be hard to digest, and too much cotton candy at the zoo.

🍼 Long car trips on winding roads are a good time to remember that your child's sense of time is very different from yours. An hour for a two year old is a *far* larger percentage of his life than yours.

🍼 Babies and small kids often fall asleep in rough weather on boats—this is their way of dealing with sea sickness.

How I remember those long drives on California's Highway 1, clutching the side of the car and my stomach as my parents remarked on the beauty of the Pacific Ocean. As an adult, I realize we were rarely on the road for more than an hour at a time, but it seemed endless. I also get seasick in a bizarre form. I'm fine on the water, but once back on dry land, I can't shake the odd, rocking feeling—as though I'm on a boat. This awful sensation lasts for the same amount of time I am on the water—an hour boat ride, an hour rocking sensation; three days on a boat, three days on land, rocking. (I'm getting queasy.)

🍼 Ginger is a natural remedy for motion sickness—it's available in powdered form in health food stores, or brew up some ginger-root tea with honey (for the child older than one year) and bring it—warm but not too hot—in a thermos.

🍼 Try anti-nausea wrist bands, available in boating shops and catalogs, outdoor equipment stores, and maternity shops (they are also useful for morning sickness). They may be too big for a small child's wrist. You can also ask your pediatrician about medication for motion sickness.

🍼 Nibbling on saltines and sipping *small* sips of water can help.

🍼 Have child focus on the horizon.

T

TANTRUMS

T is for Tantrums, Terrible Troublemakers, and Toddler Torture. Kids have their own agenda, and it may not include getting to the dry cleaner before it closes, or making the last train back to Berlin. On the road, normal stresses may seem more intense to a kid, leading to more tantrums just when you *least* have the time.

Kids have different tantrums styles. Some fling themselves down, beating their heads, screaming and flailing like wind-mills. Others are like my little cousin Wren, who slowly and dramatically lowers herself to the floor, wriggles around to make sure she is comfortable and, only then, lets it fly.

Supermarket Tantrums

Supermarkets can be disastrous. They are over-stimulating. The child is confined and not allowed to run. The humiliation potential is high—and parents are often tense. Kids **want** what they see and can't understand why they can't have it. The best solution is prevention, often including small food bribes (we talked about this in Chapter 7), but what happens when the two-year-old tornado hits, screams, and falls on the floor?

You can ignore the stares of fellow shoppers, try to calm the child, or leave your cart in the middle of an aisle and haul the child outside. This is **not** about punishment—changing the physical place changes the emotional space. Let the child cry it out. Then return with your sniffling and subdued little offspring, find the cart, and make it snappy before the time bomb goes off again.

Ten minutes to let a child "get it out of her system" is a long time in a busy day. But this is part of taking your child with you—sometimes you have to operate on Toddler Time—if you slow your pace in general, your child will generally be more serene.

Babies and little kids *hate* to be misunderstood, and, especially at the ages when their internal development is greater than their ability to ver-balize, frustration runs high. Understanding this—and taking time to really understand what a child wants, can avoid many stormy moments.

Many tantrums happen because a kid is pushed. Slow down, and let Baby help determine the pace.

Real tantrums are huge explosions of energy and frustration caused by strong desire, minimal skills, and weak internal controls (sounds like the definition of a toddler to me!). Whatever else, kids this age should *never* be punished if they fall apart like this. A tantrum is terrifying for a child—keep her safe until the storm is over. Most tantrums end with sobbing and sleep. When the beast awakes, she's usually filled with charm and ease.

U

UNWANTED ATTENTION

U is for Unwanted Attention. As the stranger in town, your child may get more than his share, especially if the "town" is across the world and he is the one blond child in a throng of brunettes, the one child of color in a crowd of Caucasians. People may stare, or try to touch his hair and skin. Little children may find this intensely uncomfortable. (You probably would, too!) Be the child's ally. Don't force him to socialize before he's ready. Let him cling to you, or remove him from reach. He'll soon feel more comfortable—and become more outgoing—if you allow him to take it at his own pace.

V

LOST VISAS, PASSPORTS, AND OTHER MISSING PAPERS

V is for Visa. No, not the credit card, I'm talking about your permission slip to get across the border to Burundi. Say you wash your hands in the airport bathroom, put your purse above the sink—and leave without it. No papers. No money. No tickets.

 Before you leave, make two copies of each of your important documents. Store one set with a friend at home, pack the other set in your luggage—away from the originals.

If it happens, calm down. Most of these things can be replaced, with varying time and hassle. Remember your core values—you've got the most precious thing in the world with you—your family.

Get on the horn and start honking. Try the Passport office, the consulate or embassy, and the airline. Things get lost—all these offices have procedures for taking care of the situation. Once a visa has already been approved—as yours was—it should take far less time to get it replaced. Worst-case scenario is a brief delay, and a headache.

W

WAVING YOUR BABY, AND WATER SAFETY

W is for "When In Doubt, Wave Your Baby." Your child is your ally. An adult in trouble is just another person—a parent with a young child in trouble brings out the humanity in all of humanity. Wiggle the baby in the air, and the World Will Work With you.

W is also for Water Safety. Water is vital to health, and it is easy to get dehydrated on the road. In many places, the water can be dangerous—it may carry amoebas, bacteria, or parasites that can make you a *very* unhappy traveler. The rule if you're served water from a mysterious source: When in doubt, dump it out. And don't eat the ice. If the drinking water is "risky," you have a number of options:

 Bottled water is available in many countries, and usually inexpensive. Make sure the top is *factory sealed* (we've heard horror stories about shopkeepers refilling old bottles.)

- Water boiled for 10 minutes (longer in the mountains) is safe to drink.

- Brush teeth with bottled, boiled, or purified water. Yes, even if your child spits it out!

- There are a number of microporous water filters available that remove bacteria and parasites. Some also eliminate viruses with iodine.

- In an area where you are unable to boil your water (like the Himalayas,) you can purify water by adding eight drops of a two-percent iodine solution to a quart of water. Wait 20 minutes. Some camping and outdoor-supply stores sell iodine treatment kits. We used this method in Nepal. "Iodinized" water has a slight taste (you might add powdered fruit juice for kids), but it's safe.

- On an extended journey or living overseas, bring fluoride pills for your child. Most countries' water is *not* treated.

X

OVER-X-CITEMENT AND X-OTIC LOCALES

X is for eXcitement, and over-stimulation. One reason to travel is to gain new stimuli, but you *can* overdo it. Some kids are extra sensitive to excitement—but all kids can be over-excited. Here's the equation: Over-excited child = hassled parent. Know your child, know yourself, know your limits, and slow down!

    X is also for eXotic. Living in California, the beaches of relatively nearby Mexico provide the occasional inexpensive tropical vacation, but Bali, on the other side of the world, seems impossibly exotic, frightening, and almost as foreign as Mars. Little do we understand (until we're slurping smoothies and fending off blanket vendors on Kuta beach) that Bali has become Australia's Mexico, riddled with surfers and hardly free from Western influences. The world has been televised. Few places are untamed. Yes, adventure still awaits, but you can go almost everywhere—"exotic" or not—with your kids and still find the comforts of home.

Y

IN THE EVENT OF YELLOW FEVER, CHOLERA, OR REVOLUTION

Y is for Yellow Fever. Yikes! Preventive vaccinations of yellow fever and cholera are not recommended for little babies, but more than that, they aren't always effective anyway. Bail out.

Safety is your first and primary concern. Yes, a revolution or a plague is interesting, but is it more interesting than watching your child grow up? Take advantage of the "children first" emergency evacuations, and get your child to safer, higher ground.

Z

TIME ZONES AND JET LAG

Z is for Time Zone, and the disorientation it can cause. Changing time zones requires a period of readjustment. Allow time for body-recovery, but change the clock immediately, and break on through to the other side. The faster you adjust your schedule, the faster your body will adjust.

Time zones are often talked about in conjunction with jet lag. A lot of jet lag is caused by dehydration—which is avoidable. Drink those fluids! (Nag, nag, nag.)

- Doing the Time Zone Shuffle will throw off feeding schedules and meal times. Make sure food is available. If you're a nursing mother, give in to the forces of nature and nurse on demand for a few days, until a new schedule is established.

- Be prepared for wild bouncing at midnight, and glazed eyes at noon. Scolding and discipline will have little effect—your child's whole *system* is off-kilter. It will pass.

- Some kids have increased incidents of night terrors after shifting many time zones.

- Most people find it easier to go West than East. (Everybody I know, except for me.)

- Children usually have an easier time than parents. (Don't they always?) Maybe because they get to *nap*, while you get to tote baggage, carry their sleeping bodies, and unpack. Life, she is not always fair. You'll have fun *anyway*, and if you're lucky you'll have somebody to care for you in your dotage.

- If you're crossing many time zones, consider sedation. (Hey! Ask your pediatrician!) This is not *just* for your travel sanity—if your child is well rested, her body will more easily make the time shift.

- Let 'em nap when they need to, but save the bedtime rituals for the All New! All Improved! bedtime.

Travel with Children

Adventuring with Children, Nan Jeffrey (Avalon Books)

Best Places to Go: A Family Destination Guide, Nan Jeffrey (Foghorn Press)

The Family Travel Guide: An Inspiring Collection of Family-Friendly Vacations, Ed. Carole Terwilliger Meyers (Carousel Press)

Outdoor Adventures with Kids, Mary Mapes McConnell, (Taylor Publishing Company)

Travel with Children, Maureen Wheeler (Lonely Planet Travel Guides)

Trouble-Free Travel with Children, Vicky Lansky (Book Peddlers)

Safety, First Aid, and Health

Baby Proofing Basics, Vicky Lansky (Book Peddlers)

The Complete Guide to Non-Toxic and Environmentally Safe Housekeeping, by Annie Berthold-Bond (Ceres Press, 1994)

Overcoming Jet Lag, Dr. Charles F. Ehret and Lynne Waller Scanlon (Berkeley Pub. Group)

A Sigh of Relief: The First-Aid Handbook for Childhood Emergencies, Martin I. Green (Bantam, Doubleday, Dell)

Staying Healthy in Asia, Africa, and Latin America, Dirk G. Schroeder (Moon Publications)

Where There is No Doctor, David Warner, with Carol Thuman and Jane Maxwell (Hesparian Foundation, PO Box 1692, Palo Alto, CA 94302)

Wilderness Medicine: Beyond First Aid, William W. Forgey, M.D. (Ics Books)

General Parenting

Baby and Child Care, Benjamin Spock, M.D. and Michael B. Rothenberg, M.D. (Pocket Books)

Becoming the Parent You Want to Be: A Source Book of Strategies for the First Five Years, Laura Davis and Janis Keyser (Broadway Books)

Child of Mine, Ellyn Satter (Bull Publishing Co.)

The Nursing Mother's Companion, Kathleen Huggins, R.N. M.S., (Harvard Common Press)

Your Growing Child, Penelope Leach (Alfred A. Knopf)

Equipment

Adaptive Parenting Equipment: Idea Book 1, (TLG, 800-644-2666)

The Complete Buyers Guide to the Best Outdoor and Recreation Equipment, Kevin Jeffrey (Foghorn Press)

Family Travel Resources

Family Travel Agents and Consultants
(800) 499-0929 (in California) or (510) 848-0929
Dan and Wendy Hallinan traveled for years with their three kids before opening their own business. They provide not only the "normal" travel agent services of air, car rental, and hotel, but also itinerary planning based on experience, bibliographies and fact sheets organized by age, place and interests; housing rental services, and an irregularly produced newsletter. They work with clients to help them "slow down." Itinerary and housing rental assistance comes free with air tickets, or you can hire them for housing bookings and consultation at $25 a well-worth-it hour.

Carousel Press
P.O. Box 6061, Albany, CA 94706
(510) 527-5849
Send a SASE to receive their annual Family Travel Guides Catalogue listing over 200 family-oriented travel guides and children's travel activity books.

Escape Artist Travel
(510) 652-3017
Travel agent Bonnie Lewkowicz specializes in travel arrangements for people with disabilities.

Lodging Resources

IntervacU.S.
PO Box 590504, San Francisco, CA 94159
(415) 435-3497
FAX (415) 435-7440
E-mail: **Intervac@aol.com**
Intervac has been helping people arrange national and international home swaps since 1953. A subscription includes listing your own home (with photo) in one book, while receiving a total of three books.

Hostelling International—American Youth Hostels
(202) 783-6161
Hostel rates range from $9 -$22 a person per night (plus membership fee). Family membership is $35 annually and includes automatic membership in Hostelling International®, access to almost 5,000 hostels in 70 countries, directory of U.S. and Canadian hostels, and assorted discounts on rentals, equipment, admissions, and other services. Call the number above, look

in your phone book for your local American Youth Hostel listing, or check out their Web Site at www.Hostelling.com.

Condominium Travel Associates
(800) 492-6636
CTA provides rental information and reservation services and/or refers callers to local booking agents for condominiums and villas in the U.S., Caribbean, Hawaii, Mexico, and Europe.

Child Care Resources

Child Care Aware
(800) 424-2246
Child Care Aware is a national initiative designed to improve the quality of child care and increase the availability of quality child care in local communities. Along with training of child care providers, Child Care Aware helps parents identify quality child care environments, and helps parents locate quality child care in their community. Call for help locating your local child care resource and referral agency. Their free brochure includes an excellent checklist for measuring the quality of a child care home or center.

Internal Revenue Service
(800) 829-1040
Wait on hold here for information on paying taxes on your nanny.

Disability Resources

Through the Looking Glass
2198 Sixth Street, Suite 100, Berkeley, CA 94710-2204
(800) 644-2666
Through the Looking Glass is a national clearinghouse for families of adults who have disabilities. Along with their resource book, *"Adaptive Parenting Equipment: Idea Book 1"* ($10 for consumers, $25 for professionals), they also publish a newsletter, "Parenting with a Disability." All of their services are free. Also see: www.lookingglass.org

Society for the Advancement of Travel for the Handicapped
347 5th Ave, Suite 610, New York, NY 10016
(212) 447-SATH
SATH is a non-profit organization dedicated to barrier-free access for travelers. They publish a regular travel newsletter, plus a variety of information sheets.

Travelin' Talk
P.O. Box 3534, Clarksville, TN 37043
(615) 552-6670
An international information network providing assistance to travelers with disabilities. They publish a comprehensive directory of individuals and agencies throughout the world who can provide information and services to people with disabilities.

Car Seats for Kids with Physical or Neurological Disabilities

Columbia Medical Manufacturing
(800) 454-6612
Tumble Forms
(800) 547-4333

Equipment

Babies Away
(800) 571-0077
Babies Away rents babies equipment—cribs, strollers, toys, rocking chairs, gates, potty seats, VCRs with children's tapes, you name it—in 31 "destination resort" locations including eight in Canada.

National Highway Traffic Safety Administration Auto Safety Hotline
(800) 424-9393
Provides information on car seat safety and recalls. Also provides a handout: *"Shopping Guide for Child and Infant Safety Seats"* which lists manufacturers, models, and price ranges of car seats meeting current federal government requirements. Can tell you which model car seats will fit in your car (there is no universal standard).

Tushies Diapers
(800) 344-6379
Even a lot of the diaper companies are offering Tushies as an alternative—gel-free, perfume-free, dye free, they are a lot healthier (if pricier) than the normal disposable. Check your natural foods markets or call for distribution information.

Overseas Travel Resources

U.S State Department Information Services

(202) 647-5225

The U.S. State Department runs a detailed 24-hour recorded hotline of overseas citizen services. Call for travel warnings and advisories around the world, disease information, information about emergencies regarding U.S. Citizens, and details on every country's tourism status, visa requirements for U.S. Citizens, and the locations of its embassy or consulate in the United States.

International Association for Medical Assistance to Travellers

417 Center Street, Lewiston, NY, 14092

(716) 754-4883

IAMAT provides a world directory of English and French-speaking doctors (trained in Europe or North America) in 125 countries and territories. Membership is free (donations encouraged.)

The Center for Disease Control and Prevention

1600 Clifton Rd. NE, Atlanta, GA 30333 USA

(404) 639-3311

The CDC is the main authority, guys, for *any* traveler health-related issues. If you're on-line, check out their Web Site at www.cdc.gov for information on immunizations, travel advisories, and detailed information on food and water safety.

Other Resources

La Leche League

(800) LA LECHE

La Leche League offers breastfeeding information and support. Call for a referral to a local La Leche League representative.

Orches

530 East 8th Street, Oakland, CA 94606

(510) 832-3835

Orches is a non-profit organization specializing in motion therapy, dance training and body health. Ergonomic and movement experts Peter Brown and Vicki Gunter are available for consultations on ergonomically-safe work environments, RSI recovery, infant and child motion development, and modes of toting little ones.

ID Your Kids

Inexpensive, waterproof, disposable I.D. Me™ bracelets with a place to write name, local address, phone, and other information on the underside. Send a SASE to Practical Parenting, Dept. ID, 15245 Minnetonka Blvd., Minnetonka, MN 55345. Cost: two for $1. (Extras are 50¢ each, maximum ten for $5 per envelope.)

Medic Alert Foundation

(800) 344-3226

If you or your child has a chronic medical condition, allergies, or is on medication, you might want to join Medic Alert. Membership benefits include an engraved Medic Alert bracelet, set-up and maintenance of a computerized medical file, and emergency response service. Initial membership costs $35, with $15 annual dues thereafter.

index